Supporting the Literacy Development of English Learners

INCREASING SUCCESS IN ALL CLASSROOMS

Terrell A. Young
Washington State University
Richland, Washington, USA

Nancy L. Hadaway
University of Texas at Arlington
Arlington, Texas, USA

E D I T O R S

INTERNATIONAL
Reading Association
800 BARKSDALE ROAD, PO BOX 8139
NEWARK, DE 19714-8139, USA
www.reading.org

KH

The International Reading Association attempts, through its publications, to provide a forum for a wide spectrum of opinions on reading. This policy permits divergent viewpoints without implying the endorsement of the Association.

Director of Publications Dan Mangan
Editorial Director, Books and Special Projects Teresa Curto
Managing Editor, Books Shannon T. Fortner
Acquisitions and Developmental Editor Corinne M. Mooney
Associate Editor Charlene M. Nichols
Associate Editor Elizabeth C. Hunt
Production Editor Amy Messick
Books and Inventory Assistant Rebecca A. Zell
Permissions Editor Janet S. Parrack
Assistant Permissions Editor Tyanna L. Collins
Production Department Manager Iona Muscella
Supervisor, Electronic Publishing Anette Schütz
Senior Electronic Publishing Specialist R. Lynn Harrison
Electronic Publishing Specialist Lisa M. Kochel
Proofreader Stacey Lynn Sharp

Project Editor Shannon T. Fortner

Art Cover Design, Linda Steere; Cover and Interior Illustration © Image Zoo/Images.com

Web addresses in this book were correct as of the publication date but may have become inactive or otherwise modified since that time. If you notice a deactivated or changed Web address, please e-mail books@reading.org with the words "Website Update" in the subject line. In your message, specify the Web link, the book title, and the page number on which the link appears.

Library of Congress Cataloging-in-Publication Data

Supporting the literacy development of English learners : increasing
   success in all classrooms / Terrell A. Young, Nancy L. Hadaway,
   editors.
      p. cm.
   Includes bibliographical references and index.
   ISBN 0-87207-569-9
   1. English language--Study and teaching--Foreign speakers.
   I. Young, Terrell A. II. Hadaway, Nancy L.
   PE1128.A2S8876 2005
   428.0071--dc22

                                                          2005023864

11/17/06

This book is dedicated to English learners and the teachers who are committed to their success.

CONTENTS

SECTION III
READING INSTRUCTION

SECTION IV
ORAL AND WRITTEN LANGUAGE

ACKNOWLEDGMENTS

The contributions of several people made this book a reality. We first wish to thank the authors of the chapters found in this volume. This book is a tribute to their scholarly expertise and great concern for English learners. We also want to recognize the support we received from the Publications Division of the International Reading Association. We are grateful to Matt Baker for his support for the project. We especially thank Corinne Mooney and Shannon Fortner for the time, skills, and guidance they devoted to this project.

Finally, we want to express our appreciation to our families. Nancy wishes to thank her husband, Art Sikes, and her parents, Boyd and Mable Hadaway, for their constant support. Likewise, Terry is grateful for the love and support of his wife, Christine; his children, Jonathan, Natalie, Emilee, and Jeffrey; and his mother, Patricia Young.

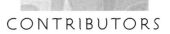

CONTRIBUTORS

Diane August
Senior Research Scientist
Center for Applied Linguistics
Washington, DC, USA

Mary Cappellini
Author and Educational Consultant
Newport Beach, California, USA

Maria Carlo
Assistant Professor of Teaching
    and Learning
University of Miami
Coral Gables, Florida, USA

Deanna Day
Assistant Professor of Literacy
    Education
Washington State University
Vancouver, Washington, USA

David E. Freeman
Professor of Education
University of Texas at Brownsville
Brownsville, Texas, USA

Yvonne S. Freeman
Professor of Education
University of Texas at Brownsville
Brownsville, Texas, USA

Deanna Peterschick Gilmore
Assistant Professor of Literacy
    Education
Washington State University
Richland, Washington, USA

Nancy L. Hadaway
Professor of Literacy Studies
University of Texas at Arlington
Arlington, Texas, USA

Teresa J. Lively
Clinical Psychologist and Former
    Bilingual Teacher
University of California, Santa Cruz
Santa Cruz, California, USA

Barry McLaughlin
Professor Emeritus
University of California, Santa Cruz
Santa Cruz, California, USA

Jill Kerper Mora
Associate Professor of Teacher Education
San Diego State University
San Diego, California, USA

Barbara Moss
Professor of Literacy Education
San Diego State University
San Diego, California, USA

Janice Pilgreen
Professor of Education and Program
    Chair of Reading
University of La Verne
La Verne, California, USA

Marsha L. Roit
Director of Professional Development
SRA/McGraw-Hill
Phoenix, Maryland, USA

Catherine Snow
Henry Lee Shattuck Professor
    of Education
Harvard University
Cambridge, Massachusetts, USA

Sylvia M. Vardell
Professor of Literature for Children
    and Young Adults
Texas Woman's University
Denton, Texas, USA

Terrell A. Young
Professor of Literacy Education
Washington State University
Richland, Washington, USA

Vida Zuljevic
School Librarian
Pasco School District
Pasco, Washington, USA

INTRODUCTION

Terrell A. Young and Nancy L. Hadaway

English learners are the fastest growing student population in the United States. Given the unprecedented surge in the number of these students, all teachers need a firm understanding of how to work most effectively with them. Unfortunately, many teachers have had little or no training focused on facilitating the English learning and literacy development of English learners (Hadaway, Vardell, & Young, 2004). To bridge the gap between students' needs and teachers' preparation, this book provides an overview of English learners, a section on broad issues in instruction and curriculum planning, and sections that address reading instruction as well as oral- and written-language instruction. Within each section, chapters focus on how teachers can help English learners develop the language and literacy skills necessary for success in today's standards-based classrooms.

Section I, "Supporting English Learners," sets the stage for the book, noting that teachers must first understand their learners before they can adequately support them. In chapter 1, "Changing Classrooms: Transforming Instruction," Nancy L. Hadaway and Terrell A. Young highlight the complex family, cultural, and language backgrounds that English learners bring to classrooms at every grade level. Then the authors offer a set of beginning considerations, drawn from research, theory, and practice, for helping teachers overcome misconceptions about working with English learners so that they will more likely meet students' needs.

Section II, "Curriculum and Planning," tackles overarching matters, such as differentiating instruction to meet diverse proficiency levels, moving beyond initial social language and building academic language, and addressing content topics through thematic instruction.

In chapter 2, "Differentiating Instruction for English Learners: The Four-by-Four Model," Jill Kerper Mora asserts that the range of language proficiency and literacy development levels in today's classrooms creates a special challenge for teachers. Teachers must determine the competence of each student in the four language arts: listening, speaking, reading, and writing. To this end, Mora has developed the Four-by-Four Model, a helpful framework for analysis and problem solving, which can be used when planning and implementing English learner programs and instruction.

Part of the planning process begun in chapter 2 with the Four-by-Four Model includes the critical area of academic language. Formal academic-language development determines how well students fare in school tasks—from interpreting literature to performing on standardized tests. Although it is well documented that students can often attain interpersonal communication skills in one to three years, it typically takes five to seven years for students to develop academic-language proficiency (Cummins, 2003). Less understood is the methodology needed to help English learners in content area classrooms attain academic-language proficiency in contexts that effectively provide access to the core curriculum. Janice Pilgreen provides such methodology in chapter 3, "Supporting English Learners: Developing Academic Language in the Content Area Classroom." Pilgreen describes and demonstrates explicit strategies that enable English learners to maximize academic-language development.

The final curriculum and planning issue of section II is presented in chapter 4, "Teaching Language Through Content Themes: Viewing Our World as a Global Village." An integrated thematic approach to instruction is excellent for organizing curriculum in general, and it is especially helpful for English learners, as language is best learned when encountered in the context of the various subject areas. In chapter 4, authors David E. Freeman and Yvonne S. Freeman illustrate the importance of thematic instruction for English learners and present suggestions for developing themes—including how to choose culturally relevant literature, how to scaffold to teach vocabulary and concepts, and how to draw from students' first languages and cultures to develop academic English. Throughout the chapter, the authors provide real-life examples of classroom teachers implementing thematic instruction.

With an understanding of students and the issues involved in working with English learners in general education classrooms, teachers can move their attention to more specific instructional concerns. Section III, "Reading Instruction," addresses comprehension strategies, vocabulary development, guided reading, and expository text structures.

Reading comprehension instruction that emphasizes modeling and thinking aloud by teachers and students, discussing text, and group problem solving provides a rich environment for learning English. Students develop flexibility with English and gain self-confidence. Several key competencies can be developed in this environment that will help students increase both reading comprehension and language development. These competencies include use of English in a flexible way, use of abstract and less "imageable" vocabulary, ability to consider contexts, ability to determine importance and unimportance, ability to elaborate in responses, and ability to engage in natural conversations. In chapter 5, "Essential Comprehension Strategies for English Learners," Marsha L. Roit discusses each of these competencies and provides instructional strategies for maximizing shared reading, vocabulary networking, expanding knowledge, and conversational opportunities.

Vocabulary and concept development are often great challenges for English learners. Although English learners may correctly pronounce the words of text selections, they often do not have the English vocabulary necessary to comprehend assigned texts at high levels. In chapter 6, "Promoting the Vocabulary Growth of English Learners," Diane August,

Maria Carlo, Teresa J. Lively, Barry McLaughlin, and Catherine Snow describe the key curricular elements of a one-year intervention, the Vocabulary Improvement Program, which enriched vocabulary knowledge and bolstered reading comprehension of Spanish-speaking fifth-grade English learners in bilingual and general education classrooms.

Guided reading is an important part of a balanced literacy program for English learners. It is the crucial link to independence. In guided reading, the teacher guides students to use the reading strategies and language structures they have been developing during instruction (shared reading and read-aloud). In order to lead English learners through a guided reading lesson successfully, teachers must know students' individual language and reading levels and must choose appropriate books that match students at both of those levels. In addition, teachers must examine whether student miscues are due to language issues and, if so, determine how to help students develop language in addition to reading strategies during guided reading. Mary Cappellini provides guidelines for modifying guided reading lessons to meet the needs of English learners in chapter 7, "Using Guided Reading With English Learners."

Section III wraps up with chapter 8, "Teaching English Learners About Expository Text Structures," by Barbara Moss. Students typically find nonfiction more challenging to read than fiction. For English learners, the challenge is even more pronounced. Moss examines the importance of teaching expository text structures and provides classroom-based examples for developing understanding of expository text types. The chapter provides an overview of the five most common expository text structures (description, sequence, compare/contrast, cause/effect, and problem/solution) and offers practical classroom ideas for developing English learners' understanding of expository text through such oral-language activities as total physical response (TPR), creative dramatics, and Readers Theatre. Moss also explains how student understanding can be developed through read-alouds, retellings of nonfiction trade-book stories, and writing. The chapter concludes with lists of nonfiction titles suitable for helping students understand the five common text types.

Section IV, "Oral and Written Language," completes the instructional focus of the book by offering strategies to enhance student speaking and writing. Strategies include letter and dialogue-journal exchanges, poetry performance, puppetry, and literature circles.

Nancy L. Hadaway and Terrell A. Young begin section IV by presenting guidelines for using letters and dialogue journals in chapter 9, "Negotiating Meaning Through Writing." The authors emphasize that the value of journal and letter writing is in their ability to involve English learners in using real and purposeful dialogue. Such writing activities help English learners "develop fluency because [the activities] are meaningful, they are responded to, and they give writers the freedom to concentrate on what they are saying rather than on how [to say] it" (Peregoy & Boyle, 2001, p. 229). Hadaway and Young illustrate the instructional potential of these interactive writing activities with excerpts of student letters and journals. They also offer extensions of letter and journal exchanges and describe how to use exchanges to assess language proficiency and to plan instruction that meets English learners' writing needs.

Oral-language development plays a powerful role in acquiring language, laying the foundation for success in written language (Hadaway, Vardell, & Young, 2002). Talk builds a syntactic base that aids reading and writing (Clay, 2002). In chapter 10, "Language Play, Language Work: Using Poetry to Develop Oral Language," Nancy L. Hadaway, Sylvia M. Vardell, and Terrell A. Young highlight the many benefits of poetry in developing oral language. They also provide guidelines for performing poems as a class, in small groups, and solo.

The discussion of oral-language development continues in chapter 11, "Using Puppets With English Learners to Develop Language." Classroom teacher Vida Zuljevic shares her successful use of puppets with bilingual Russian–English students. Zuljevic notes that puppets address the affective as well as the cognitive dimension of language learning, giving shy students and beginning English learners confidence as they "lend their voices" to the puppets.

Chapter 12 concludes section IV and the book with "Let's Read, Write, and Talk About It: Literature Circles for English Learners." Frequently English learners become fluent decoders before they are able to comprehend what they read. Literature circles offer English learners a context that emphasizes comprehension and response to reading (Samway & Whang, 1995). Discussion during literature circles "is guided by students' response to what they have read" (Schlick Noe & Johnson, 1999, p. ix). In chapter 12, Deanna Peterschick Gilmore and Deanna Day articulate the benefits of literature circles for students learning English. They provide guidelines for supporting students through the text reading and suggest ways to extend the reading experience through response activities.

In summary, *Supporting the Literacy Development of English Learners: Increasing Success in All Classrooms* offers practitioner-focused strategies for curriculum and planning, reading instruction, and oral-language and writing development with English learners. With a solid foundation to help them understand and address the special needs and strengths of English learners, teachers can move all students forward to increased success in school.

REFERENCES

Clay, M. (2002, October). *Three into one will go: Putting Humpty Dumpty together again*. Paper presented at the Canadian Regional IRA Conference, Vancouver, BC.

Cummins, J. (2003). Reading and the bilingual student: Fact and fiction. In G.G. García (Ed.), *English learners: Reaching the highest level of English literacy* (pp. 2–33). Newark, DE: International Reading Association.

Hadaway, N.L., Vardell, S.M., & Young, T.A. (2002). *Literature-based instruction with English learners, K–12*. Boston: Allyn & Bacon.

Hadaway, N.L., Vardell, S.M., & Young, T.A. (2004). *What every teacher should know about English learners*. Boston: Pearson/Allyn & Bacon.

Peregoy, S.F., & Boyle, O.F. (2001). *Reading, writing, and learning in ESL: A resource book for K–12 teachers*. New York: Longman.

Samway, K.D., & Whang, G. (1995). *Literature study circles in a multicultural classroom*. York, ME: Stenhouse.

Schlick Noe, K., & Johnson, N.J. (1999). *Getting started with literature circles*. Norwood, MA: Christopher-Gordon.

SUPPORTING ENGLISH LEARNERS

CHAPTER 1

Changing Classrooms: Transforming Instruction

Nancy L. Hadaway and Terrell A. Young

C hanging U.S. demographics have significantly altered the face of K–12 schools. The Office of Bilingual Education and Minority Languages Affairs, U.S. Department of Education, reported 3.9 million public school students as limited English proficient (LEP) in 2001, a number that is nearly double what it was less than a decade ago (Kindler, 2002). Three quarters of these students are concentrated in six states: California (1,511,646), Texas (570,022), Florida (254,517), New York (239,097), Illinois (140,528), and Arizona (135,248). However, a dramatic shift in English learner enrollment occurred in many other states between academic years 1997–1998 and 2000–2001. Nine states (Arkansas, Idaho, Indiana, Kentucky, Minnesota, Missouri, New Hampshire, Oregon, and Virginia) showed a growth in English learner enrollment of 50% to 80%. South Carolina and Georgia had increases of 127% and 210%, respectively.

Over 400 languages are reported to be spoken nationwide. Spanish is the predominant language among English learners: 79% speak Spanish, 2% speak Vietnamese, 1.6% speak Hmong, 1% speak Cantonese, and 1% speak Korean. These are followed by Haitian Creole, Arabic, Russian, Tagalog, Navajo, Khmer, Mandarin, Portuguese, Urdu, Serbo-Croatian, Lao, and Japanese.

Looking ahead, the U.S. Census Bureau (2004) estimates that 88% of the population increase between 2000 and 2050 will be children of new immigrants. With this projected increase, educators must turn their attention to English learners—who not only need instruction in their new language but who may also require extra academic assistance if schooling in their country of origin was limited. Current data, however, shows that English learners are not acquiring the skills to perform well in school. When compared to fluent English speakers, English learners tend to receive lower grades, score below the average on standardized math and reading exams, and are judged by teachers to have weaker academic skills (Moss & Puma, 1995).

This chapter provides an overview of the complex population of English learners in schools, explores how schools have addressed this group of students, and offers some recommendations for educators.

Language Diversity and Education: A Brief History

From the beginning, language diversity has been part of life in the United States. The Native American nations and the early Spanish, French, English, and African inhabitants all had unique languages. In the century after the Revolutionary War, over 5 million immigrants poured into the United States. During the first half of the 1800s, immigrants, most often from Northern and Western Europe, had a desire to maintain their first languages. This wish to preserve cultural ties spurred legislation in more than 12 states to mandate bilingual education; Swedish, Danish, Norwegian, Italian, Polish, Dutch, and Greek were included in the curriculum as both a subject of study and a medium of instruction.

In contrast, during the Great Immigration (1890–1920), Southern and Eastern European immigrants outnumbered Northern Europeans. Indeed, these "new" immigrants were judged to be so different that many states considered "English only" legislation. Students were often punished, and teachers could be fined, fired, or lose their teaching certificate, for using a language other than English on school grounds (Crawford, 1999). World War I intensified the prejudice and discrimination; 15 states passed laws mandating "English only" instruction and forbidding foreign-language instruction. World War II heightened discrimination even more, and those with a language difference were often viewed as suspect. However, the end of World War II and the Sputnik launch stirred a revival of interest in foreign-language instruction.

Since the 1960s, attention to language diversity and education has increased, and so has the controversy. In 1965, Title VII of the Elementary and Secondary Education Act (Johnson, 1965), called the Bilingual Education Act, was signed into law, establishing a U.S. federal policy focused on English learners. In response to the new Bilingual Education Act, Chinese parents in San Francisco, California, filed a class action suit claiming their children were being denied an equal educational opportunity. This resulted in the U.S. Supreme Court's 1974 decision in Lau v. Nichols:

> Where inability to speak and understand the English language excludes national origin minority group children from effective participation in the educational program offered by a school district, the district must take affirmative steps to rectify the language deficiency in order to open its instructional program to these students.

Although the Bilingual Education Act did not mandate dual-language programs only, the focus has often been on the provision of bilingual methods more than English assistance methods. However, a variety of models have been implemented to assist English learners in acquiring English and achieving in school. Linquanti (1999) highlights four major instructional methods that are characterized by the degree to which they incorporate a student's native language and by their approach to academic content delivery. Each of these four methods can be further broken down into specific configurations of instruction:

1. Instructional methods that use the native language include transitional bilingual programs (early-exit bilingual), developmental bilingual programs (late-exit bilingual), and two-way immersion programs (dual-language or bilingual immersion). Transitional, or early-exit, programs include the use of two languages during the day with a gradual transition to English only in two to three years. In developmental bilingual programs, on the other hand, students are instructed mainly in their native language with the aim to foster the growth of both languages. Finally, two-way immersion offers an opportunity for English learners to work together with their native English-speaking counterparts to learn two languages in a bilingual setting.

2. Instructional methods that use native language as support may either translate unfamiliar English vocabulary into the primary language or use the primary language to clarify lessons taught in English.

3. Instructional methods that use English as a second language (ESL) include grammar-based ESL, communication-based ESL, and content-based ESL.

4. Content-based instruction/sheltered instruction methods focus on supportive instruction in English emphasizing academic as well as general language, including specially designed academic instruction in English (SDAIE), sheltered instruction observation protocol (SIOP), and cognitive academic language learning approach (CALLA).

Current attention, rather than continuing to be focused on the expansion of special language program options, is focused on limiting the number of years students may participate in bilingual education and on limiting the number of bilingual programs in schools. For example, California's Proposition 227 (California Secretary of State, 1998) emphasizes the need for students to be taught primarily in English. The national push has also been to exit students from bilingual education classes after three years or by the end of the primary grades. In 2001, President Bush signed into law the No Child Left Behind (NCLB) Act. This legislation brings English learners into the same context of standards and accountability as their fluent English-speaking peers and requires that "all children...reach high standards by demonstrating proficiency in English language arts and mathematics by 2014" (Abedi & Dietel, 2004, p. 782). Although this is certainly a worthy objective and hopefully will assist an important population in classrooms, there are four challenges to accomplishing this goal (see Abedi & Dietel, 2004, p. 782):

1. Historically low academic performance and very slow improvement. As noted earlier, English learners may take five to seven years to master academic language. Thus, quick turnaround on test scores by specific deadlines is difficult and unrealistic.

2. Lack of measurement accuracy. For English learners, "tests measure both achievement and language ability." In other words, English learners might master the concepts but still be unable to demonstrate their understanding given the language difficulties posed by the test.

3. Instability of English learner student subgroup. English learners are a group in constant transition. Once their language mastery reaches a certain level, English learners exit ESL classes and are then counted among the students in the general education classroom. This leaves the English learners at the most basic levels of language proficiency, which drives test scores downward.

4. Factors outside of the school's control that negatively affect performance. "Schools are unable to control all the factors related to student achievement," such as parent literacy level or trauma associated with immigration.

Given the current focus, attention must be turned to the complexities noted and how teachers can best address the needs of English learners.

Understanding English Learners

In meeting current educational goals, the teacher is the key component (Reed & Railsback, 2003). Teachers must link academic instruction to the content standards set by the state and ensure that the curriculum and teaching strategies align with the English-language proficiency of their students. This goal is complicated by the fact that the majority of U.S. teachers lack the training to help culturally diverse students succeed academically (Clair, 2000). Although half of all teachers may anticipate working with English learners during their career, currently only 2.5% of teachers working with English learners have a degree or certificate in teaching English to speakers of other languages, and only 30% have received any professional development in that area (McKeon, 1994; National Center for Education Statistics, 1997). To accomplish educational goals, teachers must understand what English learners bring to the school experience, including their family, cultural, and language backgrounds.

Family, Cultural, and Language Backgrounds

The backgrounds that English learners bring to the classroom are incredibly diverse. Ovando, Collier, and Combs (2003) suggest eight background elements that are relevant to working with students who are immigrants:

1. Country of origin
2. Length of residence in the United States
3. Extent of ties to country of origin

4. Political and economic situation in the region from which they immigrated

5. Reasons for immigration

6. Other countries lived in prior to the United States

7. Amount and quality of schooling in native language

8. Languages other than English and their native language to which students have been exposed

Not all English learners fit into the immigrant category, however. Many English learners are born in the United States. Yet English learners who are U.S. natives often come from linguistically isolated communities where little English is spoken. Forty-seven million U.S. residents—nearly one in five—speak a language other than English at home (Crawford, 2002). Pockets of Spanish only, Korean only, etc., exist in many U.S. cities. English is truly a new language to these students. Their culture shock is more related to language difference than it is to a different way of viewing the world. Students who are immigrants, on the other hand, experience both a different language and a different way of life shaped by American culture.

Geographic background further compounds educational adjustment as students who lived in rural areas may have lacked access to schools or had interrupted schooling (Romo, 1993). Also, the last decade has seen a rise in immigrant movement to rural areas in the United States (which is related to employment), but high school completion rates are lower in rural areas for students who are immigrants, and the gap between rural immigrants and nonimmigrants seems to be growing (Huang, 1999).

Socioeconomic level and previous educational attainment are additional variables to consider. For instance, parents' English-language fluency can influence their occupational opportunities and, hence, their earning ability. "Immigrant youth were twice as likely as natives to live in families with an income in the lowest quartile and to have parents with less than 12 years of schooling" (Schwartz, 1996). Conversely, high school graduates from immigrant families are more likely to pursue college education when they come from homes with higher educational attainment and high educational expectations. It is not that parents with low incomes have low expectations; Azmitia et al. (1994) found that parents with low incomes had high aspirations for their children but difficulty knowing how to help them realize such goals.

The importance of family involvement in education has been well documented. Epstein's six types of parental involvement (Epstein, Coates, Salinas, Sanders, & Simon, 1997) provide a helpful template that teachers can use to connect families and schools:

1. Parenting. School staff can provide special assistance in parenting and child-rearing skills, and the district can provide training and offer background information to help classroom teachers understand and work more effectively with students' families.

2. Communicating. School staff can experiment to find the most effective methods of communication from home to school and from school to home.

3. Volunteering. Schools and teachers can increase family involvement in school and school programs by considering recruitment, training, and scheduling issues. For instance, staff may extend outreach to places of worship and neighborhood groups where parents are already involved.

4. Learning at home. Learning does not begin and end at the school door. Teachers can link families to their children's curriculum through homework and other learning activities at home.

5. Decision making. It is critical to include family members as decision makers, advocates, and members of school councils and committees.

6. Collaborating with the community. School staff need to be aware of and utilize existing services in the community to assist families with special needs.

Cultural Adjustment

The initial encounter with school requires students to work through a period of cultural adjustment. Igoa (1995) identifies six stages of adjustment:

Stage 1. The child feels mixed emotions related to the move to the new country or the move from home to school.

Stage 2. The child feels excitement and/or fear.

Stage 3. Once the child enters the school, a natural curiosity may take hold as the child tries to make sense of this new environment.

Stage 4. The conflict between the new environment and the child's existing set of rules leads to culture shock. The child may feel a sense of depression, confusion, and isolation as he or she experiences a new language and culture.

Stage 5. As the child grows accustomed to the new environment, he or she begins to experience assimilation or acculturation. Problems may arise at this phase as many school professionals believe "that children can discard their old cultural values and replace them with new ones as easily as they throw away old shoes and get a new pair" (p. 44).

Stage 6. Finally, the child moves into the mainstream; the child feels more grounded.

The important role of culture and learning is highlighted by Fillmore and Snow (2000) who assert that teachers function as "agents of socialization," supporting students through the adjustment process and socializing them to the norms, beliefs, and communication patterns of school and to the patterns of mainstream U.S. culture. Haynes (2005) provides some valuable tips for school staff to use during the initial stages of adjustment:

- Focus on the positive, on what the student *can* do. Create frequent opportunities for student success. Don't call on a student to perform alone above his or her level of competence. Prepare the other students to welcome the new student to the class.

- Pronounce the newcomer's name correctly. Learn the correct pronunciation of the name from the newcomer, and determine which part is the given name and which is the family name.

- Take the newcomer on a school tour. Arrange for parent volunteers or older students who speak the newcomer's language to take the new student on a tour of the important places in your school.

Language Acquisition

Language acquisition involves the interplay of many factors. A basic understanding of these variables can help teachers better serve English learners (Fillmore & Snow, 2000; Hamayan, 1990). One factor, the age at which the child enters the school system, plays a crucial role in becoming competent in English. Collier (1989) finds that children who arrive in the United States before age 12 with at least two years of schooling in their native country reach the 50th percentile on reading, language arts, science, and social studies tests within five to seven years in U.S. classrooms. Young children, ages four to six who have little or no schooling in their native language, do not reach the 50th percentile after six years. Without a firm foundation in the native language, young children may confuse English-language concepts with those in their first language. Adolescent arrivals may not have enough time remaining in school to master the academic-language proficiency for school achievement.

Another factor critical to the acquisition of English is first-language literacy. "Parents who read to and talk with their children in their home language help their children develop language skills in ways that will facilitate their learning of English..." (Bermúdez, 1994, n.p.). For instance, children who have been read to and who read at home, whatever the language, bring a more developed knowledge of print and print conventions to school (Krashen, 1982).

Teachers need to capitalize on the understandings about language that students bring to school, but they must also be aware of the differences between English and the native language. Gibbons (1993) makes the point that English learners may have a native language with a different "script" from English (e.g., Chinese or Arabic), with a script similar to a Roman script but with different sound–symbol relationships (e.g., Turkish), or with a Roman script that has the addition of diacritics (e.g., Vietnamese).

Beyond first-language script issues, directionality (other than left-to-right), syntax (grammar), phonology (sound), and punctuation are all variables in learning another language (Collier, 1995). The more differences there are between a student's first language and English, the greater the challenge. Conversely, the more similar the first language is to English in terms of alphabet, the more easily students' writing skills will transfer to English (Odlin, 1989).

Collier (1995) suggests that teachers keep in mind the following basic strategies to foster English-language acquisition:

- Model academic language and make connections between language and content concepts.
- Focus on strategic thinking, problem solving, and comprehension techniques that students can use.
- Emphasize activation of students' prior knowledge, respect for their native language and culture, and ongoing assessment using multiple measures.

Once teachers have a better understanding of their learners in terms of family, cultural, and language background, they can focus their attention on selecting and implementing the most effective instructional strategies.

Supporting English Learners

The Teachers of English to Speakers of Other Languages (TESOL) *Standards for Pre-K–12 Students* (2003) address the English-language development needs of English learners, noting three broad goals:

1. Use English to communicate in social settings.
2. Use English to achieve academically in all content areas (more specifically, to interact in the classroom; to obtain, process, construct, and provide subject matter information in spoken and written form; to construct and apply academic knowledge).
3. Use English in socially and culturally appropriate ways.

The research is clear that social language, targeted in the first TESOL goal, emerges in two years or so, but that academic language takes five to seven years for children who arrive in the United States between ages 8 and 11, and even longer for children ages 4 to 7 (Collier, 1987). Thus, the second TESOL goal concerning academic language is a critical one, and one that has recently become a focus.

The debate over the best techniques for helping English learners acquire academic language at the same level as their fluent English-speaking peers has been hampered by limited scientifically based research and common misconceptions about effective instruction for English learners (Harper & de Jong, 2004). Understanding these misconceptions and their implications can help all educators create a strong program to support the language development and school achievement of English learners.

Topping the list of educators' misconceptions about English learners is that their needs "do not differ significantly from those of other diverse learners" (Harper & de Jong, 2004, p. 152). From this misconception stems the belief that "exposure and interaction will result in English-language learning" (p. 153). To the contrary, the purpose of this chapter has been to delineate the special factors in the backgrounds of English learners that necessitate targeted instruction to facilitate their acquisition of English.

Although Krashen (1982) and others have advocated comprehensible input for language learning, the progression of grade-level classrooms, textbooks, and standardized assessments require students to negotiate increasingly complex and abstract concepts (Lightbown & Spada, 1990; Spada & Lightbown, 1993). Therefore, teachers must provide targeted instruction, modeling the academic language needed to perform the required tasks. Fillmore (2002) explains that academic English tends to

- be more precise and specific in reference (personal, object, concepts, time, place, relational, etc.) than everyday English;
- make greater use of vocabulary that is Latin or Greek in origin;
- be more complex syntactically;
- be more dependent on "text" than on "context" for interpretation;
- be more cognitively demanding than everyday English;
- use distinctive grammatical constructions and devices, vocabulary, rhetorical conventions, and discourse; and
- be learned in school—but not without instructional attention.

Fillmore contends that school is the logical place to teach academic language since this is often where students first encounter it. Therefore, teachers must move beyond simply presenting and discussing content; teachers must direct student attention to the language of the task and the language needed to participate in the learning activity. Gibbons (2002) refers to this as academic-language scaffolding. Such scaffolding "actually consists of several linked strategies, including modeling academic language; contextualizing academic language using visuals, gestures, and demonstrations; and using hands-on learning activities that involve academic language" (Reed & Railsback, 2003, n.p.). This focus on building academic language has particular importance for the many grade-level teachers working with English learners but without the appropriate training to do so.

Related to the misconception that exposure alone will provide for language acquisition is the idea that the interaction between English learners and their peers in group work provides adequate input and practice for English-language development. On the one hand, research indicates that small group cooperative-learning activities can be an effective vehicle for learning content and learning in a second language (Klingner & Vaughn, 1996). For instance, Muñiz-Swicegood (1994) found that students working in small cooperative groups to generate and answer questions about the reading scored better on reading comprehension measures than students using basal reading approaches. Calderon (2001) suggests that "cooperative learning is effective when students have an interesting well-structured task such as a set of discussion questions around a story they just read, producing a cognitive map of the story, or inventing a puppet show to highlight character traits" (p. 280).

On the other hand, even when given a highly structured cooperative-learning activity, English learners may not possess the proficiency needed to participate effectively in questioning, agreeing, disagreeing, interrupting, presenting an opinion, or asking for clarification or assistance (Pica, 1994; Swain, 1985, 1995). Therefore, teachers must consider both the task structure *and* the linguistic demands of classroom activities, including the language of classroom discourse and small-group participation.

Closely linked to the misconception of homogeneity across groups—that the needs of English learners are not that different from other learners and that the process of learning a first language is not that different from learning another language—is the idea of within-group similarity. In other words, all English learners develop their new language "in the same way and at the same rate" (Harper & de Jong, 2004, p. 154). Nothing could be further from the truth; the diversity among English learners in the classroom is quite challenging. And, although there are identifiable stages of language development, the many family, cultural, and language variables can either assist or cause difficulties for language acquisition.

In trying to provide some beginning assistance to grade-level teachers working with English learners, educators too often provide information that leads to the formation of misconceptions. For instance, in discussing social and academic language, a common misunderstanding is that social-language ability automatically develops first because the timeline of language acquisition is one to two years for social-language development versus five or more years for academic-language development. This timeline fails to take into account older learners who attended school in their country of origin and developed a firm literacy foundation in their native language. These students also may have studied English in their own countries where the schools generally focus on reading and writing (academic language) rather than on communicative competence (social language) in English.

Indeed, Reid (1998), in her work with English-language writers, makes a distinction between "eye" and "ear" learners or those who learned English from written text and those who learned from oral communication. She notes that the learning styles and, therefore, the instructional needs of these two groups of learners are different. In short, "we must guard against a 'one-size-fits-all' mindset, looking for the one best program for all [English learners]. Instead, the focus must be on implementation of optimal programs in local schools for local communities" (Christian, 2004, p. 5).

A final point that Harper and de Jong (2004) offer is that teachers must examine the role of language in teaching and learning. Indeed, one of the pervasive suggestions for working with English learners has been to combine the teaching of language and content. This issue has important implications for content teachers who do not view themselves as language teachers and who are largely unaware of the language demands of their discipline. As a general rule, content teachers view their role as providing the conceptual background for a specific discipline such as science or math. Further, because they have a specialization in a content area, these teachers may forget the distinctive literacy demands of the curriculum in their field.

Recent research has questioned the effectiveness of combining content and language teaching, noting that invariably this leads to sacrifices in the area of language development (Gersten & Baker, 2002). Echevarria, Vogt, and Short (2004) attempt to address these criticisms with the SIOP, which requires significant teaching skills in both English-language development and content instruction, along with clearly defined language and content objectives and modified curriculum, supplementary materials, and alternative assessments.

In order to effectively address language and content objectives, teachers must carefully consider both the language and the cognitive loads of instruction (Meyer, 2000). In terms of considering language load, content teachers can take into account the vocabulary of the discipline (the specific terms, including technical and common words) as well as the language of classroom interactions and instructions.

The cognitive load refers to the difficulty of the concepts presented in class and the level of the materials used to convey them. An example of the importance of materials in determining cognitive load is the content textbook, which often drives subject-area instruction in the intermediate grades and beyond.

The organization of a text can be classified as considerate (reader friendly) or inconsiderate (Armbruster & Anderson, 1984). A considerate text presents information so that even a reader with limited background knowledge feels that the information is relatively easy to learn. Unfortunately, most content textbooks are not considerate; thus, they increase the cognitive load for the learner. The issue of reader friendliness also extends to visual texts, such as Web-based materials that do not necessarily follow a typical, linear format and are more complex to comprehend (Zammit, 2000).

In terms of planning content, Gersten and Baker (2002) argue that "effective teachers intentionally vary cognitive and language demands to achieve specific goals. In short, when cognitive demands are high, language expectations are simplified" (n.p.). Teachers can use Figure 1.1, a tool for lesson planning, to consider instruction/content in relationship to language demands. In the figure, Quadrants 1 and 3 deal with less academic language tasks that make fewer cognitive demands on English learners. However, Quadrant 1 involves language tasks that are both easy to understand and highly contextualized. Quadrant 3 addresses language without the context that can enhance understanding. In Quadrants 2 and 4, English learners encounter academic language tasks that are challenging but essential to success in school. However, the tasks in Quadrant 2

FIGURE 1.1
Instructional Planning and Language Demands

TASKS ARE LESS COGNITIVELY DEMANDING

<table>
<tr>
<td rowspan="2">C O N C R E T E   L A N G U A G E</td>
<td>

Quadrant 1

Viewing/Listening Activity
Follow a demonstration, follow directions.

Examples
Beginning-level proficiency: Conduct a read-aloud of a short poem with concrete words. Use overhead transparencies to emphasize the words in the poem, then have students use physical actions to perform the poem.

Intermediate-level proficiency: Conduct a read-aloud of a poem using overhead transparencies to emphasize the words in the poem.

</td>
<td>

Quadrant 3

Discussion Activity
Interaction is conducted in more informal language.

Examples
Beginning-level proficiency: Using sentence strips, students put together a poem in the correct sequence and discuss it in their own words.

Intermediate-level proficiency: Students discuss the poem in their own words.

</td>
<td rowspan="2">A B S T R A C T   L A N G U A G E</td>
</tr>
<tr>
<td>

Quadrant 2

Participation Activity
Make a model, chart, or graph.

Examples
Beginning-level proficiency: Students perform the poem in small groups using physical actions. Then they illustrate the poem with a drawing for each line/phrase of the poem.

Intermediate-level proficiency: Cut the poem into individual words or lines and have students work together to "re-create" the poem in the correct sequence and then illustrate the meaning.

</td>
<td>

Quadrant 4

Translation Activity
Transform content of previous activities into academic language. State the main idea of the lesson.

Examples
Beginning-level proficiency: Students write a sentence response to the poem.

Intermediate-level proficiency: Students write a paragraph response to the poem.

</td>
</tr>
</table>

TASKS ARE MORE COGNITIVELY DEMANDING

Adapted from Chamot & O'Malley, 1987; Cummins, 1981.

involve language that is contextualized; teachers can introduce academic content through hands-on instruction that supports the understanding and mastery of these concepts. Quadrant 4 highlights the most challenging language for *all* learners. The presentation of academic content without visuals or demonstrations to assist understanding is cognitively demanding. When working in Quadrant 4, teachers need to build the appropriate background knowledge for students prior to the lesson and text assignment.

Instructional Planning and Language Demands

Throughout this discussion, we have stressed that teachers must analyze the language of their content area and classrooms. Once this task is complete, they must select critical vocabulary and build student word knowledge through effective instructional techniques. Following are some important points for teachers to consider when selecting and teaching vocabulary to English learners (Gersten & Baker, 2002):

- Limit the number of new vocabulary terms introduced in a lesson; focus on seven or fewer words.
- Work on these words over longer periods of time with multiple encounters and methods in order to teach word meanings and uses at a deep level.
- Select words that convey key concepts, are of great utility, are relevant to the bulk of the content being learned, and have meaning in the lives of students.
- Use visuals, such as graphic organizers, concept and story maps, and word banks, to give students a concrete system for processing, reflecting on, and integrating word knowledge.

Echevarria and Graves (1998) describe how this type of vocabulary instruction might look and recommend intensive five-minute segments consisting of "the teacher saying the vocabulary word, writing it on the board, asking students to say it and write it, and defining the term with pictures, demonstrations, and examples familiar to students" (p. 220).

Conclusion

"The real challenge for schools today is not the growing number of [English learners], but the school's continuing need to do a far better job of delivering instruction to them in English" (Christian, 2004, p. 5). Given the changing demographics, educators must transform instruction in all classrooms. A committed teacher with a beginning understanding of English learners' family, cultural, and language backgrounds; the cultural adjustment of both native and non-native students; and the basic principles of language acquisition can make all the difference to a child's success in school.

REFERENCES

Abedi, J., & Dietel, R. (2004). Challenges in the No Child Left Behind Act for English language learners. *Phi Delta Kappan, 85*, 782–785.

Armbruster, B.B., & Anderson, T.H. (1984). Content area textbooks. In R.C. Anderson, J. Osborn, & R. Tierney (Eds.), *Learning to read in American schools: Basal readers and content texts.* Hillsdale, NJ: Erlbaum.

Azmitia, M., Cooper, C.R., Garcia, E.E., Ittel, A., Johanson, B., Lopez, E., et al. (1994). *Links between home and school among low-income Mexican American and European-American families.* Santa Cruz, CA: National Center for Research on Cultural Diversity and Second Language Learning. (ERIC Document Reproduction Service No. ED370757)

Bermúdez, A.B. (1994). *Doing our homework: How schools can engage Hispanic communities.* Culturally and Linguistically Appropriate Services, Early Childhood Research Institute. Retrieved July 18, 2004, from http://clas.uiuc.edu/fulltext/cl00 136/chapter1.html

Calderon, M. (2001). Curricula and methodologies used to teach Spanish-speaking, limited English proficient students to read English. In R.E. Slavin & M. Calderon (Eds.), *Effective programs for Latino students* (pp. 251–305). Mahwah, NJ: Erlbaum.

California Secretary of State. (1998). *Proposition 227: English language in schools. Initiative statute.* Retrieved July 5, 2005, from http://primary98. ss.ca.gov/VoterGuide/Propositions/227text.htm

Chamot, A.U., & O'Malley, J.M. (1987). The cognitive academic language learning approach: A bridge to the mainstream. *TESOL Quarterly, 21*, 238.

Christian, D. (2004). *Advancing the achievement of English language learners.* Paper presented at the Fourth Annual Claiborne Pell Education Policy Seminar. Retrieved October 31, 2004, from http://www.alliance.brown.edu/pubs/IS2000/down loads/christian.pdf

Clair, N. (2000). *Teaching educators about language: Principles, structure, and challenges* [EDO–FL–00–08]. Washington, DC: Center for Applied Linguistics. Retrieved October 29, 2004, from http://www.cal.org/resources/digest/0008teaching. html

Collier, V.P. (1987). Age and rate of acquisition of second language for academic purposes. *TESOL Quarterly, 21*, 617–641.

Collier, V.P. (1989). How long? A synthesis of research on academic achievement in a second language. *TESOL Quarterly, 23*(3), 509–531.

Collier, V.P. (1995). Acquiring a second language for school. *Directions in language and education, 1.* National Clearinghouse for Bilingual Education. Retrieved February 14, 2005, from http://www.ncela.gwu.edu/pubs/directions/04.htm

Crawford, J. (1999). *Bilingual education: History, politics, theory, and practice* (4th ed.). Los Angeles: Bilingual Educational Services.

Crawford, J. (2002). *Making sense of Census 2000.* Education Policy Studies Laboratory, Language Policy Research Unit, Arizona State University. Retrieved October 31, 2004, from http://www. asu.edu/educ/epsl/LPRU/features/article5.htm

Cummins, J. (1981). The role of primary language development in promoting educational success for language minority students. In C.F. Leyba (Ed.), *Schooling and language minority students: A theoretical framework* (pp. 3–49). Sacramento: California State University, Evaluation, Dissemination, and Assessment Center.

Echevarria, J., & Graves, A. (1998). *Sheltered content instruction: Teaching English language learners with diverse abilities.* Boston, MA: Allyn & Bacon.

Echevarria, J., Vogt, M.E., & Short, D.J. (2004). *Making content comprehensible for English learners: The SIOP Model.* Boston: Pearson.

Epstein, J.L., Coates, L., Salinas, K.C., Sanders, M.G., & Simon, B.S. (1997). *School, family, and community partnerships: Your handbook for action.* Thousand Oaks, CA: Corwin Press.

Fillmore, L.W. (2002, October). *Issues of language differences and literacy development: What do language minority students need?* Paper presented at the Spicola Forum, Texas Woman's University, Denton, TX.

Fillmore, L.W., & Snow, C.E. (2000). *What teachers need to know about language.* Washington, DC: Center for Applied Linguistics, ERIC Clearinghouse on Languages and Linguistics. Retrieved December 12, 2002, from http://www. cal.org/ericcll/teachers/teachers.pdf

Gersten, R., & Baker, S. (2002). What we know about effective instructional practices for English-language learners. *Exceptional Children, 55*, 454–471.

Gibbons, P. (1993). *Learning to learn in a second language.* Portsmouth, NH: Heinemann.

Gibbons, P. (2002). *Scaffolding language, scaffolding learning: Teaching second language learners in the mainstream classroom.* Portsmouth, NH: Heinemann.

Hamayan, E.V. (1990). Preparing mainstream class-room teachers to teach potentially English proficient students. In *Proceedings of the First Research Symposium on Limited English Proficient Student Issues*. Washington, DC: U.S. Department of Education, Office of Bilingual Education and Minority Languages Affairs. Retrieved December 12, 2002, from http://www.ncela.gwu.edu/ncbe pubs/symposia/first/preparing.htm

Harper, C., & de Jong, E. (2004). Misconceptions about teaching English-language learners. *Journal of Adolescent & Adult Literacy, 48,* 152–162.

Haynes, J. (2005). *Creating an atmosphere of acceptance.* Retrieved February 14, 2005, from http://www.everythingesl.net/inservices/nurturing.php

Huang, G. (1999). *Sociodemographic changes: Promises and problems for rural education.* Retrieved July 18, 2003, from http://kant.citl.ohiou.edu/ACCLAIM/rc/rc_sub/vlibrary/2_e_digs/Sociodemographic.htm

Igoa, C. (1995). *The inner world of the immigrant child.* Mahwah, NJ: Erlbaum.

Johnson, L.B. (1965). *The elementary and secondary school act. Public Law 89-10.* Washington, DC: U.S. Government Printing Office.

Kindler, A. (2002). *Survey of the states' limited English proficient students and available educational programs and services, 2000–2001 summary report.* Chapel Hill, NC: National Clearinghouse for English Language Acquisition and Language Instruction Educational Programs.

Klingner, J.K., & Vaughn, S. (1996). Reciprocal teaching of reading comprehension strategies for students with learning disabilities who use English as a second language. *The Elementary School Journal, 96,* 275–293.

Krashen, S. (1982). *Principles and practices in second language acquisition.* Oxford, England: Pergamon Press.

Lau v. Nichols, 414 U.S. 563 (1974).

Lightbown, P.M., & Spada, N. (1990). Focus on form and corrective feedback in communicative language teaching. *Studies in Second Language Acquisition, 12,* 429–448.

Linquanti, R. (1999). *Fostering academic success for English language learners: What do we know?* San Francisco: WestEd. Retrieved October 25, 2004, from http://www.wested.org/policy/pubs/fostering

McKeon, D. (1994). When meeting "common" standards is uncommonly difficult. *Educational Leadership, 51*(8), 45–49.

Meyer, L. (2000). Barriers to meaningful instruction for English learners. *Theory Into Practice, 39,* 228–36.

Moss, M., & Puma, M. (1995). *Prospects: The Congressionally mandated study of educational growth and opportunity. First year report on language minority and limited English proficient students.* Cambridge, MA: ABT Associates.

Muñiz-Swicegood, M. (1994). The effects of metacognitive reading strategy training on the reading performance and student reading analysis strategies of third grade bilingual students. *Bilingual Research Journal, 18,* 83–97.

National Center for Education Statistics. (1997). *1993–94 schools and staffing survey: A profile of policies and practices for limited English proficient students: Screening methods, program support, and teacher training.* Washington, DC: U.S. Department of Education, Office of Educational Research and Improvement.

No Child Left Behind Act of 2001, Pub. L. No. 107–110, 115 Stat. 1425 (2002).

Odlin, T. (1989). *Language transfer: Cross-linguistic influence in language learning.* Cambridge, MA: Cambridge University Press.

Ovando, C.J., Collier, V.P., & Combs, M.C. (2003). *Bilingual and ESL classrooms: Teaching in multicultural contexts* (3rd ed.). Boston: McGraw-Hill.

Pica, T. (1994). Research on negotiation: What does it reveal about second-language learning, conditions, processes, and outcomes? *Language Learning, 44,* 493–527.

Reed, B., & Railsback, J. (2003). *Strategies and resources for mainstream teachers of English language learners.* Portland, OR: Northwest Regional Laboratory. Retrieved October 27, 2004, from http://www.nwrel.org/request/2003may/index.html

Reid, J. (1998). "Eye" learners and "ear" learners: Identifying the language needs of international student and U.S. resident writers. In P. Byrd & J.M. Reid (Eds.), *Grammar in the composition classroom: Essays on teaching ESL for college-bound students* (pp. 3–17). Boston: Heinle & Heinle.

Romo, H. (1993). *Mexican immigrants in high schools: Meeting their needs.* Charleston, WV: ERIC Clearinghouse on Rural Education and Small Schools. (ERIC Document Reproduction Service No. ED357905) Retrieved July 18, 2003, from http://www.ericfacility.net/databases/ERIC_Digests/ed357905.html

Schwartz, W. (1996). *Immigrants and their educational attainment: Some facts and findings.* New York: ERIC Clearinghouse on Urban Education. (ERIC Document Reproduction Service No. ED402398) Retrieved July 18, 2003, from http://www.ericfacility.net/databases/ERIC_Digests/ed402398.html

Spada, N., & Lightbown, P.M. (1993). Instruction and the development of questions in L2 classrooms. *Studies in Second Language Acquisition, 15,* 205–224.

Swain, M. (1985). Communicative competence: Some roles of comprehensible input and comprehensible output in its development. In S. Gass & C. Madden (Eds.), *Input in second language acquisition* (pp. 235–253). Rowley, MA: Newbury House.

Swain, M. (1995). Three functions of output in second language learning. In G. Cook & B. Seidlhofer (Eds.), *Principle & practice in applied linguistics:* *Studies in honour of H.G. Widdowson* (pp. 125–144). Oxford, England: Oxford University Press.

Teachers of English to Speakers of Other Languages (TESOL). (2003). *ESL Standards for Pre-K–12 Students.* Retrieved July 18, 2003, from http://www.tesol.org/assoc/k12standards

U.S. Census Bureau. (2004). *Population projections.* Retrieved September 28, 2004, from http://www.census.gov

Zammit, K. (2000). The literacy demands of visual text: Working with new learning environments. *Scan, 9,* 10–14.

CURRICULUM AND PLANNING

CHAPTER 2

Differentiating Instruction for English Learners: The Four-by-Four Model

Jill Kerper Mora

nder U.S. federal law, schools must assess whether students whose native language is not English are eligible for special education services. Schools must address any challenges to access to academic content posed by students' lack of English proficiency. In addition, Title III of the No Child Left Behind (NCLB; 2002) Act requires schools to administer an annual English-proficiency assessment for students who are classified as limited English proficient. Federal and state policy initiatives and legislation are placing great demands on public schools to achieve accelerated academic growth for all students, but most particularly for English learners. NCLB requires that English learners, as a subgroup, show adequate yearly progress in achieving proficiency, as measured by standardized tests in reading and mathematics.

The dilemma for educators in selecting approaches to instruction for English learners is as it has always been: How do educators help English learners achieve gains in knowledge of literacy and academic content while students are acquiring English? Many philosophies and program models that address English learners attempt to meet this challenge. One approach is to provide content area instruction in students' native languages (the underlying premise of bilingual education). Another approach is to accept that a delay in academic content learning is inevitable while students are immersed in English instruction. The immersion approach often leads to a focus on quick acquisition of English and assumes that, if English learning takes too long and students are not able to perform academically at a level comparable to their English-proficient peers, remedial instruction or special services must be provided to catch up students in academic content (California Legislative Analyst's Office, 2004).

There is growing recognition that teaching English learners is a multifaceted and complex task. It requires that teachers draw from multiple sources of research to inform their practice (Eakle, 2003; Fitzgerald, 1994). A different approach to educating English

Supporting the Literacy Development of English Learners: Increasing Success in All Classrooms, edited by Terrell A. Young and Nancy L. Hadaway. Copyright © 2006 by the International Reading Association.

learners is needed, one that recognizes that second-language learning, literacy development, and academic content learning can occur simultaneously through a carefully structured and sequenced curriculum and an effective use of instructional strategies that are differentiated to address the learning needs of English learners. This shift requires a move away from compensatory models of instruction for English learners (Brisk, 1998; García, 1994). Effective instruction for English learners entails a rejection of the notion that English learners merely need modifications and adaptations in the forms of instruction traditionally provided for native–English-speaking students (Gersten, 1999).

The advent of more refined and sophisticated language-assessment instruments and the practice of testing entire populations of English learners annually has provided a large body of data for research into the process of second-language learning and the relationship between progress in second-language acquisition and academic achievement (De Avila, 1997). When students' acquisition of English is followed over time through repeated assessment of their developing language skills, a picture emerges of the length of time it takes for students to achieve full proficiency in the English language to be successful as they move up through the grades in school. Language assessment provides educators with data on students' growth in their overall proficiency in English, as well as their development of different components of languages, which are referred to as the subskills of the language arts. Carroll (1961) and Harris (1969) first proposed the breakdown of components of second-language proficiency into distinct language skills in recognition of both the differences and interrelationship between two forms of language, spoken and written. These linguists described the different linguistic activities and competencies associated with decoding and encoding spoken and written language to achieve more accurate measures of the acquisition of the components of second language.

An example of assessment of language skills and the type of longitudinal data now available to educators on English acquisition in school contexts is the California English Language Development Test (CELDT). CELDT was implemented on a statewide basis beginning in 2001 (California Department of Education, 2004). This comprehensive test of language subskills and overall fluency provides researchers and educators with annual language-assessment scores that can be compared from year to year for 25% of California's student population classified as English learners. Other states have adopted similar language assessment instruments to monitor the development of English proficiency among their English learner populations (Wright, 2005).

CELDT describes students' abilities in English as a second language (ESL) using a language assessment scale of 1 to 5, with level 1 representing a beginning level and level 5 representing language proficiency almost equivalent to that of students of comparable age who are native speakers of English. The CELDT results, for more than 1 million English learners over multiple years of administration, provide longitudinal data describing the length of time it takes students to acquire proficiency in the language subskills of listening, speaking, reading, and writing (California Legislative Analyst's

Office, 2004). The CELDT data provide a profile of students' growth through scores on three subtests: listening/speaking, reading, and writing. CELDT measures the subskills because it is recognized that students acquire each of these features of language at different rates and that all of the subskills of language must be mastered for students to be reclassified as proficient in the language needed to succeed in school. These disaggregated subtest scores for listening/speaking, reading, and writing are then reported as an aggregate language proficiency score. Reclassification of English learners as fluent English proficient is based on both the subtest scores and the overall proficiency score.

The cumulative CELDT data from test administrations in 2001 through 2003 indicate that the process of acquiring full proficiency in English takes an average of six years, with a range of between 3.6 and 7.4 years being typical for English learners from different native-language backgrounds. The results of this comprehensive and large-scale set of language proficiency test scores support the call for a shift in the design of programs and curriculum planning for English learners, because the premise that English proficiency is quickly and easily acquired through short-term intensive instruction has been proven to be unrealistic (Hakuta, Butler, & Witt, 2000). The CELDT data confirm that reading and writing skills development does not parallel development of oral English skills. Prior to having data that examined the separate components of language proficiency, educators often assumed that when English learners demonstrated proficiency in comprehending and speaking English, they were able to perform at an equivalent level in academic tasks that require reading and writing English. Teachers must be able to assess all four subskills of language and direct instruction appropriately to enhance English learners' proficiency in their areas of greatest need according to their developmental levels at any given point in instruction (Mora & Grisham, 2001). In addition, curriculum standards and accountability mandates now require teachers of English learners to integrate language arts and reading instruction (ELA) with English-language development (ELD) instruction (California Department of Education, 1999). Integrated ELD/ELA instruction is a shift away from isolated English-language instruction focused primarily on the development of oral vocabulary and speaking skills and toward the simultaneous teaching of language and literacy skills.

The Four-by-Four Model

The model of instruction presented in this chapter represents a comprehensive overview of curriculum design, lesson planning, and instruction for English learners. It is based on the close link between assessment and teaching. The model is titled the Four-by-Four Model (Mora, 1998) because it addresses four developmental levels of language proficiency from beginner level to advanced ESL proficiency and four components or subskills of language and literacy: listening, speaking, reading, and writing. Second-language educators traditionally assess language proficiency using a five-point scale, with level one representing a beginning rudimentary knowledge of English and five representing English proficiency equivalent to a native speaker. Educators commonly use this five-point language proficiency rating scale to describe the characteristics of students' language proficiency across grade levels and academic settings (De Avila, 1997). The subskills of the language arts are addressed as discrete features of academic-language proficiency and also in terms of each subskill's contributions to English learners' overall ability to perform grade-level appropriate academic tasks in the language arts and content areas. Within schools or classrooms, teachers establish performance standards and set evaluation criteria using scales or rubrics for determining levels of linguistic competence (O'Malley & Valdez Pierce, 1996).

Viewing students' language proficiency in terms of the four proficiency levels and the four subskills (Carroll, 1961; Harris, 1969) provides a means of understanding the diversity in student learning characteristics in classrooms where students are acquiring English and developing literacy skills in their second language. The four levels of proficiency approximately parallel the stages of language acquisition originally described by Krashen and Terrell (1983). These are beginning level (preproduction and early production), early intermediate (speech emergence), intermediate fluency, and early advanced fluency, which are described in the following section in terms of students' ability to perform language and literacy tasks at each stage of acquisition. The model enables educators to address particular instructional needs and provide differentiated instruction. Although it is most frequently applied in grades K–6, the Four-by-Four Model also provides a framework for organizing instruction around themes to address language learning and content standards in an integrated and coherent manner in particular subject areas or content classes in secondary classrooms where teachers have older English learners who require specially designed academic instruction in English (SDAIE; Chamot & O'Malley, 1994).

The purpose of the model is to provide a means of analyzing and problem solving during planning and implementation of programs and instruction. It assumes that in every school and classroom serving English learners, a diversity of developmental levels exists among students, which requires informed decision making. Teachers make decisions regarding effective and appropriate sequencing of instruction, selection of materials and learning activities, and choice of teaching strategies to maximize students' language, literacy, and academic content learning. Therefore, the Four-by-Four Model can be applied for planning and implementing standards-based instruction at any grade level because the themes and topics are selected to fit the specific grade-level curriculum.

An underlying assumption of the Four-by-Four Model is that English-language learning, academic-skills acquisition, and content knowledge are simultaneous and fully integrated in the overall curriculum for English learners. Effective teachers of English learners are aware of the relationship between linguistic and cognitive development and students' ability to perform academic tasks that make demands on their language competence. Based on assessments of the "match" between students' skills levels and the curricular content and tasks, teachers modify and adjust their language interactions with students and the linguistic demands of learning activities and tasks (Gruenewald & Pollak, 1990). Consequently, the Four-by-Four Model is applicable as a framework for designing instruction in any of the various program models for English learner education, including bilingual education and structured English immersion (SEI).

The Four-by-Four Model can also serve as a framework for preservice preparation and professional development as teachers strive to become more effective and confident in instruction and assessment with the English learners in their classrooms (Mora & Grisham, 2001).

Figure 2.1 shows the Four-by-Four Model as a 16-cell grid. This visualization of the interrelationship of language proficiency and the academic tasks involved in the language arts serves as a guide for teachers to assess students and plan individual and group instruction and learning activities effectively.

Theoretical Foundation of the Four-by-Four Model

The theoretical foundation of the Four-by-Four Model is multidisciplinary because its fundamental principles, curriculum design, and instructional strategies stem from converging sources of theory and their research bases in the areas of linguistics, language acquisition, literacy learning and instruction, and curriculum design and instructional strategies for meeting the needs of diverse learners. Each of these disciplines provides a perspective on the complexities of curriculum design and instruction for English learners as they acquire their second language, literacy skills, and content knowledge progressively and simultaneously.

Traditionally, theories guiding instruction of second-language learners are drawn from general knowledge about teaching and learning, as well as disciplines such as linguistics, psycholinguistics, and cognitive psychology. In the past several decades, interdisciplinary efforts have emerged to address the complexities and challenges of educating English learners in specialized programs as well as within the context of mainstream classrooms. The field of linguistics has contributed to teachers' understanding of language as a system and how particular features of English are taught effectively to enhance students' competence in performing academic tasks involving speaking, reading, and writing English with increasing levels of mastery. Second-language teaching approaches, which traditionally focused on foreign-language instruction, have been created, adapted, and refined to meet the different demands of English learners in the schools. A particular area of research has emerged related to multilingual literacy and how best to address the challenges English learners face in learning to read English. In addition, the increase in demands for accountability and accurate measurements of English-language development and progress in literacy achievement has

FIGURE 2.1
The Four-by-Four Model

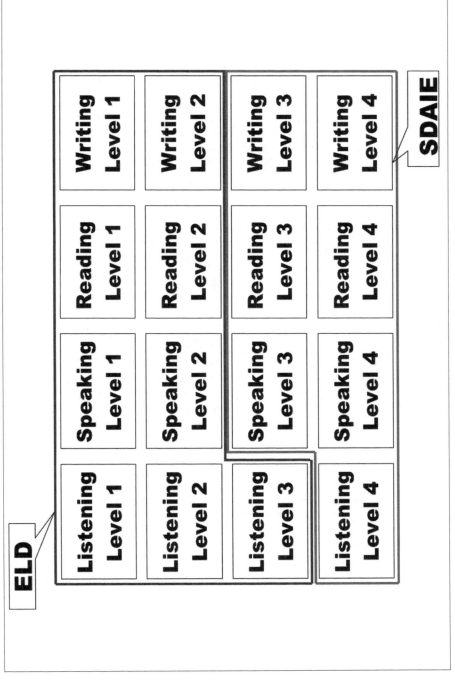

ELD

Listening Level 1	Speaking Level 1	Reading Level 1	Writing Level 1
Listening Level 2	Speaking Level 2	Reading Level 2	Writing Level 2
Listening Level 3	Speaking Level 3	Reading Level 3	Writing Level 3
Listening Level 4	Speaking Level 4	Reading Level 4	Writing Level 4

SDAIE

produced more standardized language assessment instruments that provide large-scale longitudinal data on students' progress. These data have contributed to the reexamination of theories of second-language literacy and the effectiveness of instructional approaches for teaching reading and writing to English learners (Fitzgerald, 2003). Consequently, the model for planning and implementing instruction for second-language learners links and integrates theories and research-based practices to formulate a multidisciplinary and interdisciplinary theoretical foundation.

The four areas of theory and research that support the structure, instructional design, and teaching strategies recommended in the Four-by-Four Model are (1) approaches to second-language teaching, (2) second-language literacy development, (3) language learning and cognitive development, and (4) differentiated instruction.

Approaches to Second-Language Teaching

The Four-by-Four Model is based on the rich body of approaches and strategies for teaching ESL, which has evolved over time to integrate language teaching with literacy and content teaching. Richards and Rodgers (2001) describe two major approaches utilized in modern ESL teaching: communicative language teaching (CLT) and content-based instruction (CBI). CLT is based on the premise that language is best learned when used for meaningful communication in a specific context for authentic purposes (Krashen & Terrell, 1983). The approach suggests a set of curriculum design principles and teaching/learning strategies to achieve the goal of competence in using language as a system for carrying out specific tasks through the communication process. The core principle of this approach is that teacher-designed language-learning activities require the integration of different language skills. Therefore, CLT advocates teaching oral skills along with reading and writing skills as part of authentic language-learning activities. Literacy instruction research also supports the premise that authentic tasks assist students in responding to and interpreting text in ways that both utilize and build on their existing knowledge of language as a system (Hiebert, 1994).

CBI as an approach to second-language teaching flows logically from the theoretical base and implementation of the communicative approach. The basic assumption underlying CBI is that in many academic contexts, the content of instruction is not the language per se (vocabulary, grammar, language functions, etc.); rather, the content is derived from the subject matter of the school curriculum (history, science, etc.). This is the situation for the majority of English learners who are required to learn English as they are also being taught grade-level subjects and are expected to meet content standards (California Legislative Analyst's Office, 2004; Gibbons, 2003).

These approaches to second-language teaching support the use of instructional strategies that are designed to make the language and content of instruction meaningful to English learners. Krashen and Terrell (1983) posit the theory of *comprehensible input*, which states that students must be able to connect concepts and ideas to an unknown language in order to learn the language. Without basic comprehension of the input, which includes both the language of instruction and the academic content, students perceive the unfamiliar second language only as "noise." Krashen and Terrell (1983) derived a formula (i + 1) to describe the ideal input for language acquisition. The input for the English learner should contain grammatical structures and vocabulary one "stage" or level above the student's current level of productive language ability. Language that is too grammatically complex or that contains too many unknown vocabulary words will not be comprehensible to the English learner. Very little learning of vocabulary and language structure takes place in classrooms where teachers do not modify instruction to provide English learners with comprehensible input. Consequently, effective teachers of second-language learners choose texts and instructional materials that are controlled for difficulty level and linguistic complexity so that they are simultaneously comprehensible and challenging. Teachers also modify their classroom language when presenting new concepts and skills and in their interactions with students while giving directions or facilitating completion of classroom assignments (Gruenewald & Pollak, 1990). These modifications and adjustments ensure that English learners receive comprehensible input so that their language learning and their grasp of academic content are enhanced concurrently.

English learners can move from their current level of competence by understanding linguistic input that is one level more complex and demanding than their current level. This process for ensuring comprehensibility in instructing English learners, using various strategies and approaches for lesson presentation and delivery, teacher/student interaction, and modification of texts and other instructional materials is called scaffolding (Echevarria & Graves, 1998; Gibbons, 2002; Tomlinson, 2005).

Second-Language Literacy Development

A second body of emerging research that informs the Four-by-Four Model is second-language literacy development (Bernhardt, 1991; Fitzgerald, 1994, 2003; García, 1994; Mora, 2001). Research in second-language reading supports the conclusion that students who are learning to read in a language in which they are not yet proficient face a number of learning challenges that native speakers do not. Lenters (2004) identifies a number of unique challenges facing second-language readers, including the dissimilarity of sound–symbol relationships in the readers' native language and in English, oral-vocabulary constraints, limitations due to background knowledge, and difficulties with text structure. Students who learn to read initially in English as a second language may be unfamiliar with the English sound system and may encounter features of English phonology that are different or do not exist in the native language (Freeman & Freeman, 2004). Moreover, English learners follow a different progression through the component skills of literacy learning. The results of standardized language assessments (De Avila, 1997) and state-mandated English-language development tests (California Legislative

Analyst's Report, 2004) confirm that although English learners may make rapid gains in listening and speaking abilities, they may lag in their development of reading and writing proficiency as compared to their native English-speaking or English-proficient peers. Teachers must keep in mind the fact that native English-speaking students come to the task of reading English with a full repertoire of linguistic skills as compared to their peers, whereas English learners are in the process of acquiring basic vocabulary, syntax and grammar, and phonological awareness of the sound system of English. The research in second-language literacy acquisition supports the need for careful attention to aspects of teaching and learning reading and writing skills that take into account English learners' developmental levels in oral-language skills, vocabulary, and grammar. These modifications and adjustments to instruction for students acquiring English as a second language are termed "sheltered instruction" (Krashen, 1991).

Language Learning and Cognitive Development

A third area of research that supports the Four-by-Four Model is language learning and cognitive development. Selinker (1992) examined the developing language of second-language learners as they progressively acquire higher levels of competence in using complex grammatical forms and compound and complex sentence structures. The developing but imperfect English that second-language learners produce is called "interlanguage." Several researchers address the issue of how students' interlanguage matches the linguistic and cognitive demands of academic tasks, especially those involving reading difficult texts and completing complex and abstract writing assignments (Chamot & O'Malley, 1994; Cummins, 2000; Gibbons, 2002). Theories surrounding the relationship between growth in knowledge and linguistic abilities provide teachers a perspective on whether learning difficulties are due to students' lack of language proficiency or their limited knowledge of vocabulary and concepts associated with a particular subject area or topic. Selection of appropriate teaching strategies depends on an accurate determination of whether students need targeted language instruction or learning activities focused on the subject matter.

Cummins (2000) constructs a theoretical framework to describe the interaction between the cognitive and contextual demands of learning tasks and their linguistic complexity. Cummins presents a continuum of cognitive difficulty for students with limited English proficiency as they progress through the grades and academic tasks become increasingly challenging in relationship to their linguistic resources. Research supports the premise that second-language vocabulary learning and overall language acquisition take place most efficiently when teachers provide meaningful context and communicative activities around a scenario and when learners have repeated exposure to vocabulary through instruction and group-based peer interaction (Nation & Newton, 1997; Oller, 1983). Chamot and O'Malley (1994) recommend that teachers of English learners analyze the curriculum with the students' English proficiency level in mind to determine the major concepts and relationships that are addressed, as well as the skills and processes students will employ to reach the learning objectives. The analysis includes determining the prerequisite knowledge students need to understand the subject matter.

Differentiated Instruction

The instructional design theory and practice called *differentiated instruction* (Gregory & Chapman, 2002; Heacox, 2002; Tomlinson, 2005) also supports the Four-by-Four Model. Heacox (2002) defines differentiated instruction as changing the pace, level, or kind of instruction teachers provide in response to individual learners' needs, styles, and interests. It is a way of thinking about teaching and learning based on best practices in education as well as methods for diagnosing students' learning needs and a collection of strategies to address and manage the variety of learning styles in the classroom. Second-language learning classrooms are invariably diverse and complex because English learners are at different points in their linguistic and cognitive development. Differentiated instruction is based on principles of curriculum design and used in classrooms with learners who have a diverse range of aptitudes, learning styles, levels of prior knowledge of content, and skills. Differentiated instruction emphasizes ongoing assessment as a basis for planning appropriate learning tasks for students.

The process of differentiating instruction involves determining the level of difficulty of the academic task, based on a number of factors. Learning tasks are simple or complex, concrete or abstract, single or multifaceted, more structured or less, closed or open-ended, and have differences in pacing of study and thought (Tomlinson, 2005). Considering these factors in relation to learners' levels of language proficiency allows for effective instructional planning that is tiered so as to allow students to experience success while being challenged to achieve higher levels of language mastery and content knowledge.

Guiding Principles of the Four-by-Four Model

The four guiding principles of the Four-by-Four Model are derived from a synthesis of the relevant theory and research.

1. English learners gain the subskills of language acquisition and literacy skills in a natural order. Listening and speaking (aural–oral) skills develop rapidly at the lower levels of proficiency, while reading and writing (literacy) abilities develop more gradually. It is not until the English learner reaches proficiency level 4 (see the following section, "Structure of the Four-by-Four Model") that literacy skills converge with growth in listening and speaking. Therefore, effective instruction integrates language subskills while focusing on the particular subskill that students need to master in order to progress to the next level of language proficiency.

2. As English learners progress, teachers shift the focus of instruction and instructional strategies from ELD to SDAIE. In ELD instruction, the emphasis is on language learning, vocabulary development, and listening and speaking tasks, with the academic content as the vehicle. SDAIE emphasizes content learning and literacy skills development through modifications in instructional strategies and the cognitive and linguistic demands of the task. These two instructional approaches may be employed concurrently in classrooms with a diversity of levels of English proficiency.

3. Thematic instruction provides English learners with a meaningful context for learning, as well as multiple exposures to specific concepts and their linguistic labels and descriptors. The Four-by-Four Model utilizes content area themes. Thematic instruction enhances vocabulary development. Vocabulary and concept learning occur through an organized schema as English learners link words and phrases with ideas and concepts. Vocabulary and concept learning progress simultaneously from whole to part, from concrete to abstract, and from simple to complex. Vocabulary is learned effectively and efficiently within a context based on a schematic structure.

4. In terms of the cognitive and linguistic demands of learning activities and tasks, curriculum and classroom instruction are most effective for English learners when they are provided differentiated instruction. The cognitive demands of academic instruction and learning tasks progress from concrete to abstract and from simple to complex. Teachers introduce and repeat tasks within a coherent context around a topic or theme in order to tap students' prior knowledge and build new conceptual schema. Explicit teaching of text structures enhances comprehension and provides English learners with frameworks and models to follow during reading and writing activities.

Teachers control the linguistic demands of tasks, including their syntactic and grammatical complexity and their proximity to familiar oral-language patterns. Student engagement in instruction deepens as learning tasks gradually progress from passive and receptive to active, productive participation (e.g., listening precedes speaking, reading precedes writing).

Structure of the Four-by-Four Model

The Four-by-Four Model is a matrix of four levels of developing second-language proficiency and four language development–literacy skills (listening, speaking, reading, and writing). (See Figure 2.1 on page 29.)

Student Activities

The Four-by-Four Model provides a framework for planning whole-class, small-group, and individual learning tasks and activities. Teachers group students either heterogeneously across language levels or by language level in order to address their particular needs for skills development. Students work on classroom activities focused around a "centerpiece" activity; for example, groups of students may contribute to making a mural about the theme or may write and produce a class play or other production. The lesson examples that follow, centered on the theme of oceans, illustrate how the Four-by-Four Model is applied to each language level and subskill.

Ongoing Assessment

Appropriate and effective instruction is based on frequent and ongoing assessment, including informal and formal assessment of students' progress in overall language proficiency and in the four language subskills. Assessments are based on criteria for determining students' linguistic level in listening and speaking, as well as reading inventories and writing rubrics (Helman, 2005). By assessing and analyzing English learners' learning characteristics and levels of achievement, teachers can plan thematic units with tiered teaching and learning activities that can be implemented through whole-class and small-group instruction as well as individual independent tasks and assignments. By assessing students' abilities to engage meaningfully and productively in integrated language arts activities, teachers can successfully plan thematic units and lesson presentations for each phase of students' development. Teachers place students at the appropriate language level based on both formal and informal assessments of language proficiency. (See O'Malley & Valdez Pierce, 1996, for descriptions of assessment procedures and criteria, including rubrics for scoring features of academic-language proficiency.)

Teachers who implement the Four-by-Four Model use multiple sources of data to determine students' growth in English-language proficiency, reading and writing skills, and knowledge of the academic content. Assessments focus on students' ability to use language in an integrated and holistic fashion as teachers observe students' language use in oral presentation, reading a challenging passage from a storybook or textbook, or writing a composition.

Teachers also use informal reading inventories and running records to analyze students' coordination of language-cueing systems during oral reading (Davenport, 2002). Assessments that use writing samples and a rubric of component language and composition skills are an excellent source of information about English learners' developing writing (Ferris & Hedgecock, 1998; Jacobs, Zingraf, Wormuth, Hartfiel, & Hughey, 1981).

Language Level 1

English learners with a level-1 proficiency are beginners. They are in the preproduction or early production stage of language development. In listening skills, they are learning to distinguish global meaning in order to grasp the gist of spoken language. These students are beginning to distinguish words from within a stream of speech and connect words and phrases to concepts and ideas. Their English-speaking skills are rudimentary. They are beginning to formulate sentences but may respond to questions with one-word or two-word sentences and phrases because their knowledge of English grammar and sentence structure is emerging. Their reading and writing skills are not yet developed, although these students may recognize and spell high-frequency words and familiar vocabulary words in print and may be able to decode simple texts.

Instruction for level-1 learners focuses on developing listening and sentence-construction skills for communication purposes. Teachers may give explicit instruction in distinguishing words in context, anticipating information, following simple directions, and building a basic listening vocabulary for a content theme. For example, in a thematic unit on oceans, teachers plan learning activities that require level-1 learners to pick out "ocean" words in a description of a seashore. As the description is read aloud at a normal pace, students raise their hands when they hear certain vocabulary words. Students then construct sentences to describe pictures of the seashore scene as the teacher writes the sentences on the board beside each picture. Next, students read a paraphrased passage of the description of the seashore and complete a fill-in-the-blanks worksheet or modified cloze procedure (Gibbons, 2002) using the "ocean" words they have seen in the reading passage and on the board.

Language Level 2

Level-2 learners are able to understand the main idea of concrete, context-related, and practical oral language. They can formulate basic sentences, although they must apply conscious effort to do so. They have an ample vocabulary and can use some idiomatic expressions but have difficulty talking about more complex and abstract academic topics. Level-2 learners are developing decoding skills, based primarily on familiarity with common phonetic spelling patterns and high-frequency words. Therefore, they are able to read simplified texts with comprehension, provided they have some background knowledge of the topic and do not encounter too many unfamiliar vocabulary words and complex grammatical forms. Level-2 learners can write simple sentences to create a short narrative or discourse for practical purposes, following a format or structure as a framework for their ideas.

In relation to listening, instruction for level-2 learners focuses on refining their skills to hear and understand vocabulary related to specific content areas and to understand main ideas. They can follow a series of oral directions to complete a task. They also begin to focus attention on discriminating sounds through oral-language development activities with minimal sound pairs, rhymes, songs, and other patterned forms of speech, which develop their phonemic awareness and word-discrimination skills.

These students benefit from structured speaking activities in which they formulate sentences to express ideas. These activities include retelling and paraphrasing short narratives and role-playing. Teachers pay special attention during instruction to defining and using idiomatic expressions, which are more complex because they have unusual grammatical patterns or unusual uses of vocabulary. Reading activities for level-2 learners focus on decoding and comprehending the meaning of simplified text through guided and shared reading activities (McLaughlin & Allen, 2002; Schifini, 1994). Writing activities support students to produce short, structured narratives and to work with sentence structure (Dewbury, 1994). Instructional activities include sentence transformation, in which students complete or change sentences to different grammatical forms (e.g., statements to questions, positives to negatives), and spelling of familiar vocabulary words. These learning tasks provide level-2 learners with opportunities to improve their control of English grammar and syntax in oral and written forms.

In a unit on oceans, for example, level-2 learners listen to a short narrative about waves and ocean tides. The teacher guides students in paraphrasing the narrative by writing sentences on sentence strips and having students order them as they appeared in the narrative. The students define words by using their antonyms (e.g., *high/low*, *fast/slow*, *deep/shallow*) and completing sentences using the antonyms. Students then read a longer passage about the topic. They write a one-paragraph report, in small groups or on their own, about waves and tides, using sentences from the sentence strips posted on the board.

Language Level 3

Level-3 learners have an intermediate level of English proficiency. They have developed basic communication skills and have an adequate command of functional and concrete vocabulary. Their point of growth in proficiency is in solidifying and increasing the complexity of their spoken language and learning academic language in order to perform more difficult class work and literacy assignments.

In listening, their challenge is to capture the main idea and details of the topic and to expand their understanding of content area vocabulary. They can construct sentences to express their ideas but do not yet control a repertoire of content-related vocabulary. Their spoken language contains frequent grammatical and syntactical errors, involving verb tense, complex sentence construction, and idiomatic expressions. Consequently, these learners need opportunities to practice oral expression by sharing their experiences and discussing and explaining concepts related to content. At this point, teachers correct speech patterns and pronunciation when consistent errors are present that may become permanent features of students' second language (Selinker, 1992).

Reading as a receptive language skill is the focus of instruction for level-3 learners. Extensive reading of content area and literary texts that are appropriately leveled for linguistic complexity and conceptual load is valuable for expanding vocabulary and content knowledge. Students benefit from critical reading activities and response-to-reading activities that allow them to talk about the important ideas and their reactions. An emphasis on text structures is also valuable, especially through learning tasks that focus on using patterns and structures interactively in both reading and writing. Explicit teaching of comprehension strategies is also recommended (Chamot & O'Malley, 1994; Stahl, 2004). Writing tasks for level-3 learners include basic composition and utilitarian writing, such as letters, forms, and news stories.

In the thematic unit on oceans, level-3 learners produce a letter to the editor of the local newspaper, asking the public to preserve the ecology of oceans. The teacher brainstorms with students to generate a list of do's and don'ts that describe ways to take care of the oceans. In groups, students follow a standard persuasive-letter format. They use two or three points from the brainstorm list to convince readers to preserve ocean ecology. One group member will then read each letter and respond to feedback from classmates. Next, students revise the letters and post them on the bulletin board. Students then vote to decide which letter to send to the newspaper for publication.

Language Level 4

Level-4 learners are at the early advanced stage of English proficiency. Because of their increased fluency, they are able to perform most ordinary class work but still require modifications and support in instruction to understand abstract and complex language and concepts. They may still be challenged by grade-level reading material and their writing skills are not fully developed. Consequently, literacy skills are the focus of instruction for students at level 4.

In listening and speaking, level-4 students are learning to take notes and outline information from presentations and lectures by selecting relevant facts and information. They are able to recognize unfamiliar vocabulary and capture oral definitions and explanations of more sophisticated content area terms. In speaking, they can make oral presentations and reports and contribute ideas to group discussions. They are able to explain known concepts and ideas using grammatically correct sentences with fewer errors in sentence structure, verb tenses, and phraseology, although their sentences may lack complexity. In their reading and writing, which are fairly balanced in time and focus, level-4 learners are able to perform critical thinking and analytical tasks (such as identifying characters, setting, and plot in literature). They are able to conduct basic research using multiple, but limited, resources from the class and school library and write reports and essays based on a synthesis of information, using a model or structured format.

In a thematic unit on oceans, level-4 learners listen to and summarize a description of the ecology of a tide pool. In groups they create a schematic drawing of the various factors in the environment of the tide pool and its plants and animals. Each group reads from the textbook or other resource materials about a particular tide-pool plant or animal. As a group, students show and explain to the class the schematic drawings that they select from among the ones completed by the group members. Following the presentations, students write two-to-three-paragraph reports that are later posted beside the class mural of the ecology and flora and fauna of the tide pool.

Conclusion

The Four-by-Four Model of differentiated instruction for English learners provides a framework for conceptualizing, managing, and assessing the complexities of instruction for students with diverse levels of language proficiency, literacy skills, and content area knowledge. Language is the foundation for learning, and students who are developing their knowledge in a second language need instruction that is targeted to their specific needs and challenges. Teachers must enhance learning opportunities for all students within the context of the linguistically and culturally diverse classroom.

REFERENCES

Bernhardt, E.B. (1991). *Reading development in a second language*. Norwood, NJ: Ablex.

Brisk, M.E. (1998). *Bilingual education: From compensatory to quality schooling*. Mahwah, NJ: Erlbaum.

California Department of Education. (1999). *English-language development standards for California public schools*. Sacramento: Author.

California Department of Education. (2004). *Overview of the California English Language Development Test*. Sacramento: Author. Retrieved July 25, 2005, from http://www.cde.ca.gov/ta/tg/sa/celdtinfo1104.asp

California Legislative Analyst's Office. (2004). *A look at the progress of English learner students*. Sacramento: Author. Retrieved October 12, 2004, from http://www.lao.ca.gov/2004/english_learners/021204_english_learners.htm

Carroll, J.B. (1961). Fundamental considerations in testing for English language proficiency of foreign students. In *Testing the English proficiency of foreign students* (pp. 31–40). Washington, DC: Center for Applied Linguistics.

Chamot, A.U., & O'Malley, J.M. (1994). *The CALLA handbook: Implementing the cognitive academic language learning approach*. Reading, MA: Addison-Wesley.

Cummins, J. (2000). *Language, power and pedagogy: Bilingual children in the crossfire*. Clevedon, England: Multilingual Matters.

Davenport, M.R. (2002). *Miscues, not mistakes: Reading assessment in the classroom*. Portsmouth, NH: Heinemann.

De Avila, E. (1997, November). Setting expected gains for non and limited English proficient students. *NCBE resource collection series No. 8*. Arlington, VA: National Clearinghouse for Bilingual Education.

Dewbury, A. (1994). *First Steps: Writing resource book of the Education Department of Western Australia*. Portsmouth, NH: Heinemann.

Eakle, A.J. (2003). A content analysis of second-language research in *The Reading Teacher* and *Language Arts*, 1990–2001. *The Reading Teacher, 56*, 828–836.

Echevarria, J., & Graves, A. (1998). *Sheltered content instruction: Teaching English-language learners with diverse abilities*. Boston: Allyn & Bacon.

Ferris, D., & Hedgecock, J.S. (1998). *Teaching ESL composition: Purpose, process, and practice*. Mahwah, NJ: Erlbaum.

Freeman, D.E., & Freeman, Y.S. (2004). *Essential linguistics: What you need to know to teach reading, ESL, spelling, phonics and grammar*. Portsmouth, NH: Heinemann.

Fitzgerald, J. (1994). Crossing boundaries: What do second-language-learning theories say to reading and writing teachers of English-as-a-second-language learners? *Reading Horizons, 34*, 339–355.

Fitzgerald, J. (2003). Multilingual reading theory. *Reading Research Quarterly, 38*, 118–122.

García, E.E. (1994). Linguistically and culturally diverse children: Effective instructional practices and related policy issues. In H.C. Waxman, J. Walker de Félix, J.E. Anderson, & H.P. Baptiste (Eds.), *Students at risk in at-risk schools: Improving environments for learning* (pp. 65–86). Newbury Park, CA: Corwin Press.

Gersten, R. (1999). The changing face of bilingual education. *Educational Leadership, 56*(7), 41–45.

Gibbons, P. (2002). *Scaffolding language, scaffolding learning: Teaching second language learners in the mainstream classroom*. Portsmouth, NH: Heinemann.

Gibbons, P. (2003). Mediating language learning: Teacher interactions with ESL students in a content-based classroom. *TESOL Quarterly, 37*, 247–273.

Gregory, G.H., & Chapman, C. (2002). *Differentiated instructional strategies: One size doesn't fit all*. Thousand Oaks, CA: Corwin Press.

Gruenewald, L.J., & Pollak, S.A. (1990). *Language interaction in curriculum and instruction: What the classroom teacher needs to know* (2nd ed.). Austin, TX: Pro-ED.

Hakuta, K., Butler, Y.G., & Witt, D. (2000, January). *How long does it take learners to attain English proficiency?* University of California Linguistic Minority Research Institute Policy 2000-1.

Harris, D.P. (1969). *Testing English as a second language*. New York: McGraw-Hill.

Heacox, D. (2002). *Differentiating instruction in the regular classroom*. Minneapolis, MN: Free Spirit.

Helman, L.A. (2005). Using literacy assessment results to improve teaching for English-language learners. *The Reading Teacher, 58*, 668–677.

Hiebert, E.H. (1994). Becoming literate through authentic tasks: Evidence and adaptations. In R.B. Ruddell, M.R. Ruddell, & H. Singer (Eds.), *Theoretical models and processes of reading* (pp. 391–413). Newark, DE: International Reading Association.

Jacobs, H.L., Zingraf, S.A., Wormuth, D.R., Hartfiel, V.F., & Hughey, J.B. (1981). *Testing ESL composition: A practical approach*. Rowley, MA: Newbury House.

Krashen, S.D. (1991). Sheltered subject matter teaching. In J. Oller (Ed.), *Methods that work* (pp. 143–148). Boston: Heinle & Heinle.

Krashen, S.D., & Terrell, T.D. (1983). *The natural approach: Language acquisition in the classroom*. Hayward, CA: Alemany Press.

Lenters, K. (2004). No half measures: Reading instruction for young second-language learners. *The Reading Teacher, 58*, 328–336.

McLaughlin, M., & Allen, M.B. (2002). *Guided comprehension: A teaching model for grades 3–8*. Newark, DE: International Reading Association.

Mora, J.K. (1998). *PLC 914 course reader: English language development/SDAIE*. San Diego, CA: San Diego State University Montezuma Publishing.

Mora, J.K. (2001). Effective instructional practices and assessment for literacy and biliteracy development. In S.R. Hurley & J.V. Tinajero (Eds.), *Literacy assessment of second language learners* (pp. 149–166). Boston: Allyn & Bacon.

Mora, J.K., & Grisham, D.L. (2001). !What deliches tortillas! Preparing teachers for literacy instruction in linguistically diverse classrooms. *Teacher Education Quarterly, 28*(4), 51–70.

Nation, P., & Newton, J. (1997). Teaching vocabulary. In J. Coady & T. Huckin (Eds.), *Second language vocabulary acquisition* (pp. 238–254). Cambridge, England: Cambridge University Press.

No Child Left Behind Act of 2001, Pub. L. No. 107–110, 115 Stat. 1425 (2002).

Oller, J.W. (1983). Some working ideas for language teaching. In J.W. Oller & P.A. Richard-Amato (Eds.), *Methods that work: A smorgasbord of ideas for language teachers* (pp. 3–19). Rowley, MA: Newbury House.

O'Malley, J.M., & Valdez Pierce, L. (1996). *Authentic assessment for English language learners*. Reading, MA: Addison-Wesley.

Richards, J.C., & Rodgers, T.S. (2001). *Approaches and methods in language teaching* (2nd ed.). Cambridge, England: Cambridge University Press.

Schifini, A. (1994). Language, literacy, and content instruction: Strategies for teachers. In K. Spangenberg-Urbschat & R. Pritchard (Eds.), *Kids come in all languages: Reading instruction for ESL students* (pp. 158–179). Newark, DE: International Reading Association.

Selinker, L. (1992). *Rediscovering interlanguage*. New York: Longman.

Stahl, K.A.D. (2004). Proof, practice, and promise: Comprehension strategy instruction in the primary grades. *The Reading Teacher, 57*, 598–609.

Tomlinson, C.A. (2005). *How to differentiate instruction in mixed-ability classrooms* (2nd ed.). Upper Saddle River, NJ: Pearson/Merrill/Prentice Hall.

Wright, W.E. (2005). *Evolution of federal policy and implications of No Child Left Behind for language minority students*. Tempe: Education Policy Studies Laboratory, Arizona State University.

CHAPTER 3

Supporting English Learners: Developing Academic Language in the Content Area Classroom

Janice Pilgreen

I t is a challenging task to meet the needs of all students. After all, learners are so diverse. Not only do they come to the classroom with varying degrees of educational experience, different cultural perspectives, and a broad continuum of developmental abilities, but they also arrive with an entity that is difficult to conceptualize and to assess adequately: *language*.

Language is what enables students to communicate, language is what makes collaboration possible, and using language is a way of transmitting and negotiating knowledge. But language is precisely the barrier that English learners face when they sit in the classroom.

I have been a classroom teacher for more than 22 years, and for most of those years, I was an English as a second language (ESL) teacher. I cannot tell you how many community members, social acquaintances, and even colleagues and administrators from my own school and district offered words of sympathy to me as they watched me interact with classroom after classroom of students who came from more than 53 language groups. Lucky they were, they thought, that they didn't have to work with "those kids."

Yet when we think about what English learners bring to the table, it is quite amazing. Many of them have had interesting and varied experiences in other countries. Some, as young as they are, have experienced the trauma of war, hunger, and family crisis. Most of them have developed a reservoir of knowledge that is unlike what children in the United States have developed—and this can even include literacy in multiple languages other than English.

Nieto (2004) remarks that linguistic diversity can be a "great asset to learning" (p. 216), noting that teachers' attitudes toward and expectations of English learners can have a huge impact, both positively and negatively, on student achievement. To help English learners in the context of the content area classroom, teachers must recognize the challenges these learners face and use methods that give them the greatest access to the core curriculum. Teachers need to build on what students know—and to see them as capable, contributing members of the school community.

Goals for English Learners

A primary goal for English learners is to gain enough English proficiency to carry out school tasks about as well as their fluent English-speaking peers (Peregoy & Boyle, 2005). In kindergarten and first grade, "the linguistic performance gap" between English learners and their English-speaking contemporaries is relatively small (Peregoy & Boyle, 2005, p. 62). But in the later grades, school presents increased challenges for English learners because they have more to achieve and less time in which to achieve it. Also, English learners are typically competing with fluent English speakers in the classroom. Cummins and Schecter (2003) point out that "English as a first language speakers are not standing still waiting for ESL students to catch up. Every year their literacy skills are expanding and, thus, ESL students must catch up with a moving target" (p. 8).

There is a discrepancy, too, between the challenges confronting an English learner who is beginning first grade and one who is entering fifth. When students are in the early stages of language acquisition, their main objective is to understand their teachers and peers and to make themselves understood. Much of the language they use is for social purposes, such as interacting on the playground (Peregoy & Boyle, 2005). However, especially as they proceed through the upper grades, English learners are asked to engage in higher level thinking and problem solving; they have to work diligently to acquire the formal-language competence that they need for more advanced instruction in the content areas.

English learners must maneuver their way through complex social and cognitive interactions in English, not only orally, but also in reading and writing (Peregoy & Boyle, 2005). As Cummins (1980) has shown, in order to become fully proficient, English learners need to progress beyond the level of basic interpersonal communication skills (BICS) to achieve ever-deepening levels of cognitive academic-language proficiency (CALP).

This is a distinction that is sometimes difficult to assess, particularly when students are highly verbal and seem more proficient in the target language than they really are. English learners may speak fluently (and frequently!) and appear to have a native-like command of oral language, but still be unable to read and write at grade level. Teachers must "be aware of the differences between conversational fluency and academic language proficiency," so that they can "continue to provide the academic support that ESL students may need" (Cummins & Schecter, 2003, p. 8).

Educators need a repertoire of techniques to support English learners in the goal of full English-language and literacy development—development that is at the same level of proficiency as that of fluent English-speaking peers. If students are to become capable of using both oral and written language in formal ways for academic purposes, their teachers must believe and expect that they can meet this aim and "provide social and academic support at every step along the way" (Peregoy & Boyle, 2005, p. 64). The techniques described in the rest of this chapter are part of such a repertoire and are especially appropriate for grades 3–12.

Explicit Development of Academic Language

A separate vocabulary is used by people who have been formally educated, and we sometimes refer to this category of words as "the language of school." Most educated people take for granted that such language just develops naturally. In fact, the concepts and word meanings may well be learned inductively—but in a very specific context: school.

I am speaking of such words as *title*, *chapter*, *paragraph*, *table*, *caption*, and *excerpt* and of such concepts as *note-taking*, *summarizing*, *tracing events*, *outlining*, and *comparing and contrasting*, to name only a few. Such terms constitute the language of school, or what is referred to as *academic language*.

Many teachers who work with English learners are familiar with Krashen's (1995) seminal work on comprehensible input. (See "Approaches to Second-Language Teaching" in chapter 2.) Educators first need to make their messages understandable to English learners. Only when they understand the instruction do English learners have access to what is being taught. As Krashen maintains, it is incumbent upon teachers to make lessons clear and fully comprehensible for English learners, regardless of students' level of competence in English.

Making content comprehensible is best done by providing linguistic and nonlinguistic support. Some of the linguistic aspects of simplified input that appear to be effective for promoting comprehension are slower speech rates, clear articulation, less slang, fewer idioms, and a greater use of high-frequency vocabulary (Krashen, 1995). Nonlinguistic elements include objects, visuals, videos, storyboarding, movement, role-plays, and collaborative learning (Cary, 2000).

However, English learners also need to learn the academic terms that accompany the concepts they are learning, for this is part of the knowledge that propels them over the BICS hurdle and lands them solidly in the world of CALP. Fortunately, this means that the instruction provided for the other students in classrooms does not have to be qualitatively different. Instead, teachers can use an explicit approach to teach academic concepts and their related terms that is as beneficial for fluent English-speaking students as it is for English learners.

A Confession

I did a disservice to my English learners when I was teaching developmental reading classes. I certainly demonstrated many vocabulary, comprehension, and metacognitive strategies that I'm sure they used throughout each day at school—and that they may have even transferred to higher grade-level applications as their schooling continued—but I made a huge mistake.

I did not explicitly teach the academic language that English learners need to internalize in order to manage the wide variety of reading tasks related to previewing text, understanding organizational structures, and highlighting specific chunks of text. For example, when talking about the "little title" under the "big title," I didn't mention the word *subtitle*. I frequently moved my body and arms in a sideways position as I referred to "the slanted letters" of a text (*italicized print*) or used my forefinger to punctuate "the dark letters" (*boldface print*). I never talked about *illustrations* either, only "the pictures."

In trying to make the concepts easy enough, to use language that was comprehensible, I failed to introduce many technical terms—labels that are critical for negotiating the academic pathways of school. What I did not recognize then is that the explicit teaching of academic language is crucial; students do not just "'pick it up' along the way" (Alvermann & Phelps, 2005, p. 9).

How to Start: Introducing Academic Language

In California I frequently work with teachers at various schools to provide them with practical, hands-on literacy strategies to use in their language arts and content area classes. I also direct a literacy center at the University of La Verne, where graduate-level reading-specialist candidates (who are typically full-time teachers) tutor students in grades 1 through 12. Many of these students are English learners who face challenges when reading grade-level texts. The tutors help English learners approach expository reading selections that at first may appear quite intimidating. Usually, the very first step a tutor takes is to analyze the kinds of terms that students need to know in order to maneuver through and talk about texts. A tutor typically starts with a list of terms like those presented in the first column of Table 3.1.

Many of the tutors look at the list, shrug, and say "of course" they use these vocabulary words on a daily basis in their own classrooms. But when I ask if there are any terms that they might be hard-pressed to define if students were to ask, the tutors usually admit that at least some of their responses might be a bit vague. This is primarily because it is rare for people to stop to consider definitions of terms that they have used most of their lives. The words in Table 3.1 represent the kind of school talk that educators engage in regularly. But these words are not part of the listening or speaking (not to mention the reading and writing) vocabulary of many students.

TABLE 3.1
Academic Terms for Book Parts and Corresponding Definitions

Academic Term	Definition
author index	a list of the authors referred to in a book or other text
bibliography	a list of books, articles, etc. (containing author and publisher information) referred to in a book, article, or chapter
boldface type	type that is printed in a thick, black style, or "face"
caption	a title or brief illustration appended to an illustration
chapter	a main division of a book or text
chart	a sheet of information in the form of a table, graph, or diagram
column	a vertical division of a page, chart, etc., containing a sequence of figures or words
conclusion	a summing up of any kind of text material
diagram	a drawing showing the general scheme or outline of an object and its parts; may also indicate processes related to an object or phenomenon
excerpt	a short extract from a book, text, article, motion picture, piece of music, etc.
figure	a diagram or other illustrative drawing
font size	a set of type of one size; can be any style or "face"
font/print	a set of type of one style or "face"
glossary	an alphabetical list of terms, with definitions, relating to a specific subject or text, typically placed at the end of a book
graph (line, bar)	a diagram showing the relationship, usually between two variables, each measured along one of a pair of axes
graph (pie)	a circular diagram, typically showing the relationships among specific variables
handbook	a short manual or guidebook
illustration/picture	a painting, drawing, photograph, cartoon, etc., that illustrates a book, magazine article, text, etc.
indentation	space preceding a line of type, so that the type begins farther from the margin than other lines; used to mark a new paragraph
index	an alphabetical list of names, subjects, etc., with references, typically placed at the end of a book
introduction	an explanatory section at the beginning of a book, text, etc.
italicized type	type that is printed in a style, or "face," that has sloping letters (like early Italian writing)
map	typically a flat representation of the earth's surface, or part of it, showing physical features, cities, etc.
page	a leaf of a book, periodical, etc.; what is written or printed on this
paragraph	a distinct section of a piece of writing, typically beginning on a new indented line; contains one primary (main) idea and other related ideas
passage	an extract from a book or other text piece; may consist of one or more paragraphs

(continued)

TABLE 3.1
Academic Terms for Book Parts and Corresponding Definitions *(continued)*

Academic Term	Definition
preface	an introduction to a book, stating its subject, scope, etc.; the preliminary part of a speech
quotation	a passage or remark which represents a specific statement (or part of a statement) by another person
section	a subdivision of a book, article, text, etc.
selection	may be used interchangeably with passage when used to indicate an extract; or a complete piece of text that has been chosen as the topic of reading and/or discussion
subtitle/subheading	secondary or additional title of a book, work of art, piece of music, text, chapter, article, poem, document, etc.; secondary or additional heading within these works to indicate new section
table	a set of facts or figures, systematically displayed, especially in columns
table of contents	a set of topics, listed with corresponding page numbers, indicating the different sections of a book or text
title page	a page which precedes the main part of a book or text; contains the title, author's name, date (or copyright) and, if appropriate, publisher information
title/heading	the name of a book, work of art, piece of music, text, chapter, article, poem, document, etc.
transition	a word or phrase that signals a change from one idea (or set of ideas) to the next

Let's take a look at three of the most commonly confused terms: *paragraph, passage,* and *excerpt.* Many fluent English-speaking students would have problems differentiating among the three definitions—so an English learner would have an even greater challenge dealing with such technical language. Unless these terms are taught explicitly by the teacher, that is to say, as a lesson focus and with planned repetition, students may not retain and use them correctly. Worse, they may not even understand them in the first place.

Let's say *paragraph* means "a collection of sentences that revolve around one central, or main, idea" (in expository text in particular). The main idea is contained in the paragraph's topic sentence. The topic sentence is supported by details (or reasons, or examples). How is *paragraph* different from *passage*?

A *passage* is a set of sentences, divided into paragraphs (or contained in one long paragraph). Each paragraph has its own main idea. If a passage has three paragraphs, then each paragraph has its own main idea, and the passage itself, as a whole, has a large main idea: four main ideas in all. If the passage has a title, the title most likely reflects the main idea of all three of the paragraphs put together.

Consider how *excerpt* is different from *paragraph* and *passage*. An excerpt is a section of text, which can be taken from the beginning, the middle, or the end of a larger text. An excerpt may be confusing because a good deal of the context may be missing. Readers have to use critical reading skills to make sense of an excerpt, to fill in the missing information around the edges.

One might conceivably wonder why such specificity of language is important. The fact is, in order to read, comprehend, analyze, and talk about text, readers have to be able to use these terms and see how they function. These terms help students talk about how text is organized and to see how the ideas relate to one another.

Directions such as "Please read the following passage and identify the main idea of paragraph two" are common in classrooms, usually starting as early as third grade. They are also common on standardized tests. Such directions reflect the academic language used in school.

But how do students respond to directions such as this? Do they ask what is meant by the term *passage*, and how it is different from a *paragraph*? Do they ask what a *main idea* is, how it is different from a fact, or, even more importantly, how to identify it?

No. They do what people in general do when they don't really know what is being asked of them: they guess. Many students, especially those who are learning English, are genuinely perplexed by reading assignment questions. They struggle hard to grasp the basic content of the text while simultaneously being asked to internalize and manipulate academic concepts and terms they probably haven't been introduced to, except perhaps indirectly.

Yet if teachers spent some time with students analyzing paragraphs and looking at *passages* that are made up of one, two, four, six, or more *paragraphs*, students would understand these terms. They would "get it." Even better, they would be able to read pieces of text for the big ideas, for the details, or for both. We know that "explicit instruction with regard to the structure of a text facilitates the development of important comprehension strategies" (Droop & Verhoevan, 2003, p. 101).

When working with English learners in my reading class, I failed to make clear what *boldface* and *italicized* meant. That didn't seem like a major transgression—until these students came across words that were italicized for a reason and were unable to comprehend their significance. In a piece of text from *Children of the Dust Bowl* (1992), a chapter book, author Jerry Stanley writes that the growers offered the migrants a starvation wage of two-and-a-half cents for a box of peaches—*one dollar* for a *ton* of peaches. The use of italics serves to emphasize just *how little* money was paid for *how much* fruit. Unless readers recognize the technique the author is using to highlight specific information, they miss the point.

In any case, it is absolutely critical that we teach students—and especially English learners, for whom English poses a specific challenge—the text terms that they need to understand in order to approach text in thoughtful and meaningful ways and to develop a common vocabulary that will serve them throughout their schooling.

Table 3.1 (see page 45) provides basic definitions for the academic terms listed. These terms need to become a part of every teacher's classroom vocabulary. Teachers have to remember, though, that just giving students the definitions is not enough (and there should not be a list of terms presented on Monday with a test on them on Friday). As Harvey and Goudvis (2000) assert, "For too many years we have been telling students what to do without showing them how" (p. 12).

Teachers need to show examples of captions and illustrations and model how to find important information embedded in them; choose excerpts from texts, magazine articles, diary entries, etc., and talk about what can be learned from them, both in and out of context; use the information in pie, bar, and line graphs to quantify the general information given in a chapter; and repeat academic terms over and over, bringing them up explicitly in different situations using a "think-aloud process" (Daniels & Zemelman, 2004). In short, it is necessary to provide comprehensible input—and then add the academic terms that match the concepts.

Keys to Comprehension

If we view the comprehension process as a transaction between reader and text, in which readers construct mental representations of the text by using their existing knowledge, along with the application of flexible strategies (Rupley & Willson, 1997), then it becomes very clear that the reason people read—and the way in which they read something—will determine what they get out of it. That is to say, readers set a purpose for reading and then read strategically with that purpose in mind.

For example, if I am interested in getting the overview, or the big picture, of a magazine article that interests me, I may choose to read the title, the subtitles, and perhaps even the first sentence of each paragraph—before I decide whether or not I want to read the whole article. In the same way, teaching strategies should focus on reading as an authentic process, keeping in mind that readers highlight different information for themselves as they read, based on their individual purposes for reading.

The goal is to teach English learners the processes that enable them to access many different kinds of information, including (but not limited to) *main ideas*, *details*, *sequences of events*, *implications* that authors make, and vocabulary that is defined through textual *context clues*.

For most students, these terms are abstract. I often hear teachers tell pairs of students to "read the paragraph and then tell your partner the main idea." If students ask what that means, they reply, "You know, what it's mostly about." Those directions seem pretty simple, but for an English learner who is foraging through a maze of new words, figuring out what the paragraph is "mostly about" results in a retell of every point that the student can remember—which generally consists of a mish-mash of details and very rarely even approaches the main idea.

English learners need tools for figuring out the big picture, not just prompts that use other words to ask the same question. For each reading strategy that can be taught, there are identifiable keywords that match—labels that come from the pool of academic language. Generally, the kind of information readers look for in their reading is determined by the questions they ask. Sometimes the questions are posed by teachers, sometimes they are listed at the ends of chapters, and, ideally, they are asked by readers who are reading actively.

Detail Questions

When asking students the most basic recall questions about stories and texts, teachers take for granted that students know what kind of information is needed to answer the questions. Detail questions, which begin with WH words (words that start with *w* or *h*, such as *who*, *what*, *when*, *where*, *why*, and *how*), are frequently posed during class and are often listed at the ends of chapters. Teachers sometimes forget that English learners may confuse the WH words, having not had as much time to acquire them as their fluent English-speaking counterparts.

Visual Support. One technique that I adopted, suggested by a group of elementary school teachers, is to use illustrations of answers that match the detail questions. For example, if the question starts with *who*, the icon is a stick figure, illustrating a person; if the question begins with *when*, the icon is a clock (see Figure 3.1). English learners are

FIGURE 3.1
Detail Keywords With Icons

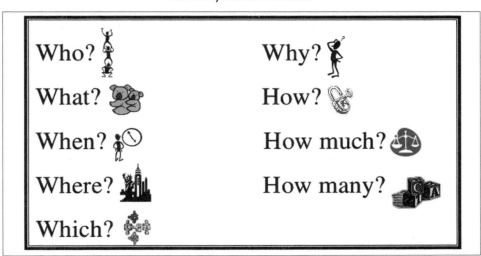

then able to visualize what the answer looks like, as soon as they see the question. The link between the exact WH word and an appropriate answer is made much faster and with a higher degree of correctness when students first practice answering questions using the icons and words in Figure 3.1.

Scanning. Along with using this pictorial aid, I taught students how to *scan* effectively. Teachers frequently assume that students know the procedure for scanning; after all, it is second nature to adults. Scanning is not really reading, in the true sense of the word; it is searching quickly (running your eyes over the page) to locate target information. For example, if you want to know someone's telephone number, you first recognize that you will be looking for a set of numbers and then you think about how the information is organized—in this case, alphabetically by name. So you think about what the person's last name is and search until you finally zero in on the exact name and number.

I have found that many English learners do not scan effectively because they don't know the procedure for getting the specific information they need. I model the following scanning procedure for them in class:

1. Identify the target information needed.
2. Look at the WH word in the question.
3. Visualize what the answer looks like.
4. Find other keywords in the question.
5. Think about how the reading is organized.
6. Scan for the target information, using keywords and the visualized answer.

Next, the students do the procedure in groups, then in pairs, and finally individually, Vygotskian-style (1934/1986). The teacher and the students collaborate until the students have internalized the task and can carry it out on their own. Once students feel comfortable, the teacher raises the bar and, as Valencia and Riddle Buly (2004) recommend, asks students to apply the procedure often, using different types and levels of materials throughout the school year.

Students might utilize the scanning procedure with the excerpt in Figure 3.2 and answer the following questions:

1. What are virtual pets?
2. When did virtual pets become a fad?
3. Why did stores have trouble keeping them on the shelves?

To answer the first question, students look at the WH word (*what*), visualize what the answer looks like (*things*), find keywords in the question (*virtual* and *pets*), notice that

FIGURE 3.2
Excerpt for Scanning Exercise

Artificial Pets

In 1997 a new toy fad swept the United States. After runaway success in Japan, tiny, cleverly packaged, hand-held electronic toys called virtual pets became a craze in America. It didn't take long for imitators to hit the market, broadening the variety and increasing availability of the virtual, or cyber-, pets. The toys were so popular, and the demand so great, stores had trouble keeping them on shelves.

Just like real pets, digital pets required loving care from their owners. They had to be kept happy and healthy and needed food, exercise, and a lot of attention. They also had to be put to bed at night and awakened again each morning. If they did not receive discipline they could become ill-mannered. The more they were neglected the more they beeped. If virtual pets were ignored completely they died. But with the push of a reset button their cyber-life instantly resumed.

From *Project Achievement Reading: Level A* (Scholastic Education Group, 1999, p. 92). Copyright © by Scholastic, Inc. Reprinted by permission.

---

the writing is organized in a *story* format, and scan for the answer (*hand-held electronic toys*). Students follow the scanning procedure again to answer questions 2 and 3.

Having a handle on how to locate specific information in their reading is very important for English learners who are overwhelmed by large pieces of text. Focusing on important details, through the use of the scanning procedure, gives students a concrete way to learn about detail questions and to practice finding target information. The scanning procedure is also useful for answering detail questions on standardized tests.

Cloze Procedure. Another method that helps students to highlight important detail information in reading selections is the cloze procedure. Originally, this technique was developed in 1950 as an assessment tool for determining what grade levels of text students could handle (Reutzel & Cooter, 2000). After reading a story or passage at a pre-designated readability level, students were asked to fill in specific blanks within a "cloze" version of the same text. In this way, educators determined if students comprehended the text at the prescribed reading level. In the original version, blanks replaced original text at intervals of every 5th or 10th word, and generally the first and last sentences were left intact.

However, a type of modified cloze procedure is now being used frequently by teachers for emphasizing content details that are especially important to the reader's understanding of a particular text. Students read a selection or passage first, and then they are given the same passage with words that have been deleted. The students' job is to fill in the missing information from memory or by using a word bank as support. Of course, the words that have been deleted (typically by whiting out words and inserting lines with a ruler on a photocopy) are those that the teacher has selected as being the most important vocabulary for the lesson, based on what is known about the students' background knowledge and the content focus.

The cloze procedure can also be used to help students learn parts of speech and grammatical forms. One effective way of highlighting the role of humans in relation to their cyber-pets (in the Figure 3.2 passage) is to delete many of the verbs and then have students replace them. Students focus on recall of the text while they are paying attention to the correct forms of the verbs. Using only the first two paragraphs of the entire selection, the cloze selection might look like that featured in Figure 3.3.

Readers not only strive to re-create the meaning of the text as they fill in the blanks with specific verbs from the word bank, but they also enjoy the challenge of trying to recall the specific answers on their own. The activity can easily be scaffolded as well, as the teacher moves from doing most of the work in the initial demonstration phase (along with a think-aloud process, "showing kids how smart readers think") to having groups and pairs work collaboratively (Daniels & Zemelman, 2004, p. 102). Eventually,

FIGURE 3.3
Paragraphs for Cloze Exercise

In 1997, a new toy fad _____ the United States. After runaway success in Japan, tiny, cleverly packaged, hand-held electronic toys _____ virtual pets _____ a craze in America. It didn't take long for imitators to hit the market, broadening the variety and increasing availability of the virtual, or cyber-pets. The toys _____ so popular, and the demand so great, stores had trouble keeping them on shelves.

Just like real pets, digital pets _____ loving care from their owners. They had to be kept happy and healthy and _____ food, exercise, and a lot of attention. They also had to be put to bed at night and _____ again each morning. If they did not receive discipline, they could become ill-mannered. The more they were _____, the more they _____. If virtual pets were _____ completely, they _____. But with the push of a reset button their cyber-life instantly _____.

Word Bank

ignored	resumed
beeped	required
died	called
neglected	swept
became	awakened
needed	were

Text selection adapted from *Project Achievement Reading: Level A* (Scholastic Education Group, 1999, p. 92). Copyright © by Scholastic, Inc. Reprinted by permission.

the word bank component can be completely discarded when learners feel that they can do it without the extra support.

Main Idea Questions

The easiest questions to answer are detail questions, which are at the recall level of Bloom's taxonomy (Bloom, Englehart, Furst, Hill, & Krathwohl, 1956). They are the questions that English learners find the least intimidating because a tangible answer can be found directly stated in the text. Having worked with students of all ages, I believe that they are uncomfortable with some of the other kinds of questions that they are asked to answer, such as main idea questions, because they have not been explicitly taught how to find the information to answer them. They also do not recognize the benefits of comprehending main ideas as they read.

When teachers talk about the "big idea" in a paragraph (or, the "gist of it"), they are speaking of the main idea. A reader who can identify the main idea of each paragraph in a passage or selection will come away with what I think of as "the jigsaw puzzle picture on the top of the box."

This may seem like a strange analogy, but if you think about trying to put together pieces of a jigsaw puzzle without knowing what the picture looks like ahead of time, you will have a very difficult time placing all the little parts in the right places. If you know what the picture will look like, it's a much easier matter to fit in each of the components. Of course, this is an issue of having a schema—a framework in your head on which to hang the new information that you acquire as you read. Schema allows a reader to make links between what is known already and the text content.

Reading a paragraph to identify the main idea—and then rereading it to assimilate all of the details—is an authentic practice. I do it when I read new text, I'm sure that many other proficient readers do it, and it would be an effective strategy for English learners to utilize as well. Students should begin by identifying the keywords of questions. The following main idea key phrases tell students that they are being asked to find the "big picture":

• Main idea	• Has to do mostly with
• Main point	• Contains information about
• Mainly about	• Good title
• Mostly about	• Possible title
• Has to do mainly with	• Alternative title

Herringbone Technique. By teaching strategies for "getting the big picture," especially strategies that students can practice in pairs or at table groups, teachers help students grasp the abstract concept of the main idea. One such strategy is the Herringbone

Technique (Tierney, Readence, & Dishner, 1990). It consists of a short graphic organizer and is a concrete way of helping English learners find the comprehensive idea in a paragraph or passage. Students answer the questions listed in the fishbone graphic organizer (see Figure 3.4). This leads to the synthesis of all the information in one newly created sentence, which becomes the main idea statement.

The two-paragraph excerpt in Figure 3.5 shows how threatening it might be to any student, much less an English learner, to be asked to identify the main idea. After all, there is a good deal of information in the text, along with some difficult vocabulary words. The following attempt by a student to answer such a main idea question clearly shows that he was not certain about what information was appropriate to share:

> EMTs are a team of people like doctors who are trained to help people in emergencies that can be severe or minor and then learn about them on the radio and go to the scene in an ambulance with four people.

However, when I modeled my own thinking as I read the text and then asked the students to help figure out the information that went into the graphic organizer, the class came up with the information in Figure 3.6. (Note that students write the main idea below the middle line rather than on it.) By putting all the detail pieces together, students get a main idea sentence such as "EMTs rush to an emergency when an accident happens in an ambulance quickly to help people who have minor or severe injuries." If the word order doesn't sound right or make sense, students then move the words around for a clearer message, such as "When an accident happens, EMTs quickly rush to an emergency in an ambulance to help people who have minor or severe injuries."

FIGURE 3.4
Herringbone Technique

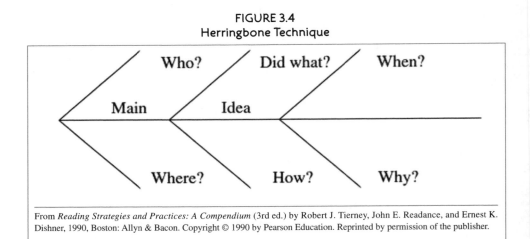

From *Reading Strategies and Practices: A Compendium* (3rd ed.) by Robert J. Tierney, John E. Readance, and Ernest K. Dishner, 1990, Boston: Allyn & Bacon. Copyright © 1990 by Pearson Education. Reprinted by permission of the publisher.

FIGURE 3.5
Excerpt for Herringbone Technique Exercise

EMTs Save Lives

Are you looking for a vocation in which your quick thinking and acting can save lives? Then you might like a career as an Emergency Medical Technician, or EMT.

When accidents occur, a team of EMTs is often the first help to arrive. An EMT is specially trained to give care and treatment to emergency victims at the scene of an accident or illness. The emergency may be anything from a severe accident to a minor cut. EMTs learn about accidents over a special radio. They hasten to the scene, often in just a few minutes. The ambulance usually carries two EMTs and the driver. A fourth person helps navigate, or guide, the ambulance driver through heavy traffic.

From *Project Achievement Reading: Level A* (Scholastic Education Group, 1999, p. 96). Copyright © by Scholastic, Inc. Reprinted by permission.

FIGURE 3.6
Class Herringbone Organizer

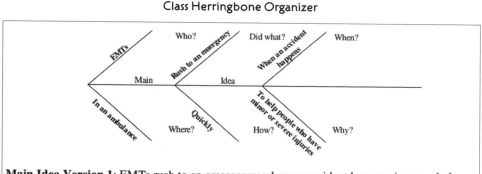

Main Idea Version 1: EMTs rush to an emergency when an accident happens in an ambulance quickly to help people who have minor or severe injuries.

Main Idea Version 2: When an accident happens, EMTs quickly rush to an emergency in an ambulance to help people who have minor or severe injuries.

The work these students did is a clear indication that "visual structures are powerful tools for comprehension instruction because they offer concrete, memorable representations of abstract thinking processes" (Barton & Sawyer, 2004, p. 338). The next step for learners, as Alvermann and Phelps (2005) suggest, is to "give them occasional follow-up passages and [have them] read for the specific task" (p. 200). Students used the Herringbone Technique with many different selections throughout the year and became more successful with it over time. They also became extremely capable of recalling the details associated with the big picture, as they had a schematic structure within which to connect the pieces.

Test Practices. Once students have begun to use comprehension strategies such as the Herringbone Technique, it becomes a simple matter to transfer their competencies to test practice situations. McCabe (2003) notes that reading scores often "reflect test anxiety to a large degree, rather than true reading ability" (p. 12). He adds that some students have had more opportunities to experience mastery in test-taking and that careful selection and use of test-like material are critical. Teachers can use easy test material (authentic pieces from class readings) and highlight short, manageable sections. As success with short portions is achieved, teachers gradually increase the length of the selections.

Taking the final main idea sentence created with the Herringbone Technique, students can now apply the information to the question "What is the main idea of the paragraph?"

A. EMTs are the most important people at an accident scene.

B. The ambulance that carries EMTs usually also carries a driver and a guide.

C. EMTs rush to accidents to help people who are injured.

D. EMTs learn about accidents over a special radio.

It is not difficult for students to identify the correct answer as *C*, as it most closely matches the sentence written with the aid of the fishbone graph. The other possible answers are either too general or represent very specific details.

Talking about such choices not only helps English learners to articulate their views on the big idea of the text piece, but it also helps them to become familiar with the way in which such concepts arise in the context of standardized tests. It is not burdensome for the teacher to provide multiple-choice practices every once in awhile, keeping in mind that the primary purpose of teaching these strategies is to boost comprehension, not simply to develop testwiseness. Most important is the "explicit modeling and discussion of the components of comprehension...on a routine basis" in order to help students become metacognitive thinkers (Barton & Sawyer, 2004, p. 338).

Sequence Questions

Another understanding that is critical to comprehension is that events have a prescribed order in which they happen, and that writers achieve cohesion by using clues, such as sequence words (which can also operate as transition words; e.g., *after, at the same time as, before, during, finally, first, in conclusion, last, next, second, then, to begin with*).

Questioning is a strategy that "propels readers forward"—when students ask themselves ongoing questions as they read, they are less likely to abandon the text (Harvey & Goudvis, 2000, p. 22). Confusion about the order of events is a roadblock that keeps English learners from moving ahead with confidence; they may ask themselves about the relationships among events but not be able to see them clearly. What many students do not understand is that the events may be told by the author in an order that is different from the way in which they actually occurred. When a writer tells the first event first and the second event second, there is not much of a problem identifying what was first and what was second (though the keywords, like those listed above, still need to be taught explicitly). But when a writer describes the events in a convoluted way, students often do not see that the events are not being told chronologically. If they are trying to comprehend the order in which the events truly happened for the purpose of understanding the story, or if they are being asked sequence questions by a teacher (or on a test), then they usually go by the order of the *telling*.

Sentence Strips + Timeline. One interactive and effective strategy to use with all students—and especially English learners, who may not be familiar with the specific discourse patterns and conventions of the English language—is called Sentence Strips + Timeline.

When utilizing an excerpt such as the one in Figure 3.7, if the teacher cuts strips of an overhead transparency and lists the events in the order in which they occur (using an overhead projector), the strips would typically appear as they do in Figure 3.8. As the teacher puts the strips on the overhead, she asks students to tell whether or not the strips show the real order in which things happened. If not, the strips are moved around to show the accurate order in which the events actually occurred. At the same time that the teacher puts the strips on the projector, students write the same information on sticky notes, which they can move around on a sheet of paper that contains a simple hand-drawn timeline. (Graphic organizers like these are also readily available through various publishers or can be constructed easily on a computer.) The teacher models, and the students follow, the process. Later, using another part of the same text—or even a different text altogether—students tell the teacher the order in which to put the strips, this time without as much assistance.

FIGURE 3.7
Excerpt for Sentence Strips + Timeline Exercise

The Night the Lights Went Out
July 13, 1977, was a stormy night in New York City. A lightning bolt struck a power line outside the city. Soon three more lightning bolts struck. At 9:34 P.M., all the lights in New York City went out. The nation's largest city was without electricity.

Most New Yorkers already knew what a blackout was like. In 1965, electric power went out in seven states in the Northeast. Now many people had to face some of the same problems once again.

And there were plenty of problems to deal with. Streetlights and traffic lights went out. Elevators stopped between stations. Airports shut down. Thousands of people were caught in places where they didn't want to be.

The blackout left many people without water, too. People living on high floors depended on water pumps. When the pumps stopped working, the water stopped as well. Refrigerators went off and food had to be thrown away. The summer heat made the problem worse.

FIGURE 3.8
Understanding Sequence of Events

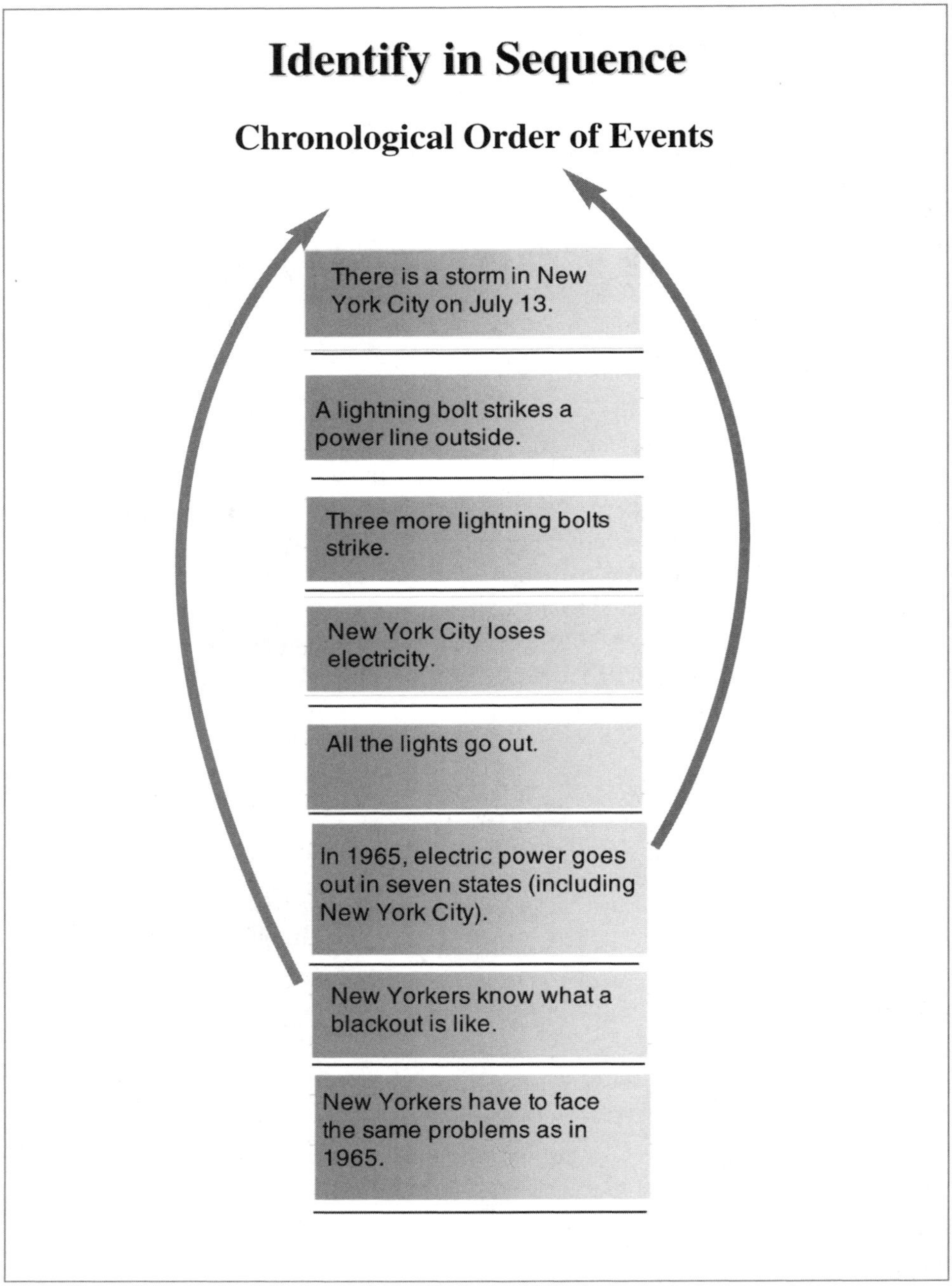

Identify in Sequence

Chronological Order of Events

There is a storm in New York City on July 13.

A lightning bolt strikes a power line outside.

Three more lightning bolts strike.

New York City loses electricity.

All the lights go out.

In 1965, electric power goes out in seven states (including New York City).

New Yorkers know what a blackout is like.

New Yorkers have to face the same problems as in 1965.

What students learn from this activity is that the first five events are told in chronological order. That is to say, they really happened in this order. However, events 6 and 7 occurred before the storm in New York City on July 13. Students have to move these two strips to the top of the page *before* the first one. Now they are putting the events in the order in which they actually happened.

Eventually, after much discussion and collaboration, the strips are in the correct order, and students can then rewrite the story chronologically. As they approach new readings in the future, they are much more likely to recognize when writers choose to introduce information in a nonchronological way, such as in flashbacks. Being able to identify the correct sequence of events is a skill required of standardized-test takers, so this strategy, which supports better comprehension during reading, can be transferred to testing contexts as well.

Conclusion

Pressley (2002) laments that "there is little comprehension strategy instruction in primary-level classrooms" (p. 181), but hopefully that trend is changing, for the primary grades are where it should begin. There are numerous sources available now that provide interactive, engaging methods for making comprehension instruction motivational and successful, not only for English learners, but for all students.

In this chapter, I've suggested that students need to recall details, find main ideas, and determine the sequence of events. Beyond this, students also need to learn to make inferences, differentiate between facts and opinions, figure out vocabulary definitions through context clues, identify causes and effects, and much, much more. In addition, as I hope I've enthusiastically emphasized, we must teach the academic language associated with concepts and strategies explicitly, not rely on students to pick them up inductively or in passing.

For English learners, the linguistic task is clearly a more difficult one than it is for other students, so the importance of teaching academic language is exacerbated. As Pransky and Bailey (2003) put it, "The challenge for teachers is to accommodate these students' needs in mainstream classrooms where, in the end, all students must learn to work confidently, productively, and successfully" (p. 382).

REFERENCES

Alvermann, D., & Phelps, S. (2005). *Content reading and literacy: Succeeding in today's diverse classrooms.* Boston: Pearson Education.

Barton, J., & Sawyer, D. (2004). Our students are ready for this: Comprehension instruction in the elementary school. *The Reading Teacher, 57,* 334–347.

Bloom, B.S., Englehart, M.B., Furst, E.J., Hill, W.H., & Krathwohl, D.R. (1956). *Taxonomy of educational objectives: The classification of educational goals. Handbook I: Cognitive domain.* New York: Longman.

Cary, S. (2000). *Working with second language learners: Answers to teachers' top ten questions.* Portsmouth, NH: Heinemann.

Cummins, J. (1980). The construct of language proficiency in bilingual education. In J.E. Alatis (Ed.),

Georgetown University roundtable on languages and linguistics (pp. 76–93). Washington, DC: Georgetown University Press.

Cummins, J., & Schecter, S. (2003). School-based language policy in culturally diverse contexts. In S. Schecter & J. Cummins (Eds.), *Multilingual education in practice: Using diversity as a resource* (pp. 1–16). Portsmouth, NH: Heinemann.

Daniels, H., & Zemelman, S. (2004). *Subjects matter: Every teacher's guide to content-area reading.* Portsmouth, NH: Heinemann.

Droop, M., & Verhoevan, L. (2003). Language proficiency and reading ability in first- and second-language learners. *Reading Research Quarterly, 38,* 78–103.

Harvey, S., & Goudvis, A. (2000). *Strategies that work: Teaching comprehension to enhance understanding.* York, ME: Stenhouse.

Krashen, S.D. (1995). *Principles and practice in second language acquisition.* London: Phoenix ELT/Prentice Hall International.

McCabe, P. (2003). What reading teachers should know about ESL learners. *The Reading Teacher, 57,* 12–20.

Nieto, S. (2004). *Affirming diversity: The sociopolitical context of multicultural education.* Boston: Pearson Education.

Peregoy, S., & Boyle, O. (2005). *Reading, writing, and learning in ESL: A resource book for K–12 teachers.* Boston: Pearson Education.

Pransky, K., & Bailey, F. (2003). To meet your students where they are, first you have to find them: Working with culturally and linguistically diverse at-risk students. *The Reading Teacher, 56,* 370–383.

Pressley, M. (2002). Effective beginning reading instruction. *Journal of Literacy Research, 34*(2), 165–188.

Reutzel, D.R., & Cooter, R.B., Jr. (2000). *The essentials of teaching children to read.* Upper Saddle River, NJ: Pearson Education.

Rupley, W.H., & Willson, V.L. (1997). The relationship of reading comprehension to components of word recognition: Support for developmental shifts. *Journal of Research and Development in Education, 30,* 255–260.

Scholastic Education Group. (1999). *Project Achievement Reading: Level A.* New York: Author.

Tierney, R., Readence, J., & Dishner, E. (1990). *Reading strategies and practices: A compendium* (3rd ed.). Needham Heights, MA: Allyn & Bacon.

Valencia, S., & Riddle Buly, M. (2004). Behind test scores: What struggling readers REALLY need. *The Reading Teacher, 57,* 520–531.

Vygotsky, L.S. (1986). *Thought and language* (A. Kozalin, Trans.). Cambridge, MA: The MIT Press. (Original work published 1934)

CHILDREN'S BOOK CITED

Stanley, J. (1992). *Children of the Dust Bowl: The true story of the school at Weedpatch Camp.* New York: Crown.

CHAPTER 4

Teaching Language Through Content Themes: Viewing Our World as a Global Village

David E. Freeman and Yvonne S. Freeman

> At this moment, there are more than 6 billion people on the planet! It's hard to picture so many people at one time—but what if we imagine the whole world as a village of just 100 people? In the global village there are almost 6,000 languages, but more than half of the people speak these 8 languages: 22 speak a Chinese dialect, 9 speak English, 8 speak Hindi, 7 speak Spanish, 4 speak Arabic, 4 speak Bengali, 3 speak Portuguese, 3 speak Russian. (*If the World Were a Village*, Smith, 2002, p. 10)

These facts come from *If the World Were a Village*, a fascinating book about what proportion of people in the world speak different languages, come from different countries, are different ages, have different levels of education, and own the world's wealth. The book is an excellent starting place for the development of a content theme in which students learn about geography, economics, science, math, and the social studies concept of interdependence. A study of the world as a global village is particularly relevant to English learners whose first languages are some of those 6,000 world languages Smith describes. Through a thematic study about the interdependence of people, animals, and nature around the world, English learners acquire language as they study academic content.

This chapter describes the importance of teaching language through meaningful content using a thematic approach. Through themes, educators can draw on performance and content standards and connect them to their diverse students' lives and interests. Integrated thematic instruction is an excellent approach for organizing curriculum in general, but it is especially critical for the academic success of English learners in the classroom. To help support students in the critical areas of reading and the acquisition of academic content, teachers need to connect students to engaging books. At least some of the books should be culturally relevant. In this chapter we discuss reasons for teaching language through content and for organizing curriculum around themes connected to standards. We conclude with an extended example of a thematic unit on global interdependence that helps readers visualize the ways that teaching language through academic content themes using culturally relevant materials can be realized.

Reasons to Teach Language Through Sustained Content

There are several benefits to teaching language through academic content. When teachers teach language through content, students learn both the important academic content they need and the academic English associated with the different content areas. As students study content, they are exposed to the language of each academic subject area in a natural context. For example, students studying insects read interesting books about insects, bring in insects to observe, keep journals about insects, do experiments with insects, and talk about all they are learning. These kinds of activities provide an authentic context for students to develop the language of science. In addition, because they are learning interesting academic content, students have a real purpose for developing a second language. Table 4.1 highlights the reasons to teach language through content.

The title of the table includes the word *sustained* because it is important to organize content teaching over an extended period of time (Pally & Bailey, 2000). For example, it is not enough for teachers to teach the language of insects by reading one book about insects, showing some pictures, and doing one activity. For students to acquire the language and the content of science by studying insects, they should read and discuss multiple books on the topic and be involved in a variety of activities. In other words, the content teaching about insects should be sustained over a period of time and, to be most effective, integrated across several subject areas.

TABLE 4.1
Four Reasons to Teach Language Through Sustained Academic Content

1. Students get *both* language and content.
2. Students learn the academic vocabulary of the content area.
3. Language is kept in its natural context.
4. Students have reasons to use language for real purposes.

Reasons for Organizing Curriculum Around Themes

Besides teaching language through sustained content, teachers should organize their curriculum around unified themes. This avoids what has been called the "cha cha cha" curriculum. In a cha cha cha curriculum, students might study insects in science, community workers in social studies, rhyming words in language arts, fractions in math, and *ea* words in spelling. The content areas are not related. The teacher finishes one area and then—cha cha cha—moves on to a new, unrelated subject. English learners often get lost in the transition, and by the time they figure out that the topic has moved from insects to community workers—cha cha cha—the teacher is moving on to a new subject. In contrast, if English learners know what the theme is as they begin study in a new academic content area, they do not waste time trying to figure out what the lesson is about. Their focus across content areas remains on the significant questions they are investigating.

In thematic teaching, the subject areas are connected. So, for example, students studying how insects affect people may read a poetry alphabet book and create their own insect poems in language arts, study where various kinds of insects live during geography, learn about how insects affect people in social sciences, observe and keep insect journals in science, investigate how insects spread or prevent diseases in health, and calculate insect reproduction rates in math.

Integrated thematic instruction provides students with repeated opportunities to learn academic vocabulary. The same terms come up in all the subject areas. Students need extensive exposure to academic vocabulary to acquire it. Nagy, Anderson, and Herman (1987) find that native speakers need to see a word several times in meaningful contexts to acquire the word meaning and function. During thematic teaching, all students see and hear the keywords connected to the topic several times. For example, during the insect unit, students hear and see the words *colony*, *adaptation*, and *migration* repeatedly as they study about insects in different subject areas. At the same time, they acquire new vocabulary as they move through the content areas. So students may acquire the names of types of insects as they locate them in geography and learn terms related to insect body parts and stages of growth during science.

Teachers can organize around themes that answer big questions. For example, one theme is the investigation of the interdependence of insects and humans. With this theme, students might investigate such questions as, "How do insects depend on humans, and how do humans depend on insects?" and "How are humans and insects alike and how are they different?" The big questions help provide unity for the theme and ensure connections among subject areas. As students move from one subject area to the next, they continue to gather information to help answer important questions.

Big questions offer teachers opportunities to connect curriculum to students' lives and engage students in learning. Often, students who are being instructed in a second language appear to have a short attention span. They don't stay focused on the lesson activities. However, as anyone who has studied a second language knows, it takes a great deal of mental energy to comprehend instruction in a language in which one has only limited proficiency. When the content of the lesson is relevant and interesting, students are more likely to try harder to understand and to stay focused.

The key for teachers is to keep students engaged and to keep providing comprehensible input to all the students in a class, especially English learners. (See "Approaches to Second-Language Teaching" in chapter 2 and "Explicit Development of Academic Language" in chapter 3 for more about comprehensible input.) In addition, when teachers teach through themes, they usually have more opportunities to differentiate instruction by organizing assignments and activities so that students, regardless of their English proficiency, can participate. Students at the beginning stages might illustrate and label key ideas instead of writing longer text. When studying the life cycle of a butterfly, for example, some students may write a description of the stages, while less proficient students may draw and label the stages. Table 4.2 highlights reasons for organizing curriculum around themes.

Connecting Thematic Content to Standards

Although the No Child Left Behind (NCLB) Act (2002) does not dictate a method for teaching English, it does state the intent to "ensure that children who are limited English proficient, including immigrant children and youth, attain English proficiency, develop high levels of academic attainment in English, and meet the same challenging State academic content and student academic achievement standards as all children are expected to meet" (p. 266).

It is important, then, that teachers connect curriculum to standards. Teachers can do this by aligning their themes with state-mandated content standards. Sometimes

TABLE 4.2
Six Reasons to Organize Curriculum Around Themes

1. Students see the big picture so that they can make sense of English-language instruction.
2. Content areas (math, science, social studies, literature) are interrelated.
3. Vocabulary is repeated naturally as it appears in different content area studies.
4. Through themes based on big questions, teachers connect curriculum to students' lives. This makes curriculum more interesting.
5. Because the curriculum makes sense, English learners are more fully engaged and experience greater success.
6. Because themes deal with universal human topics, all students can be involved, and lessons and activities can be adjusted to different levels of English-language proficiency.

teachers and administrators decide that standards impose certain "musts." Commonly heard "musts" include "Your curriculum must be aligned to the standards" and "The tests are aligned to the standards, so we must teach the standards." Rather than regarding standards as creating a set of "musts" that someone else is imposing, teachers can use the standards as a guide that provides a starting point from which to creatively meet students' needs. Akhavan (2004) describes her school's journey from being sanctioned by the state as underperforming to being recognized for providing excellent education for all students. It is a school where teachers and students, including many English learners, succeed by working together. Administrators and teachers use standards not as "a long list of bits of abstract information students are expected to know and understand during specific grade level years" (p. 9), but instead as a way to connect to student needs and help students construct knowledge. Akhavan explains that "Standards based instruction, when implemented effectively, can empower teachers to focus on children and their educational needs without zapping the essence of teaching, the excitement of learning, or taking away the energy teachers need to create effective classrooms" (p. 12).

Akhavan encourages teachers to focus on the learner, not on the subject or content. She explains how performance descriptors in standards suggest that teachers need to make their students active participants in their learning, with words such as *analyze*, *compare*, *create*, *problem solve*, and *understand*. Teachers in Akhavan's school organize thematic units around content and performance standards in ways that connect to students' lives and empower them.

Using Culturally Relevant Books

Choosing appropriate materials is also an important consideration when teaching English learners. Teachers often find that their students have greater success when at least some of the books they read are culturally relevant. Culturally relevant texts are those in which the characters, events, settings, and ways of talking and interacting are similar to the ways people talk and act and to the settings in students' communities. English learners better comprehend culturally relevant texts because of the match between the story and their lives. For students reading in a new language, it is especially important that at least some of the texts be culturally relevant. Drawn from a rubric developed by A. Freeman (2000), the cultural relevance rubric in Figure 4.1 can help teachers identify culturally relevant books. Teachers can use the rubric on their own or with students.

The Preview/View/Review Technique

In addition to drawing on students' cultural backgrounds by using culturally relevant books, teachers can draw on students' linguistic backgrounds by using the Preview/View/Review Technique (Y.S. Freeman & D.E. Freeman, 1998). This technique can

FIGURE 4.1
Cultural Relevance Rubric

---

1. Are the characters in the story like you and your family?

   Just like us .... Not at all like us

   | 4 | 3 | 2 | 1 |

2. Have you ever had an experience like the one described in the story?

   Yes .... No

   | 4 | 3 | 2 | 1 |

3. Have you lived in or visited places like those in the story?

   Yes .... No

   | 4 | 3 | 2 | 1 |

4. Could this story take place this year?

   Yes .... No

   | 4 | 3 | 2 | 1 |

5. How close do you think the main characters are to you in age?

   Very close .... Not close at all

   | 4 | 3 | 2 | 1 |

6. Are there main characters in the story who are: boys (for boys) or girls (for girls)?

   Yes .... No

   | 4 | 3 | 2 | 1 |

7. Do the characters talk like you and your family do?

   Yes .... No

   | 4 | 3 | 2 | 1 |

8. How often do you read stories like these?

   Often .... Never

   | 4 | 3 | 2 | 1 |

Adapted from Freeman, A. (2000). *Selection of culturally relevant text*. Tucson: University of Arizona.

work in classes with English learners from different primary-language backgrounds, and it can work whether or not the teacher speaks the students' languages. If the teacher, a bilingual peer, a bilingual cross-age tutor, a bilingual aide, or a parent can simply tell the English learners in their native language what the upcoming lesson is about, the students are provided a preview. During the view, the teacher conducts the lesson using strategies to make the input comprehensible. With the help of the preview, the students can follow the English better and acquire both English and academic content. Finally, it is good to have a short review during which students can use their native language. For example, students who speak the same first language could meet in groups to review the main ideas of the lesson and then report back in English. Table 4.3 summarizes Preview/View/Review, while the following scenario illustrates the technique in action.

Francisco (a fictional teacher based on teachers with whom we have worked over time) makes effective use of Preview/View/Review with his third graders. About half of his students are English learners. Most of the English learners are Latino, several of whom began school speaking only Spanish. However, Francisco also has two students whose first language is Punjabi, one student whose first language is Vietnamese, and another whose first language is Arabic. The native speakers of English include several African American and Anglo students.

Francisco understands the importance of building on the first-language skills of his English learners. Because most of his English learners speak Spanish, Francisco **previews** lessons in Spanish whenever possible. For example, he sometimes reads the Spanish version of a book (related to the theme) to his Spanish speakers before introducing the book

TABLE 4.3
Preview/View/Review Technique

Preview
First Language
A teacher, bilingual paraprofessional, or bilingual student gives an overview of the lesson or activity in the students' first language(s). (This could be giving an oral summary, reading a book, showing a film, asking a key question, etc.)

View
English (Second or Target Language)
The teacher teaches the lesson or directs the activity in English using specific strategies to make the input comprehensible.

Review
First Language
The teacher, a bilingual paraprofessional, or students working in same-language groups summarize key ideas and raise questions about the lesson in the students' first language(s).

in English. Or sometimes he reads a book in Spanish as a preview to build background concepts. At other times, Francisco simply gives a short overview in Spanish for his Spanish speakers, or he has one of his more bilingual students give the overview.

Francisco is aware that many of his students are English learners, so during each lesson (the **view**), he uses a variety of techniques to ensure that the English input he provides is comprehensible. He uses visuals, realia, hands-on activities, and group work to engage his students and help scaffold their learning in English.

At the end of a lesson, Francisco sometimes reads another book in Spanish as a **review**, or he has students who speak the same language meet together and summarize the lesson in their first language before reporting back to the class in English.

Putting It Together: Francisco's Global Interdependence Theme

This section presents an example of a theme Francisco developed that is relevant to English learners, enables them to develop language through sustained content study, and can be connected easily to standards in various subject areas. The example includes the titles of culturally relevant books in Spanish and English that Francisco uses as he teaches his lessons. At the end of the chapter, we include a bibliography of these books under "Children's Books Cited."

Francisco's theme is global interdependence. This theme connects to standards related to relationships. The class investigated the big question "In what ways do people throughout the world depend on one another, animals, and nature?" Francisco organizes the theme into six units:

1. If the World Were a Village

2. Family Members Work Together

3. Neighbors and Friends Help Each Other

4. Economic Interdependence

5. Interdependence With Animals

6. Conservation

The theme is especially relevant to the English learners in Francisco's classroom. He teaches language through content connected to standards of the various subject areas. Francisco plans for his theme of global interdependence to include social studies, science, and math standards. He uses the state content, language arts, and reading standards and draws heavily from *Performance Standards: Volume I Elementary School* (1997).

Francisco involves students in meaningful reading and writing. His daily routine includes a morning language arts block. In the afternoon Francisco teaches social studies, science, math, and enrichment subjects such as music and art. He stresses language development and academic content development for all his students throughout the day.

Unit 1: If the World Were a Village

Reading/Language Arts. Francisco introduces the global interdependence theme with the book *If the World Were a Village* (Smith, 2002) during shared reading in the language arts block. He shows students the classroom globe, and students talk about where they or their ancestors come from. Then Francisco reads to the students about how many people are in the world and how many are in the reduced global village. He reads sections of the book that tell the number of people in the global village who come from different countries, the languages they speak, their age ranges, and their religions.

Students discuss the book as a whole group. Working in pairs, they write about how the students in the class are the same as and different from the people in the global village in the book.

Francisco teaches a minilesson about capitalization, and then the student pairs check their papers to see whether they have capitalized the names of countries, languages, and religions.

Social Studies. Later that day, Francisco reads *Somewhere in the Universe* (Drew, 1988) to give students a perspective on how their own community fits into the universe, beginning with the Milky Way galaxy and moving down the hierarchy to the solar system, Earth, North America, the United States, the state, the city, and the neighborhood.

Students also read *Our Book of Maps* (2004), which shows how to make different kinds of maps and ends with a discussion of the globe. Students then find on the globe the countries they have read about, as well as countries with the largest populations and the largest number of speakers of the world's eight major languages.

Math. Students study place value and continue learning to count by tens, hundreds, and thousands. Francisco reads some of the statistics again from *If the World Were a Village* and repeats the number *6 billion* (6 billion people live in the world). He asks students to write out the number and other numbers from the book and to identify the place values. In small groups students make graphs of the countries with the largest populations.

Reading/Language Arts (continuation). The next day as a follow-up to the introduction and to help students grasp the idea of everyone in the world having a connection to others, Francisco reads to the students several books about children all over the world who, though different in some ways, have similar interests, needs, and goals: *Whoever You Are* (Fox, 1997), *This Is the Way We Go to School: A Book About Children Around the World* (Baer, 1990), and, for the Spanish speakers, *Canción de todos los niños del mundo* [Song of All the Children of the World] (Ada, 1993).

The class also reads *We're All Special* (Maguire, 1999b) and the Spanish version, *Todos somos especiales* (Maguire 1999a). The class discusses the unique gifts of each person. Students write paragraphs comparing and contrasting themselves with other children in the world.

Because the language arts standards include poetry, Francisco reads *Come to My House: Children's Poetry* (Almada & Lo-Caseio, 1999a) and its Spanish version, *Vengan a mi casa: Poesía de niños* (Almada & Lo-Caseio, 1999b), as well as *I Am of Two Places* (Carden & Cappellini, 1997a) and its Spanish version, *Soy de dos lugares* (Carden & Cappellini, 1997b). The Spanish versions serve as a preview and review for the Spanish speakers. In the books, children write poems about family traditions and their immigrant experiences.

Francisco's students talk about their native countries and traditions or those of their ancestors. Working in small groups, they write interview questions to ask family members about their family traditions and immigrant experiences. Students then use the results of the interviews to write their own poems for a class poetry book.

Social Studies (continuation). During social studies, students locate the native countries of each student's family on a large world map. Then, using colored yarn and pushpins, they connect their home country to their new home in the United States. This creates a multicolored web showing the routes each family followed to come to the United States.

Math (continuation). To review the concept of graphing, Francisco has each student write down on a sticky note what time they go to bed each night. Students then place their paper on the board over the horizontal line with times listed to create a graph. Then, students graph how many students in the class come from each country. They also graph how many members there are in their families. Francisco uses this activity as a bridge to move to the next unit, Family Members Work Together.

Unit 2: Family Members Work Together

Reading/Language Arts. To help students think about the family as a basic support group, how each member of a family makes important contributions, and how families depend on one another, Francisco reads *Take a Look at My Family* (Thompson, 1998), which describes tasks that family members perform. It ends with, "The people in my family do many different things, but I like it best when we do things together" (p. 16). Francisco reads other books that show families doing things together, including three amusing books:

- *Who Put the Pepper in the Pot?* (Cole, 1989) tells how family members helped too much and put too much pepper in mother's special stew.
- *Room for One More* (Jacobs, 2004) tells about a large extended family living together despite crowded conditions.

- *Daddy Saved the Day* (Shelf Medearis, 1999) describes a large African American family reunion and how Daddy saved the day with his music when the younger children were frightened by Aunt Angela's ghost stories.

The class also reads two bilingual books, *In My Family/En mi familia* (Garza, 1996) and *Family Pictures/Cuadros de familia* (Garza, 1990), which provide a series of vignettes about special events and experiences of Mexican American families living in the United States. Several students relate to these books and enthusiastically share similar experiences from their own families.

Students then read *My Family Tree* (Scott, 1999), which pictures and describes the members of an African American family. This book provides a base for having students work on their own family trees. They take home the project to ask their parents questions.

Social Studies. To meet a social studies standard that requires students to understand the concept of generations and the contributions of older people to society, Francisco decides to devote a whole section of the family unit to the study of grandparents. He gathers books and groups them according to topic:

- Books that show the strong connection children feel with their grandparents: *Cuando mi abuelo viene* [When My Grandfather Comes] (Costigan, 1997), *Practice Makes Perfect* (Chin, 2004b), *Los regalos de mi abuelita* [My Grandmother's Gifts] (Kratky, 1995b), and *Abuelita y yo* [My Grandmother and Me] (Kratky, 1995a).

- Books that show what grandparents teach their grandchildren: *El tapiz de abuela* [Grandmother's Rug] (Castaneda, 1997), *The Tortilla Quilt* (Tenorio-Coscarelli, 1996), *The Tamale Quilt* (Tenorio-Coscarelli, 1998), *Abuelita's Heart* (Cordova, 1997), and *El sancocho del Sábado* (Torres, 1995a) and its English version, *Saturday Sancocho* (Torres, 1995b).

- Books that show the emotions children feel when grandparents move in with their families: *Grandma Moves In* (Sigue, 1999) and *El abuelo* [Grandfather] (Cartwright, 1997).

- Books that show the specialness of visits with grandparents: *I Love Saturdays and Domingos* (Ada, 2002) and *My Grandma and Grandpa* (Giles, 1998).

Throughout the readings and discussions of these books, Francisco emphasizes how different generations depend on and support one another. To summarize this concept, Francisco reminds students of the classic tale of the little red hen. (The little red hen plants and harvests the wheat to make bread, and no one helps. Yet all the animals want to help her eat the bread.)

Francisco reads to students *Green Corn Tamales/Tamales de elote* (Rodriguez, 1994), the story of how a whole family helps to make traditional Christmas tamales. When grandmother asks, "Who will help pick the corn, shuck the corn, grind the corn, and make the tamales?" someone always says, "Not I" or "Yo no," but others do help and, in the end, through the cooperative family effort, everyone enjoys the delicious tamales.

The class also reads "Making Tamales/La tamalada" from *Family Pictures/Cuadros de familia*, in which author Carmen Lomas Garza tells and illustrates how her entire family helped make tamales. Students whose families have Mexican traditions easily connect to these readings and tell how their family members work together to make tamales. This makes other students think of special, traditional dishes their families make during special events or makes them think of projects they do together, such as building, decorating, and making costumes.

After this discussion, the class brainstorms a list of family meals and activities and the tasks each person in the family performs. Francisco writes the students' ideas on butcher paper and posts them in the room for students to refer to.

Unit 3: Neighbors and Friends Help Each Other

The family is a good place to start to get students thinking about how family members are interdependent. Social studies standards ask that students also understand the ways different community members contribute to make communities work well. The standards require students to understand and appreciate diversity within the community and consider how they, themselves, can contribute. Students also need to understand the concept of *grassroots movements* and how positive change can be effected when each person contributes.

Social Studies/Reading/Language Arts. Francisco reads *Getting to Know Your Neighbors* (Chin, 2004a). In this story two students in Mr. Etieene's multiethnic class, Yun and Berto, work on a project to discover the people in their neighborhoods who help one another. In the process, Yun and Berto contribute by connecting the community helpers they interview so that they can support one another.

Francisco reads *Los duendes y el zapatero* [The Elves and the Shoemaker] (Moguel, 1993), *El amigo nuevo* [The New Friend] (Puncel, 1997), and *Friends From the Other Side/Amigos del otro lado* (Anzaldúa, 1993) as a preview for his Spanish speakers to the reading of the books in English. All these books tell about children accepting and befriending one another. Reading *Friends From the Other Side/Amigos del otro lado*, the story of how a Mexican American girl helps a mother and her son, who have immigrated illegally, leads to rich discussion of important issues about immigration and why desperate people enter a new country.

Students can connect to social, political, and economic issues related to interdependence through literature. In *A Handful of Seeds* (Hughes, 1993), Concepción's grandmother and only caretaker dies, and she is forced into the barrio of a large city as a homeless child. Concepción has seeds from the small plot of land she and her grandmother leased, so she plants them. She knows how to care for crops, and when other homeless children befriend her, Concepción organizes them, and together they grow food for the barrio.

Another book, *Sélavi: That Is Life* (Landowne, 2004), relates the true story of the homeless children of Haiti. This book tells how a community group supported children made homeless by civil war. Unfortunately, because of political turmoil, the children lose their support, and the book ends on a sad note. Francisco uses this book and *A Handful of Seeds* as a springboard for discussions of human rights and the effects of war. Students also expand their knowledge of geography as they locate Haiti on a map.

Francisco uses three other books to extend the study of community action and interdependence. In *La calle es libre* (Kurusa, 1983) and the English version, *The Streets Are Free* (Kurusa, 1985), children in a poor Latin American barrio band together with the help of the community librarian to get land. Then they convince the community to work together to build a park. *El parque de Pedrin* [Pedrín's Park] (Mondríguez, 1992) tells of a boy and his friends who fix up a place in the neighborhood for the children to play. These two books help Francisco introduce the concept of working together to promote positive change. He wants students to understand how democracy works and how people can change rules and make life better for everyone.

To continue this theme, he reads to the class the book *Yes, We Can!/¡Sí se puede!* (Cohn, 2002)—the story of the successful Los Angeles janitor strike told from the point of view of a young Latino boy whose mother is one of the leaders—along with four books about César Chávez: *César Chávez: The Struggle for Justice/César Chávez: la lucha por justicia* (Griswold del Castillo, 2002), *Harvesting Hope: The Story of César Chávez* (Krull, 2003), *César Chávez: The Farm Workers' Friend* (Fleming, 2004), and *César Chávez: Líder laboral* [César Chávez: Labor Leader] (de Morris, 1994). The books about César Chávez encourage students to talk about the concept of justice for all. Students discuss other leaders who work or have worked to encourage people to collaborate to improve their lives, including Martin Luther King, Jr. They discuss events in Chávez's life and make a timeline of the key events.

Unit 4: Economic Interdependence

Social Studies/Reading/Language Arts. In order for students to understand trade and how people all over the world are interdependent economically, Francisco rereads *Saturday Sancocho* (in Spanish, *El sancocho del Sábado*). Students discuss how Maria Lili's grandparents have only eggs in the house, but by careful bargaining at the market, Maria Lili and her grandmother are able to exchange their eggs for bananas, potatoes, carrots, and cilantro. They even get a chicken. Thus, their eggs yield all the ingredients for a *sancocho* (a rich chicken stew).

Another book Francisco uses to help students understand economic interdependence is the content book *To Trade or Not to Trade* (Hirsch, 2004). This book explains how the kind of bargaining María Lili and her grandmother do in the market in *Saturday Sancocho* can be expanded to importing and exporting of products across the country and the world.

The students who have newly immigrated read the limited-text book *You Can Sell* (Trumbauer, 2004), which shows various community workers and the products they sell. Students discuss the products exported from their community, including produce such as strawberries, lettuce, broccoli, and artichokes. They talk about what their parents buy in the store that is not grown locally, such as rice and corn.

Unit 5: Interdependence With Animals

Francisco moves from these social studies concepts to science with a focus on ecology. In this way, he helps students understand how people, animals, and plants are also interdependent.

Reading/Language Arts. Beginning with the book *Helping Each Other* (Riley, 2004), about a blind girl and her dog who depend on each other, Francisco and his students read various books about the interdependence of animals and people, and animals among themselves. They read books about how animals help humans, such as *Animals at Work* (Graham, 1998). They also read books about how people have endangered certain animals and how to help save endangered species, such as *In Danger* (Kelly, 1996), *Mountain Gorillas in Danger* (Ritchie, 1999), *¿Por qué nos preocupa?* [Why We Worry] (Granowsky, 1986b), and *Los animales del mundo* [The Animals of the World] (Granowsky, 1986a).

In addition, students read about how people protect animals in *For the Love of Turtles* (Palacios, 1999) and how animals protect themselves through camouflage and protective outer coverings in *Spikes, Scales, and Armor* (Windsor, 1999b), *Hide to Survive* (Atkinson, 1998), and *The Hiders* (Ledington, 1999). They read about how animals live together and help each other in *That's Us* (Windsor, 1999c) and *Living Together* (Windsor, 1999a).

Science. Francisco involves students in several science projects connected to these readings. Students keep a journal to record how the fish, crabs, and snails help each other in their classroom aquarium. They observe insects in the schoolyard and keep notes on how these insects camouflage themselves.

For a final project in this unit, students divide into small groups. Each group chooses an endangered animal. They conduct research in the library and on the Internet to gather facts about the animal. Then each group develops a brochure that presents the facts about the animal and lists ways that people can work together to preserve this endangered species. Students use the computer to produce attractive brochures with pictures of the animals. The groups visit other classes at the school, give a brief talk on the endangered animal they researched, and pass out copies of their brochures.

Unit 6: Conservation

Reading/Language Arts. To bring the interdependence theme to a conclusion, Francisco and his class study conservation. This unit logically follows the study of endangered animals; many animals are endangered because of what people have done and are doing to the environment. Francisco begins the unit by reading to students *The Earth and I* (Asch, 1997). This limited-text book describes the interdependence of earth and people simply, with lines such as "The Earth and I are friends," "We play together in my backyard," and "I help her to grow. She helps me to grow." This book also explains the effects of pollution and urges people to keep Earth clean.

Students read the content book *Under the Canopy* (2004) and the fictional story *The Great Kapok Tree* (Cherry, 1996b) and its Spanish version, *El gran capoquero* (Cherry, 1996a). These books about the rainforest show how dependent the parts of the rainforest, including the animals, plants, and people, are on one another.

Students also read many books about what people can do to clean up the Earth, including the following:

- Books about cleaning up rivers: *A River Ran Wild* (Cherry, 1992) and *There's a Rainbow in the River* (Cummings, 1998).
- Books about cleaning up the environment: *What Can I Do?* (Almada, 1999), *Cleaning Up the Park* (Wetherall, 1995), and *We Clean Up* (McAlister, 1995).
- Books about recycling: *Where Does the Garbage Go?* (Showers, 1999) and *What Happens When You Recycle?* (Sharp, 1998).

Social Studies. To conclude the interdependence theme, Francisco and his students consider taking specific action themselves. Students make posters for the school and their neighborhood encouraging recycling, they write letters about endangered animals and the rainforest to senators and their local newspaper, they organize a classroom campaign to clean up a park near the school, and they collect cans and bottles to recycle.

Art. As a final project, students paint a huge mural showing how people depend on one another, as well as how people, animals, and nature are interdependent. As a title for their mural, students draw from the readings and from the first unit of their interdependence theme. They choose "We Are a Global Village."

Conclusion

Francisco organizes his curriculum around an extended theme with several related units. He teaches all of his students English through academic content study. He connects concepts from content standards to students' lives and experiences. All of his students, including the English learners, are engaged because the content is interesting and because Francisco includes books at different levels. The reading materials are accessible for all of his students.

Many of the books, especially those connected to family and traditions, are culturally relevant. Francisco uses related books in Spanish that provide a preview and review of the concepts studied in English. These books help the Spanish speakers develop concepts in their first language as they learn English. Francisco knows how to help all his students gain the important knowledge they need in order to understand academic content and to become competent readers and writers of English.

REFERENCES

Akhavan, N.L. (2004). *How to align literacy instruction, assessment, and standards and achieve results you never dreamed possible.* Portsmouth, NH: Heinemann.

Freeman, A. (2000). *Selection of culturally relevant text.* Tucson: University of Arizona.

Freeman, Y.S., & Freeman, D.E. (1998). *ESL/EFL teaching: Principles for success.* Portsmouth, NH: Heinemann.

Nagy, W.E., Anderson, R.C., & Herman, P.A. (1987). Learning word meanings from context during normal reading. *American Educational Research Journal, 24,* 237–270.

No Child Left Behind Act of 2001, Pub. L. No. 107–110, 115 Stat. 1425, Sec. 3001. (2002).

Pally, M., & Bailey, N. (2000). *Sustained content teaching in academic ESL/EFL: A practical approach.* Boston: Houghton Mifflin.

Performance standards: Volume I elementary school. (1997). Washington, DC: National Center on Education and the Economy and the University of Pittsburgh.

CHILDREN'S BOOKS CITED

Ada, A.F. (1993). *Canción de todos los niños del mundo (Song of all the children of the world).* Boston: Houghton Mifflin.

Ada, A.F. (2002). *I love Saturdays and Domingos.* New York: Atheneum Books.

Almada, P. (1999). *What can I do?* Crystal Lake, IL: Rigby.

Almada, P., & Lo-Caseio, T. (1999a). *Come to my house: Children's poetry.* Crystal Lake, IL: Rigby.

Almada, P., & Lo-Caseio, T. (1999b). *Vengan a mi casa: Poesía de niños.* Crystal Lake, IL: Rigby.

Anzaldúa, G. (1993). *Friends from the other side/ Amigos del otro lado.* San Francisco: Children's Book Press.

Asch, F. (1997). *The Earth and I.* New York: Scholastic.

Atkinson, K. (1998). *Hide to survive.* Crystal Lake, IL: Rigby.

Baer, E. (1990). *This is the way we go to school: A book about children around the world.* New York: Scholastic.

Carden, M., & Cappellini, M. (1997a). *I am of two places.* Crystal Lake, IL: Rigby.

Carden, M., & Cappellini, M. (1997b). *Soy de dos lugares.* Crystal Lake, IL: Rigby.

Cartwright, P. (1997). *El abuelo* [Grandfather]. Crystal Lake, IL: Rigby.

Castaneda, O.S. (1997). *El tapiz de abuela* [Grandmother's rug]. Boston: Houghton Mifflin.

Cherry, L. (1992). *A river ran wild.* New York: Harcourt Brace.

Cherry, L. (1996a). *El gran capoquero.* Boston: Houghton Mifflin.

Cherry, L. (1996b). *The great kapok tree.* Boston: Houghton Mifflin.

Chin, W. (2004a). *Getting to know your neighbors.* Barrington, IL: Rigby.

Chin, W. (2004b). *Practice makes perfect.* Barrington, IL: Rigby.

Cohn, D. (2002). *¡Sí se puede! Yes, we can! Janitor strike in L.A.* El Paso, TX: Cinco Puntos Press.

Cole, J. (1989). *Who put the pepper in the pot?* Boston: Houghton Mifflin.

Cordova, A. (1997). *Abuelita's heart.* New York: Simon and Schuster.

Costigan, S. (1997). *Cuando mi abuelo viene* [When my grandfather comes]. Boston: Houghton Mifflin.

Cummings, P. (1998). *There's a rainbow in the river.* Crystal Lake, IL: Rigby.

de Morris, C.S. (1994). *César Chávez: Líder laboral* [César Chávez: Labor leader]. Cleveland, OH: Modern Curriculum Press.

Drew, D. (1988). *Somewhere in the universe.* Crystal Lake, IL: Rigby.

Fleming, M. (2004). *César Chávez: The farm workers' friend.* Barrington, IL: Rigby.

Fox, M. (1997). *Whoever you are.* San Diego, CA: Harcourt Brace.

Garza, C.L. (1990). *Family pictures/Cuadros de familia.* San Francisco: Children's Book Press.

Garza, C.L. (1996). *In my family/En mi familia.* San Francisco: Children's Book Press.

Giles, J. (1998). *My grandma and grandpa.* Crystal Lake, IL: Rigby.

Graham, P. (1998). *Animals at work.* Crystal Lake, IL: Rigby.

Granowsky, A. (1986a). *Los animales del mundo* [The animals of the world]. Lexington, MA: Schoolhouse Press.

Granowsky, A. (1986b). *¿Por que nos preocupa?* [Why we worry]. Lexington, MA: Schoolhouse Press.

Griswold del Castillo, R.D. (2002). *César Chávez: The struggle for justice/César Chávez: La lucha por justicia.* Houston, TX: Piñata Books.

Hirsch, C.F. (2004). *To trade or not to trade.* Barrington, IL: Rigby.

Hughes, M. (1993). *A handful of seeds.* New York: Orchard Books.

Jacobs, R. (2004). *Room for one more.* Crystal Lake, IL: Rigby.

Kelly, A. (1996). *In danger.* Crystal Lake, IL: Rigby.

Kratky, L.J. (1995a). *Abuelita y yo* [My grandmother and me]. Carmel, CA: Hampton-Brown Books.

Kratky, L.J. (1995b). *Los regalos de mi abuelita* [My grandmother's gifts]. Carmel, CA: Hampton-Brown Books.

Krull, K. (2003). *Harvesting hope: The story of César Chávez.* New York: Harcourt.

Kurusa. (1983). *La calle es libre.* Caracas, Venezuela: Ediciones Ekaré-Banco del Libro.

Kurusa. (1985). *The streets are free.* Scarborough, ON: Firefly Books.

Landowne, Y. (2004). *Sélavi: That is life.* El Paso, TX: Cinco Puntos Press.

Ledington, S. (1999). *The hiders.* Crystal Lake, IL: Rigby.

Maguire, A. (1999a). *Todos somos especiales.* Leon, Spain: Editorial Everest.

Maguire, A. (1999b). *We're all special.* Leon, Spain: Editorial Everest.

McAlister, M. (1995). *We clean up.* Crystal Lake, IL: Rigby.

Moguel, M.R. (1993). *Los duendes y el zapatero* [The elves and the shoemaker]. Boston: Houghton Mifflin.

Mondríguez, L.R. (1992). *El parque de Pedrín* [Pedrín's park]. Boston: Houghton Mifflin.

Our book of maps. (2004). Barrington, IL: Rigby.

Palacios, A. (1999). *For the love of turtles.* Crystal Lake, IL: Rigby.

Puncel, M. (1997). *El amigo nuevo* [The new friend]. Boston: Houghton Mifflin.

Riley, G.B. (2004). *Helping each other.* Barrington, IL: Rigby.

Ritchie, R. (1999). *Mountain gorillas in danger.* Boston: Houghton Mifflin.

Rodriguez, G.M. (1994). *Green corn tamales/Tamales de elote.* Tucson, AZ: Hispanic Books Distributors.

Scott, J. (1999). *My family tree.* Crystal Lake, IL: Rigby.

Sharp, K. (1998). *What happens when you recycle?* Crystal Lake, IL: Rigby.

Shelf Medearis, A. (1999). *Daddy saved the day.* Crystal Lake, IL: Rigby.

Showers, P. (1999). *Where does the garbage go?* Boston: Houghton Mifflin.

Sigue, J. (1999). *Grandma moves in.* Crystal Lake, IL: Rigby.

Smith, D.J. (2002). *If the world were a village.* Toronto, ON: Kids Can Press.

Tenorio-Coscarelli, J. (1996). *The tortilla quilt.* Lake Elsinore, CA: Quarter Inch Publishing.

Tenorio-Coscarelli, J. (1998). *The tamale quilt.* Lake Elsinore, CA: Quarter Inch Publishing.

Thompson, J. (1998). *Take a look at my family.* Carmel, CA: Hampton Brown.

Torres, L. (1995a). *El sancocho del Sábado.* New York: Farrar Straus Giroux.

Torres, L. (1995b). *Saturday sancocho.* New York: Farrar Straus Giroux.

Trumbauer, L. (2004). *You can sell.* Barrington, IL: Rigby.

Under the canopy. (2004). Barrington, IL: Rigby.

Wetherall, M. (1995). *Cleaning up the park.* Crystal Lake, IL: Rigby.

Windsor, J. (1999a). *Living together.* Crystal Lake, IL: Rigby.

Windsor, J. (1999b). *Spikes, scales, and armor.* Crystal Lake, IL: Rigby.

Windsor, J. (1999c). *That's us.* Crystal Lake, IL: Rigby.

READING INSTRUCTION

CHAPTER 5

Essential Comprehension Strategies for English Learners

Marsha L. Roit

chools across the United States have increasing numbers of English learners entering general education classrooms. These students are expected to learn to read,
write, and speak in English. Federal mandates such as No Child Left Behind
(2002) and state standards expect that each and every student, regardless of linguistic background, not only have equal access to all areas of the curriculum but also meet
state and local curriculum standards. The challenge that teachers face every day is how
to teach linguistically diverse students to read and write in order to develop the critical
tools needed for learning across the curriculum and for participating fully in society.

Teaching reading comprehension, as noted in Anderson and Roit (1998), has the
potential to create a dual learning opportunity for English learners. Key to successful
reading comprehension is student engagement. When students are genuinely engaged in
the comprehension process, not only are they learning about strategies and using them
intentionally to make sense of text, but they are also continually using language, learning vocabulary, sharing experiences, discussing text, collaboratively solving problems,
elaborating on ideas, and engaging in meaningful conversations. Teaching reading comprehension creates the perfect environment for English learners to not only learn how
to derive meaning from text but also to learn how to talk about text and about what
they are learning. Mohr (2004) emphasizes the need for increased talk time for English
learners; reading comprehension instruction provides an ideal environment to foster discussion and accelerate English-language development.

The importance of connecting language and reading comprehension instruction
cannot be underestimated. Drucker (2003) and Allen (2002) note that while English
learners often develop conversational skills in about two years, it takes much longer to
develop the academic language so important for learning. (Also see "Supporting English
Learners" in chapter 1 and "Explicit Development of Academic Language" in chapter

3.) Comprehension instruction can support the learning of academic English in a non-threatening and supportive atmosphere.

The goal of this chapter is to provide classroom teachers with instructional strategies to teach reading comprehension to English learners. The strategies discussed in this chapter can be used for both reading and listening comprehension.

Strategies are conscious plans that people use in order to achieve a goal. This chapter focuses on two types of strategies: comprehension strategies and instructional strategies. Students need to learn and eventually use reading comprehension strategies on their own in order to monitor and make sense of text as they are reading. Reading comprehension strategies are the procedures that all readers bring to bear when they encounter difficulties reading. When something doesn't make sense, readers stop and recognize there is a problem; they use strategies to clarify confusions, inconsistencies, and complexities. For example, readers may reread difficult text at a slower pace, clarify unfamiliar words, and then reread, making connections to the known in order to better understand the less familiar. Comprehension strategies are also used to delve deeper into text, to make connections and inferences, and to draw conclusions. These strategies are the same for fluent English speakers and English learners alike.

Teachers use instructional strategies to teach students how to comprehend text. These are part of the instructional plan for teaching and should be used flexibly, depending on the needs of students. Unlike asking questions, still a commonly found methodology thought to teach comprehension, the instructional strategies laid out in this chapter emphasize teaching and student engagement. Direct explanation, modeling, scaffolding instruction, preteaching, implementing routines, organizing learning, and teaching critical linguistic structures are the keys not only to teaching students how to comprehend text but also to creating a learning environment in which students are comfortable discussing problems, sharing ideas freely, and using language confidently.

Obviously, there is an interaction between both types of strategies. The instructional strategies are the procedures used to teach reading comprehension strategies. Both categories of strategies will be discussed and then integrated into an instructional routine to support English learners as they engage in thinking about text.

Regardless of the comprehension strategy being taught or the instructional strategies being used, teachers must be sensitive to the English-language proficiency levels of their students. Hadaway, Vardell, and Young (2002) organize English learners into three English-language proficiency levels: beginning, intermediate, and advanced proficiency. At the beginning level, English learners are characterized by limited understanding and production of English. By the intermediate level, students are moving beyond mere retelling of information to explaining the why and how. At the advanced proficiency level, students are fluent with academic language and are using complex forms of English. Assessing the language abilities of students and using instructional strategies that address the specific language proficiency levels are key.

Reading Comprehension Strategies: How to Make Sense of Text

Comprehension requires the reader to interact with the text, to use background knowledge to make sense of what is being read, to monitor and check understanding while reading, and to resolve problems and inconsistencies. Strategies are the tools that readers consciously use and adapt, not only to make sense of text, but also to maximize what they are reading—to get beyond the surface level of the text. Strategies help the reader navigate through difficult text, clarify unknown vocabulary, and organize information. Key comprehension strategies include predicting, summarizing, asking questions, clarifying, visualizing or using mental imagery (Armbruster, Lehr, & Osborn, 2001), and making connections. All of these strategies need to be used flexibly and in combination, depending on the demands of the text (type of text, difficulty of the text, familiarity of the content) and the background and skill of the reader.

Strategy instruction takes time. Introducing strategies one at a time and providing students opportunities to use the strategies with different texts help students internalize strategies. The ultimate goal is to use strategies "flexibly and in combination" (Armbruster et al., 2001, p. 54). Once strategies are introduced, simple supports—such as having the names of strategies on cards in the room (Figure 5.1)—put the use of strategies front and center and emphasize their importance. Students should be encouraged to discuss the different strategies before reading, focusing on when to use strategies, why to use them, and how they can help make sense of text. Adding visual cues and the names of the strategies in students' primary languages provides additional support.

FIGURE 5.1
Strategy Cards

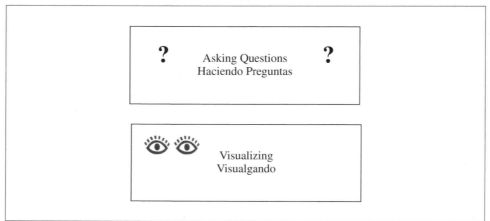

Even after English learners have been introduced to these strategies, they may be reluctant to initiate using them. This is understandable because using them involves considerable language production. Introducing and posting starter statements and questions under each strategy is a simple way to help students get started. Sample statements and questions include "What is difficult about this paragraph?" "I need to clarify..." "What picture is the author trying to create?" and "How does this connect to what I already know?" More starters that support students as they begin to use and discuss strategies can be found in Table 5.1. Statements and questions like these introduce academic language and encourage and support student participation and discussion.

As students become more and more comfortable with strategies, understand how to use strategies, and begin using the various questions and starters, additional starters can be added that not only encourage student participation but also encourage and support language development. In creating these statements, keep in mind students' levels of linguistic proficiency. For students at the beginning linguistic proficiency level, teachers should keep statements simple and encourage students to respond even if it is with

TABLE 5.1
Strategy Starters

Clarifying
- What does this...mean?
- What clues can I use to figure out the meaning of...?
- What does the author mean by...
- Why does the author write...
- How can I figure this out?

Making Connections
- The reminds me of...
- ... is like...because...
- The person in the story is like...in the story...because...
- I did...just like...in the story.
- This connects to the unit theme because...

Visualizing
- I can picture in my mind...
- I see...
- I see...after reading this part.
- From reading this, I can now see...

Predicting
- I know...so I can predict...
- The clues the author gives are...so I can predict...
- I need to make a prediction because...
- I think...is going to happen because...

single words or actions or by pointing to pictures. Students at the intermediate linguistic proficiency level should be able to use sentence stems. Teachers can start with a few statements and build throughout the year. As students begin to use strategies more independently, they can create additional statements and questions and add them to the list.

Instructional Strategies for Teaching Comprehension

While comprehension strategies provide students with the conscious plans to deal with text, instructional strategies give teachers the tools they need to teach comprehension and plan for differentiated instruction.

Strategy 1: Direct Explanation

According to Armbruster et al. (2001), effective comprehension instruction requires direct explanation. Direct explanation involves telling or describing how a strategy or skill can be used during reading. Students are not left to figure out on their own why comprehension strategies are being taught or when and how to use them; the *why* is clearly explained and the *how* is made explicit. Direct explanation of reading strategies should be done within the context of reading, using language that is consistent with students' language proficiency. For English learners, particularly those at the beginning level of language proficiency, direct explanation should be enhanced using charts, graphic organizers, pictures, and realia.

Using direct explanation to teach strategies involves telling students explicitly what strategies are going to be learned and why and how the strategies can help them make sense of text. For English learners, introduce one strategy at a time, use it while reading, and give students time to internalize the why and how of the strategy. Before reading a selection, tell students the focus strategy for the lesson; for example, "Summarizing is a strategy to use when reading. Summarizing helps us check and makes sure we understood what we read. Summarizing also helps us remember what we read. We summarize by telling the most important information."

The reading strategy of summarizing may be particularly problematic for English learners. Often there is a tendency on the part of English learners to repeat almost verbatim what they read. This is natural because students have the text in front of them and can rely on the language in the book. It is comfortable and secure. Although this is a start, it is of limited value because students may not understand what they are saying. Students need to move from this type of retelling to thinking about and identifying the most important information and synthesizing it into a concise statement. They need to get at the kernel or big idea of what was read.

For beginning-proficiency students, this may require visual supports, signal words, and restating by the teacher. Stahl (2004) finds that teaching signal words—such as *what*, *why*, *where*, *when*, and *how*, as well generic questions (e.g., What is the main idea of...?)—provides a starting point for young readers to develop a summary. These cues and structures should be explicitly taught to students. Teachers can begin by asking students to tell about what was just read: Who was the character? What happened? Where did it happen? Teachers can accept single-word answers or have students point to appropriate pictures of things from the story. Teachers write the words on the board or on chart paper and then use the single words to retell the story using complete sentences: "Oh, Anna told us that the girl picked daisies. Paolo told us that the girl picked lilies. And Richard pointed to the roses. Roses and lilies and daises are all flowers." A good summary is "The girl picked flowers."

Retelling lays the foundation for summarizing. Students need to be encouraged to move beyond this beginning stage. Working collaboratively, teacher and students can develop a summary using an explicit instructional procedure developed by Brown, Campione, and Day (1981):

- Delete the trivial.
- Delete redundancies.
- Use superordinate structures.
- Develop a topic sentence if necessary.

For more proficient students, teachers may begin by writing down what the students think should be in a summary, and then giving them responsibility for identifying trivial and unimportant information and marking it out. Once students have identified the most important ideas, they can work collaboratively to write a summary statement. For example, after a group read the book *Alexander, Who Used to Be Rich Last Sunday* (Viorst, 1987), they decided to summarize the story. They began by noting all the things Alexander spent his money on—more of a retelling than a summary. The teacher quietly wrote the students' statements on the board. When the group was done, they began to discuss each point, commenting on its importance or unimportance and crossing out the unimportant points. Then the teacher had the students work in small groups to use the remaining information to write a summary. In the end, the groups agreed on the following: "One Sunday, Alexander's grandparents gave him and his brothers some money. Alexander was tempted by all kinds of things and spent all his money. In the end he regretted it."

Strategy 2: Modeling and Thinking Aloud

Another instructional strategy is modeling or demonstrating the thinking readers use when applying strategies. Think-alouds are particularly valuable for teaching comprehension for students in general and for English learners in particular. Think-alouds involve putting into words the thinking and problem solving used to make sense of text. Think-alouds simply make public what readers do unconsciously when they apply strategies. Think-alouds initially are crafted by the teacher and are used during reading to demonstrate how to use strategies. As students understand strategies and develop their oral-language skills, teachers should encourage them to share their own thinking. Unlike asking questions, a common technique used to direct students' attention to what is important in the text, think-alouds help students to

- understand the purpose of reading,
- focus on building meaning,
- value sharing ideas,
- engage in discussion, and
- use academic language.

Developing think-alouds involves some planning:

- The teacher identifies logical points in the text to apply the different reading strategies: a particularly dense part of a text, a connection to a personal experience, a connection to something that's already been read, a point at which to visualize or imagine beyond the author's words, etc.
- Think-alouds should include the name of the strategy, why it is being used, and how it is being used.
- Think-alouds should sound natural and use language that addresses the linguistic needs of students.
- Think-alouds should provide scaffolding for English learners to help them understand and use more complex linguistic structures. Teachers must be sensitive to English learners' linguistic levels of proficiency.

Using an excerpt from the story *Rugby and Rosie* (Rossiter, 1997), the teacher can model through a think-aloud the strategy of visualizing. The story begins with a description of a boy and his dog:

Rugby is my dog. He is a chocolate Labrador, and we have had him for as long as I can remember.

He walks with me to the school-bus in the morning, and he meets me there when I get home. He follows me around when I do my chores and he sleeps beside my bed at night. He is my best friend. (n.p.)

This beginning provides a perfect opportunity to visualize or use imagery. Students can picture the characters together and sense the feelings they share for each other. Teachers should vary the think-aloud for visualizing, depending on the types of responses they expect from students at various proficiency levels.

For English learners at the beginning language level, teacher modeling or thinking aloud about visualizing might sound something like, "I read the words. I can close my eyes and see the boy and his dog. They are together at the bus and at home." For English learners at the intermediate level, teachers should provide a more elaborate model; for example, "When I close my eyes, I can visualize this boy and his dog. They are special friends. They have a loving relationship with each other. They are like best friends." This second model raises the bar because it involves making some inferences.

This type of public sharing not only provides insight into how and why to use strategies but also provides models of academic language. As students themselves begin thinking aloud, they begin to use the names of strategies, explain why they are using them, and share their thinking.

Find stories that have obvious places for using strategies. For example, in *Angel Child, Dragon Child* (Surat, 1983), the author tells the story of a Vietnamese student who came to the United States without her mother and how she and her fellow students resolve problems and develop mutual understanding and respect. Making connections is a natural strategy to use with this story because it encourages discussion and enhances students' understanding of both the strategy and the story.

By thinking aloud, teachers are able to model what comprehension is about: making sense, solving problems, using multiple strategies, and reflecting on text. Thinking-aloud gives students the opportunity to hear teachers restate selection content in manageable language. Once thinking aloud is turned over to students, teachers have an open window to students' thinking and are able to monitor their students' growth and identify where they need additional support. Throughout the process, teachers need to use the language of learning—think-aloud, visualize, summarize, and the like—and to gradually expect students to use this language as well.

Strategy 3: Scaffold Learning

Scaffolding moves learners beyond their comfort zone to take greater and greater ownership of the thinking and problem solving involved in reading. When students are first learning to engage in text, to use strategies, to monitor their comprehension, and discuss the selection, they need considerable instructional support. Teaching one strategy at a time, the teacher gradually turns responsibility for modeling and thinking aloud over to students. This shift from the teacher doing all the work and thinking to the students doing the thinking is key.

Gambrell and Mazzoni (1999) describe a three-stage model in which the teacher initially assumes the responsibility for using strategies. During the second stage, the teacher and students share responsibility as the teacher prompts students to take more and more responsibility for initiating the use of strategies. In the third stage, students become responsible for applying their knowledge of strategies while reading. This scaffolding helps ensure the transfer of learning and student ownership of comprehension strategies.

Instructional language used to scaffold the use of strategies must be related to the English-language proficiency level of students. Teachers must constantly be evaluating students and increasing expectations of student performance. Students have a tendency to stay in their comfort zone; teachers have a responsibility to move students to more sophisticated levels of thinking, to the use of academic language and greater independence. Table 5.2 includes examples of think-alouds for students at the beginning, intermediate, and advanced language-proficiency levels.

Ongoing assessment is inherent to recognizing when students are ready to take on more cognitive responsibility for using strategies. As students take on more responsibility for thinking, teachers need to adjust the scaffolding.

TABLE 5.2
Scaffolding Strategy Instruction: Visualizing

Beginning Level	Intermediate Level	Advanced Level
Modeling	*Prompting*	*Student Thinking*
Teacher models: "The author makes a picture with words. If I close my eyes, I see a boy and his dog."	Teacher models: "I close my eyes and I can visualize the boy and his dog. They are friends. They do everything together. What do you see?" (Modeling at this level relies less on the illustrations in the text and more on interpreting the author's words.)	Students take ownership of thinking aloud: "As I see the boy and dog, they have a special relationship. They are together almost all the time and love doing all kinds of things together. They work together and they play together."
• The teacher supports this modeling with pictures of the points being visualized. While modeling, the teacher puts up the pictures.		
• The teacher gives students the stem "I see..." as a scaffold, and the students complete the statement with words or pictures.	• The teacher encourages students to share their own mental pictures so that students feel free to add what they see the boy and dog doing together or how the boy and dog feel about each other.	• The teacher may need to scaffold learning by cueing students as necessary.
	• The teacher may still need to support students by combining the sentences that students give.	• Students initiate strategy use, create their own pictures, and make inferences based on what they have read and what they know about friendship in general.

Strategy 4: Teaching Useful Linguistic Structures

Adams and Dutro (2005) emphasize the importance of teaching critical linguistic patterns and structures that students need to understand and use in order to discuss text. Examples of linguistic structures are as follows:

- First, after, then, finally (temporal order words)
- The cause is..., and The effect is....
- The main idea of the paragraph is..., and One detail in the paragraph is...
- I want to...like a....
- The...behind the...is....

These linguistic structures create a meaningful context for introducing and practicing both academic and text-specific vocabulary that is critical for comprehension.

The use of linguistic structures supports not only text comprehension but also the development of vocabulary and academic language. Teachers need to scaffold the instruction of these syntactic structures just as they do for comprehension strategies. Tables 5.3, 5.4, and 5.5 provide examples of linguistic structures that can be explicitly taught to students. The teaching of these structures supports the development of vocabulary, the use of strategies, and the discussion of texts. Student responses may range from pointing to pictures (beginning-level response) with the teacher incorporating the information into the linguistic structure to advanced use of the structures orally and in writing.

TABLE 5.3
Linguistic Structures That Support Comprehension and Vocabulary Development

Classify
- ...are..., but...are....

Sequence
- First, I read about....
- Then, I read about....
- Last, I read about....

Compare
- ...is like...because....

Compare/Contrast
- ...is like....
- ...is different from...because....

Cause and Effect
- If..., then...will happen.
- Because..., the....

TABLE 5.4
Linguistic Structures That Support Strategy Use

Making Connections
• This reminds me of...when I...
• ...is like...in the story...
• ...reminds me of something I once did. It was...

Predicting
• The author wrote...so I predict...
• ...and...have already happened, so I predict...will happen next.

Visualizing
• I see...
• I can visualize...
• From what the author wrote, I can picture...

Table 5.5
Linguistic Structures for Discussing Text Types

• This story reminds me of...
• My favorite part is...
• I liked...because...
• I didn't like...because...
• This story reminds me of...
• I liked the part where the author wrote...
• This story is like...because...
• I learned about...in this story.
• I like it when the author wrote...

Strategy 5: Developing Elaborate Responses

Teaching linguistic structures helps students focus on identifying and using important information. English learners are surrounded by a plethora of information waiting to be learned. Teaching linguistic structures helps them sort out and use information, but students need to move beyond these structures to more elaborated responses. As students become comfortable using different structures, they need to extend the use of the structure by adding details, combining short sentences, and using complex sentences. Students need to be moved out of their comfort zone into using more elaborate responses. As noted in Table 5.6, scaffolding can encourage students to extend simple sentences into more elaborate ones. Often students are quite ready to do this on their own; sometimes all they need is simple cueing from the teacher: *Can you tell me...?* (*why, when, where,* etc.).

TABLE 5.6
Scaffolding Strategy Instruction: Elaborating on Responses

Beginning Level	Intermediate Level	Advanced Level
Teacher models: "What did I read about first? Next? Last?" (Students may answer with one word.)	Teacher models: "What did I read about first? Next? Last?" (Students are able to answer using simple sentences.)	Teacher models: "What are the important ideas in this selection?" (Students answer with complex sentences that incorporate the main ideas.)
• Scaffold by reading the first part again and saying, "I read about...first."	• Scaffold by putting up the words *first, second,* and *last.*	• Scaffold as necessary by having students give a simple sentence.
• Place a picture next to the word *first.*	• Write a single-word response and have students use it in a simple sentence.	• Help students extend by asking them to tell *where, how, why, when,* or *who.*
	• Encourage English learners to combine ideas using *and.*	

Strategy 6: Organizing Materials to Support Concept and Vocabulary Development

English learners need multiple opportunities to develop concepts and internalize vocabulary. By thoughtfully organizing reading materials into themes in which stories are logically sequenced to build on each other, teachers can help students learn critical vocabulary through multiple exposures in multiple contexts (Carlo et al., 2004). In this way, students are able to expand their understanding of basic concepts related to a theme (Mohr, 2004; Schmitt & Carter, 2000). But beyond the obvious advantages themes have for developing vocabulary and concepts, themes provide contextualized opportunities for students to develop ideas, incorporate new vocabulary into discussions about the selections and the theme, learn through different text types, and make connections across selections. (See chapter 4 for more about themes.)

Theme reading should not be limited just to student materials. Teachers should regularly read aloud to students theme-related stories to provide opportunities for building concepts (Freeman & Freeman, 2000). In a unit on camouflage, a teacher decides to introduce the unit by reading aloud *Who's Hiding Here?* by Yoshi (1987). The book has carefully crafted, colorful pictures; short rhythmic narratives; and repetitive elements. It introduces basic concepts that students will encounter later as they read selections about camouflage. The book also provides instructional opportunities to meet the needs of English learners at all three levels of linguistic proficiency.

For students at the basic level, the teacher uses the book to preteach basic theme vocabulary related to colors, names of animals, and the concept of hiding or camouflage. For students at the intermediate level, the book encourages thinking about camouflage and the different forms it takes. Students at the advanced level write about what they already know about camouflage and write questions they want answered through the reading. Students of different English-proficiency levels don't always need different materials; they need teachers who use the materials differently.

Strategy 7: Preteaching

Preteaching, or front loading (Dutro & Moran, 2003), is key to successfully engaging English learners during reading instruction. Preteaching gives students a head start by preparing them for what they will encounter. Preteaching can focus on developing critical background information. It can give students opportunities to discuss content or be an opportunity to teach vocabulary, focusing on difficult text elements. It can also be a way to introduce strategies.

Carefully structured preteaching gives students something else that is critical: a sense of success, a feeling of "I can do it." If preteaching is to be beneficial, the teacher has to identify content, vocabulary, linguistic elements, comprehension strategies, and text organizers that may be problematic for English learners at different proficiency levels.

Returning to the unit on camouflage, the teacher identifies critical linguistic structures that students need to understand in order to both comprehend the upcoming reading selections and to discuss the reading selections:

- ...is the same as...
- ...can hide by...
- ...changes...to hide from other animals

Vocabulary instruction is logically connected to these structures as well and gives students needed support for incorporating newly learned vocabulary into their discussions. For example, if *octopus* and *color* are vocabulary words, students might fill in the blanks as follows: "The octopus can hide by changing color." Using this pattern for other animals and forms of camouflage provides valuable practice using linguistic structures, and helps students focus on using key unit-related words and concepts.

To support discussion, the teacher focuses on the following linguistic elements:

- Today I learned...
- I was surprised to find out...
- Something interesting on page...was...

To support teaching the strategies of making connections and summarizing, the teacher preteaches the following linguistic elements:

- This reminds me of...
- On this page I read...

The preteaching of vocabulary and linguistic structures helps ensure students' successful student engagement in the actual lesson.

Strategy 8: Using Instructional Routines

The instructional routine of thinking before, thinking during, and thinking after reading has several distinct advantages when working with English learners. The routine provides consistency and helps students focus their attention on using strategies and learning new content. In addition, it helps students to identify what is important and to set expectations; it becomes an organizer students can use when they are reading any text.

For teachers, a comprehension routine facilitates instruction. Once the routine is introduced, teachers can focus on teaching comprehension. An additional benefit of using a routine is that it maximizes instructional time, which is the precious commodity teachers always wish they had more of. Key to the before-, during-, and after-reading routine is to have students do the thinking. This routine can be used whether the teacher is reading the selection, with the focus on listening comprehension, or the students are reading the selection. Scaffolding, modeling, and thinking aloud are integral to the routine, and student engagement increases with preteaching.

Before Reading. Students need to be engaged in thinking before reading—to think about and discuss what they already know and build background about the theme and selection:

- Activate background knowledge—existing knowledge about the theme—to develop a conceptual hook upon which to make connections.
- Build background by reading aloud carefully selected materials that provide exposure to the theme. This can be done during preteaching.
- Teach critical concepts and vocabulary. Use graphic organizers to connect newly learned vocabulary with concepts and words introduced in read-aloud selections.
- Preteach if necessary and discuss characteristics of literature to be read.
- Develop critical linguistic structures. For example, if the selections are organized temporally, teach words such as *first, then,* and *finally.*

During Reading. Students need to be engaged in thinking while reading—to use strategies, solve problems, and discuss the meaning of text:

- Model thinking aloud while reading in order to solve problems and make sense of text.

- Scaffold instruction to move students toward using strategies on their own. Prompt them during reading and remind them to check the strategy cards (see Figure 5.1 on page 82) and use the cues on the cards if they need help.
- Encourage students to ask questions when they don't understand something. Model solving the problem. If students are ready, have them think aloud about how to solve the problem. Discuss problems and their solutions.
- Develop focus questions to help students center on the big ideas in the selection and the selection's connection to the unit theme.

After Reading. Students need to reflect on text after reading—to think about what they have read, connect what they have learned to what they already know, and expand their knowledge base:

- Build language and comprehension by discussing what was read.
- Scaffold learning by providing pictures and realia at the basic level for students to use.
- Encourage single-word responses or pointing to pictures or specific parts of the story in the actual text.
- Use discussion starters, such as "I liked...," to make responding manageable for beginning-level students.
- Encourage students to talk about characters, favorite parts, problematic words, and ideas at the intermediate level.
- Have advanced students discuss intentions, make inferences, and evaluate ideas.
- Discuss strategies and how they help the students solve problems.
- Talk about the type of literature and connect it to other selections of the same genre.
- Reread the selection with a specific focus in mind. Students can do this in small, collaborative groups, and each group may have a different focus question that they discuss after rereading a selection.

Conclusion

In this era of "leave no child behind," instructional time must be maximized. Reading comprehension instruction provides an opportunity not just to teach reading comprehension strategies but to teach strategically in order build content and support language development, thereby helping linguistically diverse students become confident and successful learners.

REFERENCES

Adams, M., & Dutro, S. (2005). *Open Court Reading English learner support guide*. Columbus, OH: SRA/McGraw-Hill.

Allen, R. (2002, Fall). Acquiring English: Schools seek ways to strengthen language learning. *Curriculum Update* [Electronic newsletter of the Association for Supervision and Curriculum Development].

Anderson, V., & Roit, M. (1998). Reading as a gateway to language proficiency for language-minority students in the elementary grades. In R.M. Gersten & R.T. Jimenez (Eds.), *Promoting learning for culturally and linguistically diverse students: Classroom applications from contemporary research* (pp. 42–54). Belmont, CA: Wadsworth.

Armbruster, B.B., Lehr, F., & Osborn, J. (2001). *Put reading first: The research building blocks for teaching children to read*. Bethesda, MD: Partnership for Reading.

Brown, A.L., Campione, J.C., & Day, J.D. (1981). Learning to learn: On training students to learn from text. *Educational Researcher, 10*, 14–21.

Carlo, M.S., August, D., McLaughlin, B., Snow, C.E., Dressler, C., Lippman, D.N., et al. (2004). Closing the gap: Addressing the vocabulary needs of English-language learners in bilingual and mainstream classrooms. *Reading Research Quarterly, 39*, 188–215.

Drucker, M.J. (2003). What reading teachers should know about ESL learners. *The Reading Teacher, 57*, 22–29.

Dutro, S., & Moran, C. (2003). Rethinking English language instruction: An architectural approach. In G.G. García (Ed.), *English learners: Reaching the highest level of English literacy* (pp. 227–258). Newark, DE: International Reading Association.

Freeman, D.E., & Freeman Y.S. (2000). *Teaching reading in multilingual classrooms*. Portsmouth, NH: Heinemann.

Gambrell, L., & Mazzoni, S.A. (1999). Principles of best practice: Finding the common ground. In L.B. Gambrell, L.M. Morrow, S.B. Neuman, & M. Pressley (Eds.), *Best practices in literacy instruction* (pp. 11–21). New York: Guilford.

Hadaway, N.L., Vardell, S.M., & Young, T.A. (2002). *Literature-based instruction with English language learners, K–12*. Boston: Allyn & Bacon.

Mohr, K.A.J. (2004). English as an accelerated language: A call to action for reading teachers. *The Reading Teacher, 58*, 18–26.

No Child Left Behind Act of 2001, Pub. L. No. 107–110, 115 Stat. 1425, Sec. 3001. (2002).

Schmitt, N., & Carter, R. (2000). The lexical advantages of narrow reading for second language learners. *TESOL Journal, 9*(1), 4–9.

Stahl, K.A.D. (2004). Proof, practice, and promise: Comprehension strategy instruction in the primary grades. *The Reading Teacher, 57*, 598–609.

CHILDREN'S BOOKS CITED

Rossiter, N.P. (1997). *Rugby and Rosie*. New York: Dutton Books.

Surat, M.M. (1983). *Angel child, dragon child*. Ill. D.M. Voh. New York: Scholastic.

Viorst, J. (1987). *Alexander, who used to be rich last Sunday*. Ill. R. Cruz. New York: Simon & Schuster.

Yoshi. (1987). *Who's hiding here?* New York: Simon & Schuster.

CHAPTER 6

Promoting the Vocabulary Growth of English Learners

Diane August, Maria Carlo, Teresa J. Lively,
Barry McLaughlin, and Catherine Snow

The number of 5- to 24-year olds in the United States who speak a language other than English at home has increased dramatically in the past 20 years—from 6 million in 1979 to 14 million in 1999 (National Center for Education Statistics, 2004). Despite excellent programs and devoted teachers, many English learners have difficulty succeeding in American schools because they are not reading at the level necessary for school success (Moss & Puma, 1995). One reason they lag behind in reading is their lack of word knowledge (Fitzgerald, 1995; Jimenez, Garcia, & Pearson, 1996; Nagy, 1988). In fact, in one study, vocabulary knowledge is found to be even more important to test performance among fifth- and sixth-grade Latino students than prior knowledge of content (Garcia, 1991).

This chapter describes key curricular elements of a one-year intervention, the Vocabulary Improvement Program (Lively, August, Carlo, & Snow, 2003), designed to enrich the vocabulary knowledge and bolster the reading comprehension of Spanish-speaking, fifth-grade English learners in bilingual and general education classrooms. Although the focus of the intervention is English learners, the program is also designed to benefit students in the classroom whose first language is English. The program is appropriate for students in fourth through sixth grades.

The research study that supports the effectiveness of the Vocabulary Improvement Program is reported in detail in *Reading Research Quarterly* (Carlo et al., 2004). Measures used to assess the program are described in chapter Appendix A on page 106. The results of the research indicate that, although there were no treatment gains on the Peabody Picture Vocabulary Test (PPVT; Dunn & Dunn, 1997), English learners in the Vocabulary Improvement Program improved on several measures of vocabulary and comprehension. Students did better in generating sentences that conveyed different meanings of multimeaning words, in completing cloze passages, in tests of knowledge of word meanings, and on measures of word association and morphological knowledge. On a cloze test, used to evaluate comprehension, students showed significant improvement, but the impact on comprehension was much lower than on word learning. It is clear from these results that the program led to improved knowledge of the words studied.

Research Foundation of the Vocabulary Improvement Program

The Vocabulary Improvement Program reflects a model of the complexity of word meaning. Knowing a word implies knowing many things about the word—its literal meaning, its various connotations, the sorts of syntactic constructions into which it enters, the morphological options it offers, and a rich array of semantic associates, such as synonyms and antonyms (see Nagy & Scott, 2000, for a review). These various aspects are related to depth of word knowledge, or how well a student knows the meaning of a word, which is as important as learning many words (breadth of word knowledge). English learners have been shown to be impaired in depth of word knowledge, even for frequently occurring words (Verhallen & Schoonen, 1993). Thus, it is important to develop depth of word knowledge as well as breadth of word knowledge.

The basic principles that guided the design of the Vocabulary Improvement Program are related to practices that have been shown to be effective in previous work (Beck, McKeown, & Omanson, 1987; Beck, Perfetti, & McKeown, 1982; Craik & Tulving, 1975; Stahl, 1999; Stahl & Clark, 1987; Stahl & Fairbanks, 1986). These practices suggest that effective vocabulary instruction includes both definitional information and contextual information about each word's meaning, and that effective instruction actively involves students in word learning and provides multiple exposures to meaningful information about each word. Effective vocabulary instruction also involves teaching within-word parts (i.e., prefixes, suffixes, roots) (Stahl, 1999). Finally, targeted instruction in cognate use and morphological relationships between Spanish and English helps English learners whose first language is Spanish to acquire English word knowledge (Garcia & Nagy, 1993; Nagy, Garcia, Durgunoglu, & Hancin-Bhatt, 1993).

Developing the Program

The vocabulary improvement activities were initially drawn from the research literature on vocabulary acquisition previously cited (Beck et al., 1982, 1987; Craik & Tulving, 1975; Stahl, 1999; Stahl & Clark, 1987; Stahl & Fairbanks, 1986) and from teacher suggestions further developed through pilot testing and extensive teacher–researcher collaboration to make them applicable to bilingual and general education classrooms composed of English learners and fluent English-speaking students.

Prior to implementing the Vocabulary Improvement Program, teachers from the four sites where research was to take place (two schools in Santa Cruz, California; one school in Boston, Massachusetts; and one school in Falls Church, Virginia) met with researchers at the University of California at Santa Cruz to discuss pertinent research and best practice in developing vocabulary and to lay the groundwork for developing the intervention. Following the meeting, a core group of teachers and researchers met in Virginia to develop and field test the program. During the year of pilot testing (1997–1998), there was an initial 5-week pilot of the materials. Based on observations and weekly debriefings with teachers, researchers and teachers revised the materials into two 6-week segments that were pilot-tested between January and June of that year.

Prior to the first year of the program, teachers and researchers from the four sites met again, this time at Harvard University, to discuss first-year findings and to further refine the curriculum. For example, *Fables* (Lobel, 1980), used during the pilot year of the program, was replaced by the theme of immigration in three time periods: early settler, early 20th century, and present. This theme was selected to connect to students' heritage and experience, as well as to conform to district and state social studies standards.

Moreover, in keeping with these standards, which demand exposure to nonnarrative reading, additional genres were introduced, including diaries, textbook accounts, firsthand documentation of the immigrant experience, and newspaper stories. Researchers also replaced several activities that were not as engaging as envisioned. Supplementary Spanish-language materials (in both written and audiotape versions) were provided for the Spanish speakers to preview before the general lesson sequence began. The revised materials were more challenging and at a higher level, as well as better designed, than the previous year's.

What the Program Teaches

The Vocabulary Improvement Program was implemented in fifth-grade classrooms and consisted of 75 lessons. Each lesson lasted approximately 40 minutes. Classroom teachers were trained by the researchers to deliver the instruction. In accordance with research indicating that words are best learned from rich semantic contexts, target vocabulary words were selected from brief, engaging reading passages.

The program focused on a relatively small number of vocabulary items (12 each week) that students at this level were likely to encounter repeatedly across texts in different domains. Although the program focused on only a few words each week, activities helped students make semantic links to other words and concepts, and thus attain a deeper and richer understanding of a word's meaning. From the activities, students also learned other words and concepts related to the target word. In keeping with the research-based best practice previously cited, the lessons also taught students to infer meanings from context and to use roots, affixes, cognates, morphological relationships, and comprehension monitoring.

The lessons were grouped into weekly units (five lessons per week), and each weekly unit followed a similar format. On Monday, generally the first lesson of each unit, the teacher introduced the story and helped students predict the story line and connect the story to their background knowledge. Through teacher-directed classroom discussion, students learned the definitions of the 12 target words and how to infer word meaning from text for a subset of the words. They reviewed the meanings of low-frequency words (e.g., *sunflower*) and displayed compound words on a word wall. During the second day of the unit, students worked in heterogeneous cooperative groups on word-context activities to build depth of word meaning. They were given approximately 14 pairs of sentences. Students had to select the correct target word, based on the sentence context, and explain why they had selected that particular word. Following is an example of a pair of sentences used in this activity:

> Immigrants were typically not rich when they first arrived in the United States. Some became <u>prosperous</u> and successful after years of hard work and sacrifice.

Students had to select *prosperous* from a list of the week's target words.

The third day was devoted to building depth of word meaning through engaging activities that encouraged students to process new word meanings. For example, in one deep-processing activity students interviewed one another using questions that contained the target words (e.g., "What has caused the most <u>torment</u> in your life?" "Name three things that commonly <u>arouse</u> a teacher's anger."). The fourth day, students worked on cognates and morphological relationships and took an assessment on the week's target words so that teachers could monitor their progress. During the fifth day, students learned to use other tools to develop vocabulary, including using affixes, roots, cognates, and comprehension monitoring. (The activities are more fully described in the section "A Close Look at Four Types of Activities.")

Important Program Features

The Vocabulary Improvement Program included some extremely important features. First, the program encouraged teachers to use the vocabulary building strategies they learned during the daily lessons in subject-matter instruction throughout the day. Minilessons were developed for teachers to help them accomplish this. Minilessons included, for example, how to help students infer meaning from text; attain richer, deeper understandings of word meanings; use cognates; understand polysemy or multiple word meanings; and use roots and affixes. Each minilesson began with a brief description of the research base for the strategy and provided several complete examples from the program that exemplified the strategy.

Second, most of the activities combined teacher-directed instruction and cooperative group learning, a format that worked well with heterogeneous groups of students. At the beginning of a lesson, the teacher explained and modeled the activity, and students had the opportunity to practice the activity as a whole group. This was followed by cooperative group work. At the conclusion of each lesson or concurrently with the group work, the teacher pulled the class together and they reported on their work, with teacher feedback and help if necessary.

Third, students' first language, in this case Spanish, was used to bolster their vocabulary knowledge and text comprehension. Prior to each week's lesson, which was delivered in English, students could preview the week's text selection and target vocabulary in Spanish by listening to a tape developed for this purpose. (The program provided tape recorders and headsets.)

Moreover, lists of the target words, with definitions in Spanish and English, were sent home every week to be posted on refrigerators. (The program provided the magnets as well as the lists.) Some of the homework assignments entailed students asking parents about family immigration experiences. These conversations took place in the language used at home.

Fourth, almost all the lessons involved collaborative cooperative learning between English learners and English-only students. For example, in context activities that require students to select the correct target word to complete a sentence, heterogeneous groups of students worked together to arrive at the correct answer. Some of the cooperative group work, most notably the lessons on cognates, depended on the expertise of the English learners. Teachers were instructed to call on English learners as well as their fluent English-speaking teammates, and no credit was given to a group unless the student selected could provide the correct answer and explain why the answer was correct. This is one of the strongest features of the program in that it provides opportunities for English learners to converse in English with fluent English-speakers. It also provides opportunities for English learners to share their expertise with fluent English-speaking classmates.

Fifth, homework assignments reinforced class learning. For example, in the Word Wizard activity, students noted uses of target words outside of class (e.g., at home, on TV, with friends), presented these "found" sentences to their classmates, and posted them in a class book or website. As homework, students also generated new sentences, completed crossword puzzles, and worked on context activities that used target words.

Sixth, students were assessed on the target words each week, and this enabled teachers to monitor the instructional progress of all students.

Finally, built-in review units every five weeks gave students opportunities to consolidate what they had learned.

A Close Look at Four Types of Activities

The Vocabulary Improvement Program uses four types of activities to build students' word knowledge:

1. Context activities

2. Deep-processing activities

3. Cognate activities

4. Structural analysis activities

A sample curriculum is included in chapter Appendix B beginning on page 107.

Context Activities

According to Stahl (1999), because most words are learned from context, vocabulary instruction should simulate learning from context. To this end, each unit begins with an exercise in which students infer the meaning of specific words from the text of the week. The selected words deliberately provide enough cues for students to determine the meaning.

On the second day of the unit, students further develop their inferencing skills by working in small, heterogeneous groups on context activities. Each group is charged with figuring out the correct target words for sentences that support the words' meaning. When called on, students explain why the answer makes sense. Note that students have already learned the definitions of the target words. This activity is intended to give students practice inferring meaning from text and to build depth of word meaning. In the following examples, students locate the target words by context:

I think my teacher symbolizes Columbia. She represents the country, language, and the country's traditions.

When the new boy was asked a question in English, he felt foolish and embarrassed. The teacher humiliated the boy accidentally because he didn't know the boy had recently come from the Dominican Republic.

Teachers also help students use inferencing strategies outside of the specific vocabulary lessons. Because some passages don't have enough clues to help students figure out what a word means, teachers teach students to follow these steps:

1. Note context clues (if any).

2. Determine if there are enough context clues to figure out a target word's meaning and, if so, provide a plausible meaning and explanation for why the meaning is plausible.

3. Ask a friend or use a dictionary if the context does not support the word's meaning.

Throughout the day, teachers model this process with a variety of sentences that have different levels of supporting context.

Deep-Processing Activities

One of the most difficult tasks of vocabulary instruction is having students process new words at a deep level. By this we mean having students make semantic links to other words and concepts and thus attain a deeper and richer understanding of a word's meaning. Beck and colleagues (1982, 1987) suggest that one way to have students make these connections and process words more deeply is to ask questions about target words that require students to have a clear understanding of the meanings and then have students write sentences that use the words in related ways.

The Vocabulary Improvement Program modifies this strategy by selecting the target words from the program's own text, teaching students the word meanings prior to the activity, and engaging students in activities to use the words in novel ways. For example, in one activity students are paired. One student pretends to be famous and one student pretends to be a magazine reporter. The reporter's job is to ask questions of the famous person and write down the answers on a worksheet. After a few moments, students exchange places. The following are sample questions that include target words:

Name three situations that might make you feel some <u>anxiety</u>?

What are three words that describe your <u>heritage</u>?

Name four of your family's <u>values</u>?

What is an experience that could <u>transform</u> your life?

What are three things that you would like to <u>obtain</u> this year?

Name two things that you do <u>periodically</u>?

In another activity, students must decide whether people with certain characteristics would act in a certain way; for example:

1. Which of these things would a <u>reformer</u> be likely to do?
   (a) go to the park for a picnic
   (b) work to change rules that are not fair to a group of people
   (c) notice something isn't fair and say, "Oh well, I can't do anything."
2. Would an <u>idealistic</u> person sponsor an unfair contest? Explain why or why not.

The program also adapts well-known games in order to build depth of word meaning. For example, in charades, students have to act out a target word's meaning for their team; in word bee, team members work together to define a target word they have been given and then present the definition to classmates for approval; in word substitution, team members have to replace a target word with another word or phrase that means the same thing; in word guess, the team that needs the fewest clues to guess a target word wins.

To help students process words more deeply outside the vocabulary lessons, teachers are trained to use similar strategies in a less structured way. For example, if teachers encounter the word *degree* in science, they might ask for the definition of the word in its scientific context as well as the definition in other contexts (e.g., math, literature, geography). They might then ask students to think up new sentences on the spot using various definitions of the target word.

Cognate Activities

Cognates are words that have similar spellings in English and the learner's native language, in this case Spanish, and are related in meaning. Cognates are a rich source of information for some English learners, including those whose first language is Spanish. Research finds that when students' English vocabulary knowledge is controlled, their Spanish vocabulary knowledge and post-hoc ability to recognize cognates significantly predicts their English reading comprehension, indicating that students make use of cognate relationships in English reading (Nagy et al., 1993).

To help students learn more about cognates, the teacher divides them into heterogeneous groups. Each group reads a passage in Spanish and tries to define the underlined words (those that have English cognates). Based on the cognates, each group tries to explain what the story is about. In each group, fluent English-speaking students receive help from their English-learner classmates. In another activity, heterogeneous groups of students read a passage in English and circle all the English words they think have Spanish cognates and, based on their knowledge of Spanish, define the English word. Again, the fluent English-speaking students receive help from their Spanish-speaking peers. See Figure 6.1 for a sample passage in English with cognates highlighted.

FIGURE 6.1
Sample Passage With Cognates Highlighted

In newer tenements, running water came from a convenient faucet above the kitchen sink. This sink was <u>used</u> to wash dishes, clothes, and kids. Water had to be heated on the kitchen <u>stove</u>. Since bathing was <u>difficult</u> at home, most immigrants went <u>regularly</u> to <u>public</u> bath houses.

Tenement <u>apartments</u> had no <u>refrigeration,</u> and <u>supermarkets</u> had not yet been <u>invented</u>. Kids were sent on daily errands to the baker, the fishmonger, the dairyman, or the produce stall. They would rush down rickety tenement stairs, a few pennies clutched tightly in their hands. Since there were no shopping bags or fancy wrappings either, they would carry the bread home in their arms, the herring in a big <u>pan</u> [false cognate] from mother's kitchen.

From Freedman, R. (1995). *Immigrant kids* (p. 23). New York: Puffin.

Structural Analysis Activities

Some reading researchers (Dale & O'Rourke, 1986; Nagy & Anderson, 1984; Stahl, 1999) argue that one of the best ways to expand students' vocabulary is through structural analysis, or helping students figure out the parts of words and what the parts mean. For example, the word *unfruitful* comprises the prefix *un-*, the root *fruit*, and the suffix *-ful*. Other words, such as *snowman*, are compounds of two words.

Because students enjoy word play and games with words, a number of the program games teach roots and affixes. For example, in Roots Rummy, teams create words by combining roots and affixes (e.g., *demo-graph-er*; *phono-graph*; *tele-graph*; *photograph*; *bio-graph-er*). In Roots Sort, teams sort words with the same root (e.g., *television*, *telephone*, *telegraph*, *telescope*) and then try to figure out what the root means. In Suffixes, teams add *-er*, *-ment*, or both to word roots and then develop sentences using the new words.

In teaching structural analysis it is good to keep several issues in mind. The Vocabulary Improvement Program avoids "phantom" prefixes, such as *re-* in *reality*. Teachers help students so they don't look for "little words in big words" (leading to such mistakes as finding *moth* in *mother* and *fat* in *father*). The program exercises recognize that some suffixes are relatively easy to teach, such as *-ness* and *-ity*. Others, such as *-tion*, have meanings that are more abstract and are difficult to convey. In addition, when possible, the program begins with words that are already familiar to students.

Conclusion

The goal of the Vocabulary Improvement Program research project was to develop, implement, and examine the effect of a vocabulary enrichment program on the word knowledge and reading comprehension of English learners. Findings suggest that English learners make gains in vocabulary development and reading comprehension over time if they receive an enriched program of vocabulary instruction. Moreover, such a program can be implemented in heterogeneous classrooms and also benefit the fluent English-speaking students in these classrooms. Ideally, such a program is in place throughout the years of primary schooling.

REFERENCES

Beck, I., McKeown, M.G., & Omanson, R.C. (1987). The effects and uses of diverse vocabulary instructional techniques. In M.G. McKeown & M.E. Curtis (Eds.), *The nature of vocabulary acquisition* (pp. 147–163). Hillsdale, NJ: Erlbaum.

Beck, I.L., Perfetti, C.A., & McKeown, M.G. (1982). Effects of long-term vocabulary instruction on lexical access and reading comprehension. *Journal of Educational Psychology, 74*, 506–521.

Carlo, M.S., August, D., McLaughlin, B., Snow, C.E., Dressler, C., Lippman, D., et al. (2004). Closing the gap: Addressing the vocabulary needs of English-language learners in bilingual and mainstream classrooms. *Reading Research Quarterly, 39*, 188–215.

Craik, F.I.M., & Tulving, E. (1975). Depth of processing and the retention of words in episodic memory.

Journal of Experimental Psychology: General, 104, 268–294.

Dale, E., & O'Rourke, J. (1986). *Vocabulary building.* Columbus, OH: Zaner-Bloser.

Dunn, L.M., & Dunn, L.M. (1997). *Peabody Picture Vocabulary Test—Third edition: Manual.* Circle Pines, MN: American Guidance Services.

Fitzgerald, J. (1995). English-as-a-second-language reading instruction in the United States: A research review. *Journal of Reading Behavior, 27,* 115–152.

Garcia, G.E. (1991). Factors influencing the English reading test performance of Spanish-speaking Hispanic students. *Reading Research Quarterly, 26,* 371–392.

Garcia, G.E., & Nagy, W. (1993). Latino students' concepts of cognates. In D.J. Leu & C.K. Kinzer (Eds.), *Examining central issues in literacy research, theory, and practice* (42nd yearbook of the National Reading Conference, pp. 367–373). Chicago: National Reading Conference.

Jimenez, R.T., Garcia, G.E., & Pearson, P.D. (1996). The reading strategies of bilingual Latino/a students who are successful English readers: Opportunities and obstacles. *Reading Research Quarterly, 31,* 31–61.

Lively, T., August, D., Carlo, M., & Snow, C. (2003). *Vocabulary Improvement Program for English language learners and their classmates.* Baltimore: Brookes.

Moss, M., & Puma, M. (1995). *Prospects: The Congressionally mandated study of educational growth and opportunity* (First-year report on language minority and limited English proficient students, prepared for the U.S. Department of Education). Cambridge, MA: ABT Associates.

Nagy, W.E. (1988). *Teaching vocabulary to improve reading comprehension.* Urbana, IL: National Council of Teachers of English.

Nagy, W.E., & Anderson, R.C. (1984). How many words are there in printed school English? *Reading Research Quarterly, 19,* 304–330.

Nagy, W.E., Garcia, G.E., Durgunoglu, A., & Hancin-Bhatt, B. (1993). Spanish-English bilingual children's use and recognition of cognates in English reading. *Journal of Reading Behavior, 25*(3), 241–259.

Nagy, W.E., & Scott, J. (2000). Vocabulary processes. In M.L. Kamil, P.B. Mosenthal, P.D. Pearson, & R. Barr (Eds.), *Handbook of reading research* (Volume 3, pp. 269–284). Mahwah, NJ: Erlbaum.

National Center for Education Statistics. (2004). *The condition of education, 2004.* Retrieved July 16, 2004, from http://nces.ed.gov/programs/coe

Stahl, S.A. (1999). *Vocabulary development.* Cambridge, MA: Brookline Press.

Stahl, S.A., & Clark, C.H. (1987). The effects of participatory expectations in classroom discussion on the learning of science vocabulary. *American Educational Research Journal, 24*(4), 541–555.

Stahl, S.A., & Fairbanks, M.M. (1986). The effects of vocabulary instruction: A model-based meta-analysis. *Review of Educational Research, 56*(1), 72–110.

Verhallen, M., & Schoonen, R. (1993). Vocabulary knowledge of monolingual and bilingual children. *Applied Linguistics, 14,* 344–363.

CHILDREN'S BOOKS CITED

Freedman, R. (1995). *Immigrant kids.* New York: Puffin.

Lobel, A. (1980). *Fables.* New York: HarperTrophy.

Appendix A: Description of Measures

The Peabody Picture Vocabulary Test Revised (PPVT-R; Dunn & Dunn, 1997) was used to assess breadth of vocabulary knowledge. A polysemy production task was used in which students were asked to generate as many sentences as possible conveying the different meanings of the polysemous words. The words in the fifth-grade polysemy task were *ring, place, settle, pitch, back*, and *check*.

Reading comprehension was assessed with multiple-choice cloze passages with content words deleted at random. Students read three stories with six cloze items per story. Ten of the deleted words were taught in the intervention. A word mastery test was designed to determine if the vocabulary words directly taught were successfully learned. The test consisted of 36 target-word, multiple-choice items. Each target word was followed by four short definitions. Students were asked to select the definition that best described the word. A word association task measured depth of word knowledge by tapping into students' knowledge of paradigmatic and syntagmatic word relations. The task consisted of 20 target words, half of which were included in the curriculum. Each of the target words appeared in the center of a page, with 6 other words printed around the periphery. Students were asked to draw lines from the target word to the 3 peripheral words most closely connected to it. Specifically, students were asked to pick 3 of the words that "always go with the word in the middle." For example, the word *debate* has immutable associations to the words *rival, discussion*, and *opinion* but only circumstantial associations to the words *president, television*, and *fight*. Students' knowledge of English morphology was assessed with a paper and pencil adaptation of Carlisle's (1988) extract-the-base task. Our task consisted of 27 items (fewer than a third were intervention words) that required the student to provide the base form of a derived word. Students heard the derived word (e.g., *discussion*) followed by a lean sentence context (e.g., "What did he want to _____?") and were asked to provide the word that fit in the sentence (i.e., *discuss*). The items varied in the transparency of relationship between the derived and base forms. Some items involved no phonological or orthographic change (e.g., *remark/remarkable*); some involved a phonological change but no orthographic change (e.g., *nation/national*); some involved an orthographic change but no phonological change (e.g., *furious/fury*); and some involved both changes (e.g., *migration/migrate*).

Appendix B: Example of Vocabulary Improvement Program Curriculum, Grades 3–5

Text for Lesson

Excerpt from "Immigrant Kids at Home" in *Immigrant Kids* by Russell Freedman, 1995, New York: Puffin.

> Leonard Covello remembers his family's first American home: Our first home in America was a tenement flat near the East River at 112th Street.... The sunlight and fresh air of our mountain home in Lucania (southern Italy) were replaced by four walls and people over and under and on all sides of us until it seemed that <u>humanity</u> from all corners of the world had <u>congregated</u> in this section of New York City: The endless <u>monotonous</u> rows of tenement buildings that shut out the sky; the clanging of bells and screeching of sirens as a fire broke out somewhere in the neighborhood; <u>dank</u> hallways....
>
> It was Carmelo Accurso who made ready the tenement flat and arranged the welcoming party with relatives and friends to greet us upon our arrival. During this celebration my mother sat dazed unable to realize that at last the <u>torment</u> of the trip was over and that here was America....
>
> Many immigrants had to take in boarders to help pay the rent. Five or six people might sleep in one crowded room. Children <u>commonly</u> slept three and four to a bed....
>
> On hot summer days, the <u>stifling</u> tenement rooms became unbearable. Whole families spilled out of their apartment, seeking <u>relief</u> up on the roof or down in the street, where there was some hope of catching a cool breeze. Kids took over fire escapes and turned them into open-air clubhouses. They put up sleeping tents of sheets and bedspreads and spent summer nights outside, as <u>elevated</u> trains roared past a few feet away.
>
> Every immigrant neighborhood had its boys' gangs. <u>Rival</u> gangs exchanged challenges and <u>ultimatums</u>. Sometimes they fought <u>pitched battles</u> in the streets—using sticks and stones as weapons, and garbage-can covers as shields. Each gang ruled its own territory. Members of rival gangs were not welcome, and an <u>unfamiliar</u> face on the street always <u>aroused</u> suspicion.... (pp. 21–26)

Teacher Strategies: Helping Students Infer From Text

Teacher: *Meaning can be inferred for the word* humanity. *When you reach* humanity, *say to yourself, sometimes you can figure out what a word means by skipping over it and finishing the sentence. Or you can reread the sentence while thinking about what the word might mean. Let me remind you how this works by reading the sentence with humanity in it. The sunlight and fresh air of our mountain home...were replaced by four walls and people over and under and on all sides of us until it seemed that humanity from all corners of the world had congregated in this corner of New York City. Let's see, earlier in the sentence it talks about people on all sides of them. Do you think humanity has something to do with groups of people? What do you think it might mean?* [Takes student responses.] *Let's look up the definition to see if we're close.*

Curriculum adapted from Lively, T., August, D., Carlo, M., & Snow, C. (2003). *Vocabulary Improvement Program for English language learners and their classmates.* Baltimore: Brookes. Used with permission.

Using Words in Context

Prepare for Lesson

Place students in heterogeneous language groups, ideally four or five students.

Introduce the Lesson

Using the activities below, read the first sentence aloud to the class.

Say: *Your job is to figure out which word fits in the blank using the clues that are in the sentence. When everyone in the group knows the correct word and why it fits, raise your hands. I'll call on one of the first groups ready. You will get a point if you get the correct answer* [you may choose not to give points]. *Remember, everyone in your group must know the answer and why it is correct.*

Review the Lesson

• Ask one child for the correct answer and to explain why it is correct.

• You may need to be creative in finding ways to encourage English learners to participate.

• Continue until the lesson is completed, giving each group one point for each correct answer (you may choose not to use points).

Student Activities

rival unfamiliar stifling ultimatum torment monotonous pitched battles humanity elevated aroused common congregate relief dank

1. Many new immigrants come from places that are not well known to some Americans. These <u>unfamiliar</u> places become more familiar to them with time.

2. He was given a final offer by the judge. The <u>ultimatum</u> given to the man was to either stop his life of crime or be put in jail for many years.

3. Many of the Vietnamese immigrants endured terrible suffering on their dangerous ocean journeys. Their <u>torment</u> did not end when they were put into refugee camps.

4. The heat inside tenement buildings is often suffocating. Some people don't have money to buy air conditioners, which would help with the <u>stifling</u> heat.

5. Athletes from the schools in Jamaica Plain and Roslindale are competitors in baseball and basketball. These <u>rival</u> teams have exchanged wins and losses every year.

6. After José got a job, he felt free and went out and bought his mother some flowers. After so much worrying about paying his bills, José felt a tremendous sense of <u>relief</u>.

7. There was a fierce battle between the two teams for the championship. These <u>pitched battles</u> often occur between athletic competitors.

8. The houses in that neighborhood all look the same; it's pretty boring architecture. This <u>monotonous</u> design was created by an architect with no imagination.

9. The world's population is concerned with saving the planet. All of <u>humanity</u> want to protect their environments.

10. The worker painted the sign while sitting on a platform high off the ground. The <u>elevated</u> position allowed him to see all of New York City.

11. Many tenement buildings are dark and damp. These <u>dank</u> living quarters are uncomfortable for the people who live there.

12. Many immigrants from the same country gather together for religious holidays. They often <u>congregate</u> at the local church.

13. It was usual for the Italians to meet at the local church. It was also <u>common</u> for them to see each other in the neighborhood stores.

14. The man's strange behavior was sensed by the policeman. It was easy to see why the man had <u>aroused</u> the policeman's curiosity; he knew this man to be a criminal.

monotonous	congregate	relief	ultimatum	dank	pitch	unfamiliar
rivals	elevated	arouse	stifling	common	torment	humanity

1. He is such a generous person; his friends say he has tremendous <u>humanity</u> because he gives so much to the poor.

2. Sammy Sosa swung hard, but he missed the <u>pitch</u>.

3. Knowing that he could get a loan to go to college helped <u>arouse</u> Roberto's interest.

4. At some parties, the guests like to <u>congregate</u> in a person's kitchen.

5. An iguana is a rare animal. A dog is a <u>common</u> animal.

6. After passing the state exam, Adela felt a tremendous sense of <u>relief</u> and pride.

7. Many Americans are <u>unfamiliar</u> with the customs and religions of other countries.

8. That person should take speaking lessons. He gave such a <u>monotonous</u> speech, I almost fell asleep.

9. Because she did such good work, they <u>elevated</u> her salary by giving her a raise.

10. I received an <u>ultimatum</u> from my father; either do all of my homework or lose my television privileges.

11. There is great emotional suffering and <u>torment</u> felt by some immigrants when they leave their families behind.

12. Although the boxers are <u>rivals</u> in the ring, they are friends outside the arena.

13. The windows didn't open and the air conditioner didn't work; there was nothing we could do about the <u>stifling</u> heat, so we went outside.

14. After the roof leaked all night, the house smelled moldy and <u>dank</u>.

Expanding Meaning: Deep Processing

Prepare for Lesson

Divide students into heterogeneous language groups of four or five students.

Review the Concept: Deep Processing

Say: *You have already learned many of the definitions for this week's vocabulary words. Remember that definitions alone don't teach you everything you need to know to **really** understand what a word means. In today's activity you will be asked to think about how one word's meaning relates to another word's meaning. Does anyone remember what this is called? That's right, it is deep processing.*

> For example, remember when I asked you to think about a <u>reformer</u>:
> Which of these things would a <u>reformer</u> be likely to do?
>
> A. Go to the park for a picnic.
>
> B. Work to change rules that are not fair to a group of people.
>
> C. Notice that something isn't fair and say, "Oh well, I can't do anything."

Say: *When you think about each of these possibilities you ask yourself whether a reformer would or would not be likely to do each thing. This makes you think more about reformers and gives you a richer and deeper picture of what <u>reformer</u> means.*

Introduce the Lesson

Say: *Now you will work in your groups with questions similar to the one we just talked about. Your job is to read each question and talk with your group to decide which answer is correct and why. Remember, you must be able to explain **why** you chose your answer.*

Review the Lesson

Using the activities below, ask students for their answers. Ask students to <u>explain how they chose their answers</u>. The thinking process needed for an explanation is more important than a correct answer.

Student Activities

1. Would you rather <u>congregate</u> with your friends in a <u>dank</u> place or a <u>stifling</u> place? Explain why.

2. What has caused the most <u>torment</u> in your life?

3. What gave you <u>relief</u> from the <u>torment</u>?

4. Would your soccer <u>rival</u> be more likely to: teach you some skills to help you play better; try his/her hardest to get the ball away from you during a game; call you up and ask you to come over to play video games? What else might a rival do?

5. Name three things that <u>commonly arouse</u> a teacher's anger.

6. What is the most <u>monotonous</u> thing you do each day? How could you change it so it wouldn't be so <u>monotonous</u>?

7. Name 3 <u>elevated</u> things you have seen.

8. Which of the following is an <u>ultimatum</u>?

   A. What a beautiful day!

   B. I am so tired, I wish I could go home now!

   C. If you don't finish your work, you cannot watch TV tonight!

   What makes it an <u>ultimatum</u>?

9. If you see an <u>unfamiliar</u> person at your front door, should you:

   A. Invite him/her into your house to wait until your parents come home.

   B. Keep the door closed and ask him/her to return when your mom is home.

   C. Go outside to talk to him/her.

10. Name 2 places that <u>humanity</u> tends to <u>congregate</u>.

Tools to Develop Vocabulary: Cognates

Prepare for Lesson

Divide students into four heterogeneous language teams.

Introduce the Concept: Cognates

Say: *Remember that when you are learning another language, it sometimes helps to look for similarities in how words sound or are spelled. If you were in a country or neighborhood where all the signs were in Spanish, which word would you look for if you wanted to find a police station?* Teléfono, policia, *or* parque*? Who remembers what words are called that have similar spellings in English and Spanish and are related in meaning? Remember, there are also* false cognates. *False cognates are words that have similar spellings in English and Spanish, but are NOT related in meaning. Does anyone remember a false cognate? What does the Spanish word* red *mean?* Red *means "net" in Spanish!*

Introduce the Lesson

If this appears to be too difficult for your students, you may need to work as a whole group and look for the cognates in the following activity. You might emphasize the cognates as you read. (Refer to Figure 6.1 on page 103 of this chapter for a text sample.)

1. Say: *For this activity I will give each team a passage to read. Your job is to look for the words that have Spanish cognates. When you find a word that you think is a cognate, write the word and the Spanish cognate on the worksheet. Discuss the meanings of the Spanish cognates you find to make sure that they **do** have the same meaning as the English word in the fable.*

2. When all teams have completed their worksheets, collect the worksheets and write the words and their cognates on the board.

3. Ask students for meaning of both words to decide if they are true or false cognates.

4. Prompt for additional clues if students have not found them all.

CHAPTER 7

Using Guided Reading With English Learners

Mary Cappellini

Today's classrooms are full of an increasingly diverse population of children. Not only do they include children who speak a variety of languages, which makes teaching them English challenging, but they also include a range of readers, which means teaching them to read in English is even more difficult. Yet teachers are responsible for the literacy development of *all* students, regardless of their language or reading levels.

Because teachers may have students reading at all levels, from emergent readers to fluent readers, and these students may be anywhere from a beginning level to advanced level of English proficiency, they cannot possibly meet all their students' needs in one whole group. It is through guided reading, when teachers meet with small groups of students of the same instructional reading level, that teachers can best meet the needs of individual English learners, helping them become proficient readers and speakers of English.

Guided reading is an important part of a balanced literacy program for English learners. It is the crucial link to independence; the teacher guides students to use the reading strategies and language structures that they have been developing through instruction in shared reading and read-aloud, and throughout the literacy block, while now reading a book on their own. Whereas the teacher does the modeling in read-aloud and has students join in when comfortable in shared reading, in guided reading students are in the role of reader. All students in the small group take on the responsibility to read a new text on their own, with the support of the teacher guiding the lesson.

In this chapter, the following issues are addressed:

- Why guided reading is so important for English learners
- Why it is important to help English learners use the three cueing systems, to develop strategies and language patterns to help English learners use the cueing

Supporting the Literacy Development of English Learners: Increasing Success in All Classrooms, edited by Terrell A. Young and Nancy L. Hadaway. Copyright © 2006 by the International Reading Association.

systems effectively, and to assess their miscues to understand both their language and reading ability

- How to effectively lead a guided reading lesson for emergent, early, early fluent, and fluent readers, with an emphasis on discussion to build students' oral language, academic vocabulary, and higher level comprehension strategies
- How to look closely at language levels, as well as reading levels, when choosing books to match the needs of students, and how to choose books with rich language that supports English learners as they read more challenging texts

Why Guided Reading Is Important for English Learners

English learners need many opportunities to practice the strategies and language patterns they are learning. Guided reading provides plenty of opportunities for practice with the guidance of an expert. Because guided reading is in a small-group setting, it allows English learners to receive support not only from the teacher, but also from peers, whether fluent English speakers or English learners. The discussion that occurs in the context of a guided reading lesson allows students to not only highlight what they know about using reading strategies but also allows them to talk, think, and discuss in a nonthreatening situation. This is critical for the development of students' reading strategies and oral language.

Teachers also benefit from small-group guided reading, because they can observe firsthand what students are able to do while reading new texts for the first time, which is difficult to do in a whole-class group. Teachers can diagnose individual strategy and language pattern use in order to then plan for further instruction. They can also sit with one student at a time during the lesson to learn more about that student's ability and to assess whether or not the student is able to use all three cueing systems (see the next section titled "Using All Three Cueing Systems: Developing Strategies and Language").

In order to successfully lead English learners through a guided reading lesson, teachers must know students' language levels and reading levels, and they must choose appropriate books that match both of those levels. By using ongoing assessments, running records, reading inventories, and informal language assessments, teachers can determine the types of lessons to plan for students (Cappellini, 2005; Routman, 2000).

Using All Three Cueing Systems: Developing Strategies and Language

In order to gain meaning while reading, proficient readers use all three cueing systems: the *semantic*, which uses background knowledge and experience, as well as information like photographs, graphics, or illustrations, to make sense of the text; the *syntactic*, which uses knowledge of language structures and patterns to figure out if the word sounds right in the sentence; and the *graphophonic*, which uses knowledge of phonics and spelling to see if the prediction made looks right and matches the word on the page. All three cueing systems work in conjunction with one another, and readers need all three to be successful (Clay, 1991; Goodman, 1996; Wilde, 2000).

It is important for teachers to encourage and remind their students, their developing readers and language learners, to use all three cueing systems to meet challenges in the text as they read. By helping English learners develop reading strategies and language structures, teachers can help them use the three cueing systems that proficient readers use to read and figure out unknown text. Teachers can encourage English learners to use all three cueing systems by suggesting the strategies from Table 7.1.

There are three questions that help students check their predictions and help them self-correct, a very important strategy for becoming an independent reader. If English learners cannot answer any of the three questions while reading a text, then they need help developing the cueing systems, which will enable them to answer those questions. The questions are as follows:

1. Does it look right? (graphophonic cueing system)

2. Does it sound right? (syntactic cueing system)

3. Does it make sense? (semantic cueing system)

Students' knowledge of English and how it works is a key factor in using the cueing systems to gain meaning while reading. Are English learners' understanding of language structures and patterns developed enough in English for them to be able to use cues to help themselves? If they aren't, then teachers need to help students develop them.

TABLE 7.1
Strategies to Help Students Use the Three Cueing Systems

• Look at the picture.
• Look at the word.
• Look at the beginning letter.
• Think about what would make sense.
• Use what you already know about the topic.
• Think about what you know about the word.
• Look at the rest of the letters to check your prediction.
• Slide through the word to sound it out.
• Read on to figure it out.
• Reread the line.
• Reread the page.

From Cappellini, M. (2005). *Balancing reading and language learning: A resource for teaching English language learners K–5.* Portland, ME: Stenhouse; Newark, DE: International Reading Association.

English learners are at a disadvantage if they aren't developing language that will help them use all three cueing systems to gain meaning (Cappellini, 2005).

Assessing Miscues to Understand Reading and Language Ability

Teachers need to assess the miscues that English learners make and decide whether or not the miscues are based on a lack of language structures that might impede meaning. As teachers analyze student miscues, they need to keep the focus on comprehension. Does the miscue still make sense? If so, the student is doing a good job of constructing meaning (Wilde, 2000).

It really doesn't matter if an English learner reads "They *sees* the stars" instead of "They *see* the stars," because it is obvious that the student understands the word and the meaning of the sentence. This miscue helps the teacher assess the student's language ability, however, and lets the teacher know that the student needs help perfecting subject–verb agreement in the third person. Instead of worrying about the miscue, which does not impede the student from gaining meaning, the teacher can think about planning a shared reading lesson with a language focus on subject–verb agreement, which will help develop the student's knowledge of syntax. The miscue also gives the teacher a better indication of the student's language proficiency, which is probably at the intermediate level, and alerts the teacher of the need to continually develop language proficiency as the student starts to read more challenging texts.

If language proficiency does not progress, the English learner may have more difficulty understanding complicated sentences. The more the student reads, however, the more the student is exposed to vocabulary and language patterns that will improve reading as well as language (Krashen, 2003).

Emergent and Early Guided Reading Lesson: Emphasis on Talk

Teachers can help emergent and early readers use their new language and reading strategies in the context of guided reading lessons with an emphasis on talk and discussion. Emergent readers learn to track from left to right, use background knowledge to predict, use picture clues to help gain meaning, use beginning letters to sound out words, use predictable patterns in the text, can identify some high-frequency words, and can predict the ending. Early readers use all of these strategies as well as chunking words or blending sounds to figure out more difficult words, cross-checking with all three cueing systems, self-questioning while reading to see if it makes sense, and rereading or reading on to try to gain meaning, to name a few more of the strategies used while reading longer texts (Cappellini, 2005; Routman, 2000).

The format of a 15-to-20-minute lesson for emergent and early readers is designed to allow them to be successful reading an unseen text at their instructional level. Regardless of the grade level of the students, if they are at the emergent or early stage of reading, the following format should be used (Cappellini, 2005):

- Introduction: Teacher solicits language
- Orientation: Teacher guides students through first viewing of the text
- First reading: Students read the text by themselves
- Discussion: Students respond to the text
- Students reread the text (on their own or in buddy reading)
- Students respond to the text on their own

Introduction: Teacher Solicits Language

The purpose of the introduction is to prepare students for what they will encounter in the book. By tapping into students' prior knowledge with a discussion about the book, teachers encourage students to start thinking and talking about, and anticipating, the reading. This discussion is critical in setting the scene for English learners, who might encounter new language structures and new vocabulary or be challenged to use new reading strategies while reading.

The introduction begins by the students looking at the cover of their books. The teacher asks students to predict what the book is about and to share any personal experiences they have regarding the topic or the title of the book. Through students' predictions and discussion about the picture on the cover, the teacher naturally draws out any language students have that is related to the book, and even specific vocabulary that may be in the text. Through careful questioning, based on the teacher's knowledge of the language used in the text, the teacher solicits vocabulary that students will need to know.

Many English learners have experiences that they can share in their primary language, and the teacher should encourage them to share what they can in their native tongue (especially if the teacher and some of the other students understand these students' primary language). This supports the English learners and validates that their knowledge of the topic is important, regardless of the language in which it is presented. The teacher also encourages other students to translate some of the specific words that the English learners say in order to help them learn English in the context of the discussion (and because the vocabulary is used in the book).

One example of an introduction that supports English learners uses the emergent nonfiction book *Elena Makes Tortillas* (Bowes, 1997). I used this book with a group of first graders in a school in Southern California with a predominantly Latino population. Students are naturally drawn to the photograph on the cover of the book of a Latino girl mixing *masa* (a flour mixture), and this group was no exception. They smiled at the cover when I handed them their copies. When I asked if they knew how to make tortillas, almost all of them said "*sí*—yes!" Then they answered, some in Spanish, some in English, that they made them with or learned from "*mi mamá*" (my mom) or "*mi abuela*" (my grandma).

Just by looking at the cover, before we even opened the book, a rich discussion ensued, with students explaining how they make tortillas. Crystal told me, "You need *harina* and you need *agua*" (flour and water). "Water," said Martín, who took it upon himself to translate for Crystal. Crystal tried to show me how to mix it and make a ball with the flour, but Esmeralda, and even José, would barely let her finish. They all started pressing their hands together, like many American students do when they play patty-cake. I laughed and asked them to describe in words some of the things they were doing with their hands.

José said, "Press."

Martín said, "Make a ball."

And I asked, "How do you do that?"

Then Esmeralda said, "Roll like a ball."

"Oh," I said, pleased. (I was trying to solicit the verb *roll*, which I knew was in the text.)

I asked the students to help me look through the book to see if we could read how Elena makes her tortillas. They were motivated and interested to compare their techniques. And little did they know that they just told me in their own words most of the lines in the text—how Elena makes tortillas.

Most English learners I share this book with love it, mainly because they personally relate to the experience of Elena. I have always found that when interest is high, the discussion is effortless. Teachers might ask the following questions, though, when students do not have the same experiences:

- What is she doing in the picture?
- Do you know how to make tortillas?
- How did you learn to make tortillas?
- How do you make tortillas?
- What do you need to make tortillas?
- Do you think Elena can make the tortillas by herself?
- Why or why not?
- What do you like to eat with tortillas?

Orientation: Teacher Guides Students Through First Viewing of the Text

After setting the scene in the introduction, the teacher guides students through the text, from the title page on, with an orientation of the whole book. The teacher guides students to use all of three cueing systems and reminds them to use strategies that will help them. The orientation is not only an opportunity to look at the pictures but also to look at the text and to think about what might make sense. The teacher encourages students to find words on the pages that match their predictions, what they see in the pictures, and what they think the author would say. The teacher has students use their knowledge of language, language patterns, and verb tenses to try to solicit the correct language that the author chose for the page. If the text is in the present progressive tense, for example, the teacher asks, "What is she doing?" or "Where is he going?" This models the tense used and hopefully encourages students to respond in that tense in order to be successful reading it. This is very important for English learners who may be in the same reading group but may have different levels of English-language proficiency.

In the lesson with the book *Elena Makes Tortillas*, the pictures match the limited text beautifully, so when Elena first uses flour, then water, the students predicted from the picture what she was doing. Then I had them point to the words on the page. As the book went on, the students were thrilled to see Elena do what they do when they make tortillas, yet they didn't always have the exact word for *roll*, *pat*, and *press*. On each page, I had students check their prediction with the words on the page. In some instances, one student helped the rest of the group with the words. All of the students, however, then pointed to the words without any problem.

It is the teacher's job during the orientation to ask leading questions that are carefully shaped to solicit the vocabulary that students need in order to be successful at reading each page on their own.

First Reading: Students Read the Text by Themselves

Once the teacher has guided students through the text, the teacher then asks students to close their books, go back to the beginning, and read the text by themselves. Often the introduction and orientation of an emergent or early text takes more than half the time of the lesson for English learners because of the emphasis on language development as well as strategy use.

It is very important for English learners to talk and think out loud, and use the language that they are learning, as they are going through a new text. If the orientation is successful, students breeze through their first reading of the text. Also, because the books at the emergent and early stages are often very short, many students finish reading them in a minute or less. That leaves plenty of time for more discussion and follow-up and for students to read the book again.

During this first reading on their own, students individually read the book, trying to construct meaning, and this gives the teacher an opportunity to see and hear the strategies students are using by themselves. The teacher may decide to sit in closer to one or two students during the reading in order to help those individuals use specific strategies to construct meaning on their own. The teacher may also just observe the whole group as they read and take notes or anecdotal records about students. The key at this time is to let students read; the teacher helps them if they need it.

For early-stage texts, which are longer than emergent titles, the reading of the text takes more time, and this gives the teacher more time to work with individual students on their reading strategies. The teacher listens to a student read and, if the teacher hears a mistake, draws the student's attention to it at the end of the text line. The teacher then repeats what the student says and asks if it makes sense.

For example, while reading *The Big Surprise* (Leighton, 1997), Melissa, a second grader and an early reader with an intermediate level of English, read, "Will you still love me *with* the new baby is born?" instead of "*when* the new baby is born." I asked Melissa if it sounded right. She said yes. I had her look at the word *when* and asked her if that looks like the word *with*. She still said yes, so I asked her what sound does *with* end with. Although the *th* sound might have been difficult for Melissa because she was a Spanish speaker, she still said it easily. I asked Melissa what letters make that sound, and she said, "*t-h*." Then I pointed again to the word and asked if she saw the "*t-h*." She said, "No, it's an *n—when!*"

While I was helping Melissa with reading strategies, to help her make sense of what she was reading, the other students were reading quietly on their own. I was able to instruct Melissa to use her knowledge of phonics and the graphophonic cueing system, and I was able to diagnose her need to develop her language structure in order to use her syntactic cueing system to self-correct better. After I had Melissa reread the line to see if it made more sense, I left her and moved on to another student. When one or two students finished faster than the other two in the group, I had them turn to each other and buddy read or let them reread the text on their own while they waited for the others to finish. This is especially helpful, because it allows the group to stay together and doesn't put undue pressure on a student that may need more time to figure out the text.

Discussion: Students Respond to the Text

After all students finish reading the text individually, the teacher leads them in a brief discussion about their personal reactions to the text. Individual responses and interpretations of the text are essential, especially because English learners are often just gaining confidence in sharing their opinions with a group.

During the emergent guided reading lesson of *Elena Makes Tortillas*, the students couldn't stop talking about the last page and all the great things they eat with their tortillas when they make them. They also talked about how Elena makes tortillas the same way as they do. But Esmeralda shared how her mother presses the tortillas by hand, not in a press, as Elena does.

In the early guided reading lesson of *The Big Surprise*, all the students shared how they were surprised, just as the sisters in the book were, that the mother had twins. I then shared that I have twins. Melissa shared that her mom just had a baby and that she felt the same as the girl in the book—she was not sure if her mom was still going to love her.

This brief discussion validated all of the students' use of language and their opinions. It gave them the opportunity to use their new language for a real purpose, and it also gave them time to share strategies that they used to help themselves. A teacher may need to verbalize the strategies that students used while they got stuck so that all members of the group might be reminded to use them, like asking if it made sense, or rereading the line, or using their knowledge of phonics to check their predictions. This helps students think about using effective strategies while they read.

Students Reread the Text (on Their Own or in Buddy Reading)

As mentioned previously, if some students finish reading before others, they can turn to a partner and reread the text or they can reread the text on their own. Often there is time within the guided reading lesson to have all students buddy read. If time does not permit this, then students can take the book back to their seats and read independently or read to each other in their literacy centers while the teacher pulls a new guided reading group. Students learn by listening to each other read, by helping each other, and by sharing the text. They can place their books in their individual book boxes to revisit and read again during independent reading.

Students Respond to the Text on Their Own

There are numerous responses students can make to a text. Often a short discussion led by the teacher motivates students to come up with their own written, oral, or artistic responses to a text. Still, the best response to a book is to read it again. This response should not only be accepted, it should be validated if it is the only response a student wants to make to a particular text.

Early Fluent Guided Reading Lesson: Sustaining and Expanding Meaning

The format of the early fluent guided reading lesson is very much the same as it is for the emergent and early readers, but because the texts are longer, the discussion within the lesson also takes longer, and the focus starts to shift to use the use of strategies that expand meaning. Often, early fluent readers spend a lot of time just trying to sustain meaning while reading, because they are starting to read more challenging texts with more and more unique vocabulary and complex sentence structures.

There is no way to introduce all of the vocabulary that each of the English learners in a group may not know, because all of them come with such diverse backgrounds and language levels. Teachers need to help English learners develop their vocabulary while they are reading and provide them with the strategies that fluent readers use when they come across words they do not know. Teachers can focus, therefore, on helping students figure out unknown vocabulary in context.

One focus, then, for early fluent readers is to have them practice learning new words or phrases in context. Unlike the emergent and early readers, early fluent readers are ready to jot down their thoughts during the guided reading lesson. Teachers can use a focus sheet, which especially helps fluent readers but is also good to introduce to early fluent readers. The focus sheet in Figure 7.1 asks students to list new words or phrases that they want to learn, what they know about them already, how they are used in context, and what they think the word means (Cappellini, 2005). In the context of the lesson and the small-group setting, each student's words and phrases can be shared and students can help one another learn the new words and phrases by locating them in the text.

In follow-up lessons teachers can give students a blank journal and encourage them to keep their own word banks as they continue their own reading. Listing the words

FIGURE 7.1
Focus Sheet: Figuring Out New Words or Phrases

Name _____

Title of Book _____

Genre _____

Author _____

New Words or Phrases	What I Know About Them	What I Think They Mean	How They Are Used

From Cappellini, M. (2005). *Balancing reading and language learning: A resource for teaching English language learners K–5*. Portland, ME: Stenhouse; Newark, DE: International Reading Association.

and including what they already know about them and what they think they mean validate students' background knowledge. It also encourages them to try to figure out the words in context. The example in Figure 7.2 presents a page from Adriana's journal. Adriana is a third-grade English learner whose journal includes words from two books she read in guided reading and then on her own: *Whale Watching* (Cappellini, 2000b) and *Sam and Kim* (Cranefield & Long, 2001). By having students keep their own word banks in a journal format, teachers help them remember words, recognize them when they are reading new texts, and possibly use them in their own writing. By recording

FIGURE 7.2
A Journal Word Bank

New Words or phrases	What I know about the words	What I think they mean
Book— Whale Watching		
p.8 surface	Surface of a table	top of something
p.9 water spraying up	like a hose	water shoots up
p.9 blowholes	blow a bubble	blow out of hole
p.15 shallow	shalow pool	not deep
Book— Sam and Kim		
p.13 predators	emeny, mean animal	will eat other amimals
p.14 endangered	could die	in danger
p.15 damage	bad, can't use	hurt

the page number where the word was found, students avoid having to copy down how the word was used in context but can use the book as a reference if needed.

Early fluent readers need to focus on developing higher level strategies that help them expand meaning while they are reading just as fluent readers do (Fountas & Pinnell, 2001). Because these students are transitional readers, teachers need to strike a balance between helping them sustain meaning and helping them expand meaning (Szymusiak & Sibberson, 2003; Cappellini, 2005). The next section discusses how to help fluent readers expand meaning. Because all English learners come with unique backgrounds, they do not fit into one neat category, so hopefully teachers will also see how the following fluent lesson on expanding meaning could also be appropriate for early fluent readers of all language levels. It is important for teachers to take the framework of the lessons and fit them to individual readers' needs regardless of the students' grade level (Routman, 2000).

Fluent Guided Reading Lesson: Focus on Higher Level Comprehension Strategies

As students become fluent readers, they independently sustain meaning and need more help with higher level strategies. The important part of planning a guided reading lesson for fluent readers is to group students according to similar needs, not just based on reading levels or language levels. Teachers may have numerous students that are fluent readers, but only a few, for example, that are still having trouble summarizing a text. Or there may be students that need to focus on inferring.

At this stage it is critical for teachers to analyze English learners beyond level of speech, oral fluency, and basic level of comprehension to get at deeper comprehension levels (Cappellini, 2005). Many students fool their teachers. They might sound like good readers or be able to provide a literal description of the text, but when asked to analyze the meaning or tell the author's intent, many students are not able to do so. By looking closely at students' ability to use higher level comprehension strategies, teachers can group students according to their needs (Fountas & Pinnell, 2001).

Planning for fluent guided reading is often more challenging than planning for emergent, early, or even early fluent guided reading lessons, because the needs of students vary and change so frequently, and thus, so do the groups. Table 7.2 presents an outline for leading a 25-to-30-minute guided reading session for a group of four to eight fluent readers.

In a guided reading group of fourth-grade fluent English learners that were reading below grade level, I used the book *The Big Catch* (Cappellini, 1996) to focus on the higher level strategy of understanding the author's intent. I hoped this would help the students analyze the text and deepen their understanding of the message of the book. The focus sheet in Figure 7.3 helped students fine-tune their thinking during the reading.

TABLE 7.2
Outline of a Guided Reading Lesson for Fluent Readers

To Prepare
- Group students based on similar needs.
- Decide which strategy to teach based on individual needs.
- Choose the book that will best help students use the target strategy while reading.

To Begin
- Review the strategy that students will practice using during reading; introduce the focus sheet.
- Guide students through an introduction of the text, tapping their background knowledge.
- Orient students to the book and have them look at its components, especially if nonfiction.

During Reading
- Guide students through the text with a set purpose, having them read a few pages at a time silently.
- If some students finish sooner than others, have them use the focus sheet to write down their findings, based on the purpose of the reading.
- While students are reading silently, sit close to one at a time to listen to them read individually in order to support their reading and assess individual ability.

To Discuss Text
- Have students discuss what they found in or learned from the text, depending on the focus and strategy used. Have students share their focus sheets.
- Have students compare their findings to help them in comprehension.

Reproduced with permission from Cappellini, M. (2005). *Balancing reading and language learning: A resource for teaching English language learners K–5.* Portland, ME: Stenhouse; Newark, DE: International Reading Association.

To begin the lesson, I solicited students' background knowledge about fishing and their experiences with the sea, and asked for their predictions about the book. Then I shared that I wrote the story based on my experiences fishing with my dad as a young girl. Their task, I explained, was to figure out the purpose of the story. In order to understand the purpose, or the author's intent, they needed to understand the main character (or two), the problem that they have, and what change the characters go through that helps them solve the problem.

Students read the first couple of pages silently to see if they could find the problem in the story and to see if they could also find out something about the main characters. They wrote down their findings on the focus sheet. As students continued reading and the story developed, they learned more about the main character, Michael, and his dad, and they recorded their findings on the focus sheet. We stopped and discussed what they wrote a couple of times. When students saw Michael's attitude change, both in his outlook on the situation and in his actions, they realized the problem was going to be solved. The students were then able to go back to the beginning and answer the first questions: "What is the purpose of the story?" "What is the author trying to say?"

FIGURE 7.3
Focus Sheet: Studying the Author's Intent

The Big Catch

Studying the Author's Intent

What was the purpose of the Story?
What was the author trying to say?

How you and your dad can do cool things
PROBLEM: together.

Michael didn't want to go fishing

CHARACTER Michael What I know about the Character	What I learned about the character
he's kind of borded of going fishing	He finds other things to do
What is the character like in the beginning of the story?	How does the character change?

CHARACTER What I know about the Character	What I learned about the character
Dad He loves to go fishing. Hes patience.	He He is strong
What is the character like in the beginning of the story?	How does the character change?

SOLUTION:
The dad cot somthing
Michael found sea amimals and he was
What did I learn from the story? excited.
What was the author trying to say?

It can be fun to go fishing because you
can find cool stuff besides the big fish.

Although the focus sheet may seem complicated, its components are important. It is important to talk to students about the connection between the problem, the solution, and the main characters rather than always discussing them separately, as if they can be separated. An author creates the story plot with some purpose in mind—to teach something or to share a message or to offer hope in a situation where otherwise there isn't any. By intertwining the characters with the problem they face and the solution that occurs (usually because of their actions), the author weaves the message seamlessly into the plot. This focus is best taught first in a read-aloud so that the teacher models how to analyze the author's intent. Then students can practice using this strategy during the guided reading lesson (Cappellini, 2005; Fountas & Pinnell, 2001; Hahn, 2002).

During the guided reading lesson of *The Big Catch*, students discovered right away that Michael does not like to go fishing because he and his dad never catch anything. It is evident in Yesenia's written response that, even though she is an English learner, she had no problem understanding the author's intent. Yesenia is correct in her analysis of the text's characters, problem, and solution. Michael discovered a whole world of sea life on the rocks and in the tide pools as his dad was fishing, and he loved passing the time with his dad, sharing all of his new discoveries. Although the editor changed the ending to have the dad actually catch a huge fish, thus the title, it wasn't really necessary because Michael enjoyed his exploration and his time with his dad regardless.

After the group shared their discoveries and discussed what they learned from the story, I still wanted to see if they understood my intent that it did not really matter if Michael's dad caught a big fish or not. I asked them one last question: "Do you think Michael's dad really needed to catch the big fish?" Yesenia answered this way: "No, 'cause what you really should do is to have fun. Michael had fun anyway 'cause he found lots of cool things and he was fishing with his dad." She understood the author's intent even with the changed ending, and I learned that she not only uses higher level thinking strategies but also native expressions in her speech.

Choosing Books for Guided Reading With English Learners

There are numerous books, both fiction and nonfiction, to choose from for fluent readers, books that cover a range of genres besides the one described in the guided reading lesson for fluent readers. When choosing guided reading books for fluent readers, teachers need to know the purpose for choosing them—what strategy do the English learners need to work on? Which book would best match that strategy? Books for all levels of guided reading must be thoughtfully selected and matched to the strengths and needs of all the English learners. Careful selection of the text is dependent on what is considered a challenge and what is considered a support for individual students. In order to match the books accordingly, the teacher must first be aware of the following:

- the developmental reading level of individual students,
- the developmental language proficiency of students,
- the reading strategies that students are using effectively, and
- students' individual interests and experiences.

Knowing the books well enables teachers to guide students through the texts almost effortlessly. Knowledge of the challenges and the supports the text holds for the readers, as well as knowledge of students' individual needs, helps teachers successfully lead a guided reading lesson. There should be enough supports in the book to help students feel confident as readers, and there should also be enough challenges to push them a little farther than their comfort zone—encouraging them to take risks as they are becoming confident readers and English-language users (Cappellini, 2005; Fountas & Pinnell, 1999).

The same book may be more challenging for some students than for others because of the language structure or the content of the book. Each text holds its own supports and challenges for different readers based on the readers' experiences, reading levels, and language levels (Peterson, 2001). If a book is too challenging for a particular reader, which could be because of a variety of reasons, then the teacher needs to pick a new book for that student.

Enriching Vocabulary and Selecting Texts

Guided reading exposes English learners to rich language and academic vocabulary as they start to read more challenging texts on their own. The texts are chosen for students to be supported by the teacher, not to be read independently. Therefore, students are not supposed to know all the words, which is important to remember. There will be many words that English learners do not know, but in the context of wonderfully designed guided reading texts, with great illustrations or photographs, rich language patterns, and often repetitive texts, students have the opportunity to learn new English vocabulary. Many English learners already know what the pictures and concepts are that they are reading about, even though they may not know the exact words in English. They aren't necessarily learning a new concept but rather learning a new label for the idea.

For example, in a guided reading lesson with a group of emergent readers, a beginning speaker named Mayra already knew what that "red thing" was in the picture of the book *A Friend for Me* (Buxton, 2001), even though she didn't have the exact name for it. "To take dog for walk," she said. She then learned the new word *leash* for a concept she already had. (See Cappellini, 2005, for more detail on such lessons.)

Allowing students to tap into their background knowledge and relate to their experiences in their primary language helps them become successful readers and speakers in English (Krashen, 1996). Concepts transfer—students just need to learn the new vocabulary words in English. Cummins (1989, 2003) calls this the "common underlying principal," in which concepts or ideas are stored not by an individual language but by the idea itself. Therefore, students do not have to learn over again what a *leash* is or what it is used for but rather the new name for it in English. This is important for teachers to remember, because often we think a book is too difficult for students if they don't know an exact word.

By encouraging students to think of what a word might mean in their native language (e.g., "*patience*—like *paciencia* in Spanish"), teachers can help students quickly and successfully transfer their knowledge to English. The example of *patience/paciencia* is an English/Spanish cognate, and there is much research on the success of using cognates to develop vocabulary of native Spanish-speakers learning English (Bear, Templeton, Helman, & Baren, 2003; Cummins, 2003; Freeman & Freeman, 2002). Teachers can have students keep a list of the cognates they discover during a guided reading lesson or keep a class list on a chart for all to read (Cappellini, 2005; Rodríguez, 2001). This helps students develop their academic vocabulary, which Cummins (2003) notes is critical to their success in becoming fluent English speakers. (Also see "Cognate Activities" in chapter 6.)

English learners need to be exposed to as much rich vocabulary as possible in the context of a supportive guided reading lesson, not less. Teachers shouldn't shy away from selecting texts with difficult vocabulary for them. English learners need to catch up to their fluent English-speaking peers in order to be successful. Unless teachers continually challenge English learners with interesting and exciting texts that expose them to new academic vocabulary, they will never catch up. Choosing decodable texts and books designed primarily to build on high-frequency words aren't the best books for English learners to use for guided reading. Decodable texts might help students practice their knowledge of phonics, but they are not helpful for getting students to use a variety of strategies and practice using all of the cueing systems to construct meaning, which is the key to guided reading. Books that build on high-frequency words might be great practice materials for reading high-frequency words, but they do not help English learners use strategies to deal with challenging vocabulary and detailed plots, let alone get them interested in reading exciting stories.

Utilizing Sentence Structures: Matching Language Level

Guided reading also gives English learners opportunities to practice language structures that they are learning in English. If they are at the beginning or early-intermediate proficiency level of English, students can practice reading simple repetitive sentences in present tense in emergent books such as *I Play Soccer* (Cappellini, 2000a; e.g., "I kick the ball. I pass the ball."). Or if students are at the early-advanced proficiency level of English, they can practice reading longer sentences with two clauses and sentences with adjectives before the noun (which is unlike Spanish grammar) in fluent books such as *Sam and Kim* (e.g., "The green sea turtle was badly hurt by the net, and it couldn't go back to live in the ocean.") (Cranefield & Long, 2001). The important thing for teachers to remember is to provide students with opportunities to practice language structures at their instructional language levels, not just at their developmental reading levels.

If students are not ready for the past tense yet, then reading sentence patterns in the past tense will be too difficult for them, and they won't be able to use all of their reading strategies effectively because their language structures aren't developed enough. That does not mean, however, that teachers need to choose texts at a lower reading level. It just means that they need to carefully select texts within students' reading levels that are appropriate for their language levels (Cappellini, 2005). There are thousands of guided reading books, published by numerous publishers, that provide lots of opportunities for selecting the "just right" book for all English learners. (See Cappellini, 2005, and Fountas & Pinnell, 1999, 2001, for suggestions.)

Conclusion

Guided reading is a wonderful technique to use with English learners at all levels of language and reading development. It makes instruction easier for teachers, allowing them to plan flexible groups based on students' strengths and needs. It allows teachers to teach to individual students, rather than trying to fit one text to the needs of many diverse students in a classroom. Guided reading benefits English learners because they not only are able to practice their reading strategies, but they are also able to practice their oral language through the rich discussions that occur in the small-group setting. When teachers know their students well, know their students' language proficiency levels as well as their developmental reading levels, and know how to analyze student miscues, they have enough information to plan an effective guided reading lesson. Guided reading lessons should catch students at the cusp of their development and guide them on their path to becoming proficient readers and speakers of English.

REFERENCES

Bear, D., Templeton, S., Helman, L., & Baren, T. (2003). Orthographic development and learning to read in different languages. In G.G. García (Ed.), *English learners: Reaching the highest level of English literacy* (pp. 71–95). Newark, DE: International Reading Association.

Cappellini, M. (2005). *Balancing reading and language learning: A resource for teaching English language learners K–5*. Portland, ME: Stenhouse; Newark, DE: International Reading Association.

Clay, M.M. (1991). *Becoming literate: The construction of inner control*. Portsmouth NH: Heinemann.

Cummins, J. (1989). *Empowering minority students*. Sacramento: California Association for Bilingual Education.

Cummins, J. (2003). Reading and the bilingual student: Fact and friction. In G.G. García (Ed.), *English learners: Reaching the highest level of English literacy* (pp. 2–33). Newark, DE: International Reading Association.

Fountas, I.C., & Pinnell, G.S. (1999). *Matching books to readers: Using leveled books in guided reading, K–3*. Portsmouth, NH: Heinemann.

Fountas, I.C., & Pinnell, G.S. (2001). *Guiding readers and writers grades 3–6: Teaching comprehension, genre, and content literacy*. Portsmouth, NH: Heinemann.

Freeman, Y.S., & Freeman, D.E. (2002). *Closing the achievement gap: How to reach limited-formal-schooling and long-term English learners*. Portsmouth, NH: Heinemann.

Goodman, K. (1996). *On reading: A common-sense look at the nature of language and the science of reading*. Portsmouth, NH: Heinemann.

Hahn, M.L. (2002). *Reconsidering read-aloud*. Portland, ME: Stenhouse.

Krashen, S. (1996). *Under attack: The case against bilingual education*. Culver City, CA: Language Education Associates.

Krashen, S. (2003). Three roles for reading for minority-language students. In G.G. García (Ed.), *English learners: Reaching the highest level of English literacy* (pp. 55–70). Newark, DE: International Reading Association.

Peterson, B. (2001). *Literary pathways: Selecting books to support new readers*. Portsmouth, NH: Heinemann.

Rodríguez, R.A. (2001). From the known to the unknown: Using cognates to teach English to Spanish-speaking literates. *The Reading Teacher, 54,* 744–746.

Routman, R. (2000). *Conversations: Strategies for teaching, learning and evaluating*. Portsmouth, NH: Heinemann.

Szymusiak, K., & Sibberson, F. (2001). *Beyond leveled books: Supporting transitional readers in grades 2–5*. Portland, ME: Stenhouse.

Wilde, S. (2000). *Miscue analysis made easy: Building on student strengths*. Portsmouth, NH: Heinemann.

CHILDREN'S BOOKS CITED

Bowes, C. (1997). *Elena makes tortillas*. Photog. M. Gould. Wellington, New Zealand: Learning Media.

Buxton, J. (2001). *A friend for me*. Ill. W. Rivers. Wellington, New Zealand: Learning Media.

Cappellini, M. (1996). *The big catch*. Ill. L. Porter. Crystal Lake, IL: Rigby.

Cappellini, M. (2000a). *I play soccer*. Ill. G. Crespo. New York: Bebop Books/Lee & Low.

Cappellini, M. (2000b). *Whale watching*. Photog. M. Cappellini & K. Evans. Wellington, New Zealand: Learning Media.

Cranefield, J., & Long, D. (2001). *Sam and Kim*. Wellington, New Zealand: Learning Media.

Leighton, M. (1997). *The big surprise*. Wellington, New Zealand: Learning Media.

CHAPTER 8

Teaching English Learners About Expository Text Structures

Barbara Moss

English learners in today's schools face many challenges. In addition to navigating a new culture and learning to speak a new language, these students face the demands of a school curriculum that is dependent on the ability not only to speak English, but also to read and write the academic English found in textbooks at every grade level.

The development of content/academic-language proficiency is a critical concern for teachers of English learners. Although these students often acquire social communicative language skills within a couple of years, development of academic-language skills takes much longer (see chapter 3). In fact, it may take English learners five or more years to acquire the academic-language proficiency needed for success in content area classrooms (Thomas & Collier, 1995). All too often students are given one or two years of English as a second language (ESL) instruction, during which time they have achieved communicative competence. At this point they are mainstreamed into typical content area classes, such as science, social studies, and mathematics. Although students sometimes have access to sheltered content classes, all too often they are expected to "sink or swim" in classes not specially designed to meet their needs.

Because the language of subjects (such as social studies, science, and math) becomes more academic and less closely related to the language of everyday communication, English learners frequently experience difficulty in these classes. They may have difficulties reading their textbooks and understanding the vocabulary unique to particular subjects. They may also be less familiar with the type of text structures found in the disciplines. Many students who are native speakers of English encounter these same problems with content area subjects. These problems, however, become even more intense for English learners who have not yet acquired the language proficiency needed to succeed in understanding subject-matter content. For this reason, English learners may encounter difficulty in understanding class lectures and discussions, let alone text-book readings. If these learners are to succeed in learning academic content, they need teachers who understand the nature of expository text and who employ strategies designed to facilitate student understanding of expository texts. This chapter answers the following questions:

- Why should teachers teach English learners about expository text?
- What challenges do expository texts pose for English learners?
- How does exposition differ from narrative?
- What are the most commonly encountered expository text structures?
- What oral language, reading, and writing strategies can be used to familiarize English learners with these structures?

Why Teach About Exposition?

If today's English learners are to achieve success in learning the content associated with academic subjects in American schools, it is imperative that their teachers help them understand the expository text that will comprise the vast majority of the reading they do as they progress through the grades. Consider this fact: According to Venezky (1982), by sixth grade 85% of school reading tasks require the ability to read nonnarrative, or expository, text.

Students' failure to develop an understanding of expository texts can have serious consequences for schools and teachers in this age of educational accountability. The requirements of the No Child Left Behind (2002) legislation demand that all students with limited English proficiency become proficient in English and that they demonstrate that proficiency on standardized tests designed to measure progress in both reading and mathematics. No Child Left Behind requires school districts to demonstrate annual yearly progress toward the ultimate goal of proficiency in reading and math through student performance on standardized tests. These tests must be administered annually to all students, including limited-English speakers, in grades 3–8. According to the law, all students must achieve proficiency in mathematics and science by 2013–2014, or the schools they attend can be taken over by the state or privatized.

The standardized tests used to measure today's English learners' school success or failure contain a significant amount of expository text. According to Daniels (2002), 85% of standardized-test content is expository. As part of No Child Left Behind, the National Assessment of Educational Progress (NAEP) is used to compare reading scores across the United States. The most recent version of the NAEP (Grigg, Daane, Jin, & Campbell, 2003), for example, comprises 50% expository text at the fourth grade level and more than 70% by the eighth grade. Clearly, then, students' success in school is tied to their ability to understand expository text.

Instruction in reading expository text, and expository text structures in particular, is crucial for all students, but especially for English learners. These common expository text structures include description, sequence, comparison/contrast, cause and effect, and problem/solution, and are regularly found in expository text of all kinds—whether a textbook, website, or other source. According to Hadaway, Vardell, and Young (2002),

> English learners bring special needs to the language acquisition process that are different from—or at least more pronounced than—those of native English speakers. These include four critical differences: a lack of command of English vocabulary, a lack of proficiency in English text structure, a lack of appropriate content background, and a lack of knowledge of American culture. (p. 31)

Helping students to understand expository text and its structures can facilitate vocabulary and content learning, as well as an understanding of American culture.

Why is the need for the ability to read and write expository text so crucial for today's English learners? First, the literacy demands of a technological society require that students not only be able to read and write in the print world, but also in the digital world (Schmar-Dobler, 2003). The literacy demands of Internet use, for example, are significant. Using the Internet requires that students access information quickly, sift through large amounts of text, evaluate content, and synthesize information from a variety of sources (Schmar-Dobler, 2003). All of these skills, however, depend on students' ability to read the text found on websites, most of which is expository (Kamil & Lane, 1997).

Second, an understanding of expository text is essential to success in learning the content in academic disciplines such as social science, English, and science. The chief goal of ESL programs in the United States is to help students succeed academically in content area classrooms where English is the medium of instruction. Under the best of circumstances, it takes four to seven years for English learners to reach national norms on standardized tests in reading, social studies, and science, but academic instruction cannot be delayed until students master basic skills in English (Collier, 1989). This being the case, it appears critically important that instruction in expository text structures occur fairly early for all students, but particularly for English learners. As Peregoy and Boyle (2001) note,

> Assisting English learners with expository text structures is especially critical because content area texts become longer, more complex, and more conceptually dense from the third grade and up through high school and college. Text structure knowledge can help students grapple with these challenging texts, promoting reading comprehension and learning in science, social studies, and other content areas. (p. 240)

Expository text provides all learners with domain knowledge critical to their understanding in science, social studies, and even mathematics. *Domain knowledge*, or deep knowledge about a particular topic, requires long-term immersion in an area of study. This critical form of prior knowledge about a content area enhances vocabulary understanding as well as comprehension. As Hirsch (2003) notes, "If we don't know the domain, we can't construct a meaningful model of what's being said" (p. 17). By developing students' domain knowledge at the elementary level, teachers help to ensure later success with the increasingly demanding texts found in content at the upper grades. Furthermore, reading instruction that provides an in-depth, long-term focus on a specific knowledge domain not only improves general vocabulary but also improves reading fluency and motivation. Finally, domain knowledge can contribute to improved standardized test scores, because it can provide background knowledge for topics addressed in text passages. As students interact with expository texts in all content areas, they begin to see how information in that content area is organized and to develop an understanding of the text structures authors use to structure information in the various disciplines.

What Are the Challenges of Expository Texts?

Understanding expository text structures can be challenging for all students, native and nonnative speakers alike. Studies show that students have far less familiarity with expository texts and their underlying structures (Chambliss, 1995; Goldman, 1997) than with narrative texts. Knowledge of the structures of different text genres develops over time for students; older students have greater understanding of different text types than younger students (Goldman & Rakestraw, 2000). Despite this fact, students of all ages generally report that reading expository text is more difficult than reading narrative (Langer, 1985).

English learners generally have less awareness of expository text structures than native speakers. This may be a result of a number of factors. First, English learners have less exposure to expository text simply because of their lack of familiarity with the range of texts in English. Second, because text structure conventions vary from language to language, English learners may not have exposure to these text types in their native language, let alone in English. Furthermore, research (Carrell, 1984) suggests that an understanding of particular English text structures may be a function of familiarity based on commonly found text structures in students' native languages. Carrell found, for example, that Arabic students remember information best from expository texts with comparison structures, while Asian students remember best from texts with problem/solution or cause/effect structures.

Classroom exposure to expository text is limited for all students, especially in the primary grades. Duke (2000), for example, found that very little informational text was available in the first-grade classrooms she studied, whether displayed on walls or in classroom libraries. Most importantly, she found that students in these classrooms spent on average only 3.6 minutes with informational text per day. While basal readers are used in approximately 85% of elementary classrooms (kindergarten through grade 5) (Baumann, 2000), students aren't likely to encounter much informational text in them (Flood & Lapp, 1986; Hoffman et al., 1994; Moss & Newton, 2002). A 1999 study, for example, concluded that only 20% of the pages of basal readers in second, fourth, and sixth grades were devoted to informational literature (Moss & Newton, 2002).

Generally speaking, whether native speakers or English learners, students are not taught how to read expository text. Students need exposure to informational texts, but they also need instruction that familiarizes them with its organization and structure. In a study of more than 100 hours of observations in primary literacy classrooms, there was not a single instance of teachers modeling strategies for reading expository text (Fisher & Hiebert, 1990). Despite this, there is considerable evidence that *teaching* common expository text structures (such as description, sequence, compare/contrast, cause/effect, and problem/solution) facilitates reading and writing of exposition (Block, 1993; Goldman & Rakestraw, 2000; McGee & Richgels, 1985; Raphael, Kirschner, & Englert, 1988).

Students who learn to use the organization and structure of informational texts are better able to comprehend and retain the information found in them (Goldman & Rakestraw, 2000; Pearson & Duke, 2002). As Peregoy and Boyle (2000) note,

> All English learners can benefit from text structure instruction. By showing students the elements, organization, and sequencing that make up a "good essay," a "good story," or a "good argument" English teachers can immediately boost the quality of their students' reading and writing. (p. 240)

How Does Exposition Differ From Narrative?

Exposition is the language of information. Textbooks, newspapers, encyclopedias, and websites all use exposition to communicate to readers. Narrative, conversely, is the language of story. Authors create stories by using a narrative format. The different purposes of the two text types help to drive the decisions that authors make as they craft their work in each genre. While the main purpose of expository text is to inform, describe, or report, the main purpose of narrative text is to tell a story. When authors write information books, they conduct research to gain information on the topic at hand. They organize the information as logically and interestingly as they can, using different expository text structures. When authors write a story, they create people and events from their imaginations and craft these into stories using a narrative structure that teaches the reader about the characters and conveys the action (Moss, 2004).

The different purposes of the two text types contribute to differences in the physical appearance between informational text and narrative. Stories contain paragraphs of prose that continue one after another, unless interrupted by illustrations. Long works of fiction are usually divided into chapters. Illustrations may be used to extend the meaning of the text.

Informational texts, however, may contain boldface headings and italicized or boldface vocabulary terms. Visuals (including photographs, graphs, cross sections, and timelines) help to clarify, explain, or extend text information. Maps not only help readers to pinpoint locations but also provide a spatial picture of the progress of an event.

Certain linguistic conventions also define each type of text. When creating stories, for example, authors most frequently write in first or third person. They use devices such as dialogue, past tense, specific settings, and a prose paragraph style. They usually arrange the story in chronological order and structure the story according to a particular pattern referred to as story grammar. This typically includes characters, a setting, a problem (or conflict), a climax or high point to the action, and a resolution. This predictable structure forms a framework that readers encounter over and over again.

Expository texts, like narrative, have their own structures, but these structures are far less predictable than story structure. Authors of informational materials focus on a particular topic and present that topic, usually at the beginning of the book. Important ideas may be signaled through topic sentences, and these big ideas may be linked to smaller ones through language. Authors may use one or more organizational patterns, including description, time order, cause/effect, explanation, examples, or a combination of these. They often use present tense and employ technical vocabulary related to the topic. Table 8.1 illustrates some of the differences between narrative and expository texts.

TABLE 8.1
Comparison of Narrative and Expository Text Features

Narrative	Expository
Contains characters, plot, theme, and setting events, actions, behaviors.	Explains or sets forth information; reports in story form.
Seeks to entertain.	Seeks to inform.
Uses illustration to extend text meaning.	Uses illustration to clarify or explain.
Written in past tense.	Written in present tense.
Written in first person.	Written in third person.
Organized in time sequence.	Organized by topic, cause/effect, problem/solution, or listing.
Uses dialogue.	Uses information-giving words.
Uses prose paragraph style.	Uses headings and titles.
Uses descriptions and repeats vocabulary.	Uses technical vocabulary that is not repeated.
Elaborate writing style.	Terse writing style.
Concrete concepts related to experiences.	Abstract concepts.
Reader gets meaning from events and characters.	Reader gets meaning from information.
Reader suspends disbelief.	Reader assumes information is accurate.
Plot holds reader's attention.	Reader attends to organization of information.
Reader may read material quickly.	Reader uses flexible, slower reading rate.

From Moss, B. (2003b). *Exploring the literature of fact: Children's nonfiction trade books in the elementary classroom.* New York: Guilford. Reprinted with permission.

What Are the Most Common Expository Text Structures?

Description, sequence, compare/contrast, cause/effect, and problem/solution (Meyer, 1985) are the five most commonly found expository text structures. Signal words, or cue words, alert readers to the presence of these patterns and help guide them through texts. Sometimes, however, signal words are implied rather than stated.

Description text structures provide details about a person, place, thing, or phenomenon. No signal words are associated with this pattern.

Sequential text is arranged chronologically. In a sequential text, words such as *first*, *second*, *next*, *then*, *after that*, and *finally* guide the reader through the text.

Texts that use a compare/contrast pattern compare characteristics of two people, places, or things. Signal words such as *same as*, *similar to*, *different from*, *but*, and *yet* signal a compare/contrast structure to the reader.

Cause/effect structures are used to identify causes and their outcomes. Science text is often written using this structure. Signal words such as *so*, *because of*, *since*, *in order to*, *cause*, and *effect* signal this structure.

Finally, the problem/solution structure alerts the reader to the presentation of a dilemma and its solution through signal words such as *problem*, *solution*, *cause*, *since*, and *as a result*. Table 8.2 describes the five text structures, the signal words that go with them, and graphic organizers that can help teachers demonstrate them.

The five text structures work on two levels. Sometimes text patterns provide the macrostructure, or overall structure for a particular book, as in the case of information trade books for primary-grade students. At the microstructure, or paragraph level, however, authors may use many, or even all, of these structures within a given book, chapter, or even on a single page. Furthermore, many expository texts incorporate features of narrative as well as exposition. In addition, signal words are often implied rather than stated.

Teaching Common Text Structures

Teaching English learners about text structures helps them to predict and confirm meaning in a passage, thereby enhancing their comprehension. By carefully tailoring instruction to students' levels of proficiency in English and building background for text content and structures, "teachers can significantly increase their students' chances for success in reading English" (Peregoy & Boyle, 2000, p. 240). In a review of research on comprehension instruction, Pearson and Fielding (1991) found "incredibly positive support for just about any approach to text structure instruction for expository text" (p. 832).

Activities incorporating oral language and listening, as well as reading and writing, can facilitate understanding of expository text structures for English learners at all grade levels from kindergarten through high school. The teaching of expository text structures can begin as early as kindergarten and become increasingly sophisticated as students move through the grades and acquire greater facility with speaking, reading,

TABLE 8.2

Text Structure	Uses	Graphic Organizers	Trade Book Examples
Description	Presents a topic and provides details that help readers understand characteristics of a person, place, thing, topic, or idea. No specific signal words are typically associated with description. When authors delineate a topic (e.g., birds, California, oceans), they use description.	Semantic maps resemble a spider web that groups information by category.	*Bats* (Gibbons, 1999), *Eyewitness Juniors Amazing Snakes* (Parsons, 1990), *Ant Cities* (Dorros, 1988)
Sequential	Involves putting facts, events, or concepts in order of occurrence. Signal words such as *first, second, third, then, next, last, before, after,* and *finally* indicate order of events. Authors use sequence when giving directions (e.g., for an experiment) or explaining (e.g., the stages in an animal's life cycle).	Series-of-events chains use boxes and arrows to illustrate a sequence of events and the steps in the sequence.	*My Puppy Is Born* (Cole, 1991), *How Kittens Grow* (Selsam, 1971), *The Buck Stops Here* (Provensen, 1990)
Compare/Contrast	Involves identification of similarities and differences among facts, concepts, people, and so on. Signal words include *same as, alike, similar to, resembles, compared to, different from, unlike, but,* and *yet.* Authors use this structure to compare and contrast (e.g., crocodiles vs. alligators, life in ancient times vs. life today).	Venn diagrams use interlocking circles to illustrate similarities and differences between two things. Individual characteristics appear in the left and right sections, and common characteristics appear in the overlapping sections.	*Fire, Fire* (Gibbons, 1984), *Gator or Croc* (Fowler, 1996), *Outside and Inside You* (Markle, 1991)
Cause/Effect	Includes a description of causes and the resulting effects. Cause/effect is often signaled by *if, so, so that, because of, as a result of, since, in order to,* and the words *cause* and *effect.* When authors explain effects (e.g., of an oil spill) or reasons (e.g., for animal extinction), they use this structure.	Cause/effect maps use circles or squares with connecting arrows to illustrate relationships among causes and resulting effects.	*What Makes Day and Night?* (Branley, 1986), *What Happens to a Hamburger?* (Showers, 1985), *How Do Apples Grow?* (Maestro, 1992)

(continued)

TABLE 8.2
Common Expository Text Structures *(continued)*

Text Structure	Uses	Graphic Organizers	Trade Book Examples
Problem/Solution	Shows development of a problem and its solution. Signal words include *problem, solution, because, cause, since, as a result,* and *so that.* Authors use this structure to explain (e.g., why inventions are created, why money was invented, or why to buy a particular product).	Problem/solution outlines illustrate visually the problem-solving process by defining components of a problem and possible solutions reflective of each.	*A River Ran Wild: An Environmental History* (Cherry, 1992), *Cars and How They Go* (Cole, 1983), *If You Traveled on the Underground Railroad* (Levine, 1988)

Adapted from Figure 1 in Moss, B. (2004). Teaching expository text structures through information trade book retellings. *The Reading Teacher, 57,* 710–718.

and writing English. Each text structure should be taught individually so that students can master one structure before learning another. Structures such as sequence and compare/contrast may be easier for students to grasp, while description, cause/effect, and problem/solution may be more challenging (Moss, 2004). By providing differentiated instruction for students at different levels of English acquisition, teachers can provide much-needed exposure to these structures. Teachers can incorporate text-structure instruction into a variety of oral- and written-language activities.

Oral-Language Activities

Oral-language activities can familiarize students, especially those who are just developing communicative competence, with the linguistic features of expository texts. For beginning English learners, everyday activities that are familiar to daily living can be most effective in boosting exposure to expository text structures. Through informal, engaging learning experiences, students begin to internalize these structures and use them in their own conversations, thereby developing understanding of the structures' purposes related to oral communication as well as to reading and writing.

Total physical response (TPR) (Asher, 1982) requires that students listen to commands and respond to them nonverbally, much like the children's game Simon Says. TPR lessons are very active and engage students in listening to the teacher repeatedly before actually doing the actions. First the teacher demonstrates the meaning of the commands by both saying the command and modeling the behavior (e.g., saying "stand up" while rising to stand). Then the teacher uses the commands but does not do the physical demonstration. Then the teacher may use familiar commands but add new commands. Finally the teacher uses the commands without the demonstration (Hadaway et al., 2002).

Books that illustrate various text structures can be adapted for use with TPR. Responses may not always involve physical actions but may involve students matching photos, sequencing pictures, or holding up word and sentence strips in response to teacher commands. For example, after listening to an information trade book involving the life cycle of a frog, students could sequence pictures taken from the book into proper order.

Transferring activities (Hadaway et al., 2002), in which students receive information in one form and transfer what they have learned into a different format, are an excellent way to attune English learners to text structures through oral conversations. As with all such activities, teachers need to model the process before students engage in it. After hearing a description of a bat based on a read-aloud of *Bats* (Gibbons, 1999), students can, for example, sketch what they heard. This can sensitize them to the descriptive text structure. Following this, they can compare their drawings to their partners' and talk through the differences and similarities. In this way students can get experience in listening to the descriptive structure and engaging in talk involving compare/contrast.

Direction-giving is an excellent activity for attuning students to sequential text structures. The teacher can give students a map and have them follow directions by tracing a route with a pencil. The teacher may use signal words (such as *first, second, next*, and *then*) to reinforce the sequential structure. Students can then take turns giving directions to one another, employing these same commonly used signal words.

Still other oral activities might involve students in conversation practice. Teachers can involve students in practice conversations by posing a problem and engaging students in a discussion of its solution. Discussions of everyday problems and solutions (such as losing lunch money or missing the bus) can help acquaint students with text structures involving problem and solution by engaging them in talk that involves the use of language associated with the structure. Through these activities and many others, students can begin to comprehend the various typical text structures.

Shared Reading

Shared reading experiences are an ideal way to develop intermediate-level English learners' understanding of expository text structures. During shared reading experiences, teachers and students read the same text. Teachers can model reading strategies by having students follow along in an informational Big Book or other type of text. By making the text visible to all students, whether through a Big Book on an overhead projector, teachers can demonstrate the ways in which authors use text features, such as tables of contents and headings, to alert readers to various text structures.

For example, Amanda Craig's third-grade students were involved in a study of animals as part of a science unit. In shared reading, Amanda used the Spyglass book *Tame and Wild* (Auch, 2002). She introduced the macrostructure of the book by engaging students in a discussion of what the words *tame* and *wild* refer to. Amanda then used the table of contents to demonstrate how to find the glossary in the book. She showed students the glossary, and then read the meaning of *tame* aloud. She talked about how the words *tame* and *wild* are opposites, thereby developing the idea of contrast.

At this point, Amanda placed a transparency of the table of contents on the overhead projector. She showed students the entries in the table of contents, which included "Cats and Lions," "Cattle and Yaks," and "Dogs and Wolves." She pointed out to students that each of the chapters in the book involves comparisons of animals. She also pointed out that tame animals were listed first in each chapter, and wild animals were listed second.

Amanda then showed students the layout of the book. She showed students that each entry in the table of contents corresponds to a heading in the book. She then helped students discover that the tame animal was always described on the left side of the page, and the wild animal on the right side. Following this, Amanda assigned students in pairs to buddy read one or two chapters of the book. Students then used Venn diagrams to record the similarities and differences between the two animals in the chapter.

Informational Book Read-Alouds

Today's informational trade books are an ideal resource for teaching expository text structures to English learners because they offer clear organization and are often written in a more student-friendly fashion than textbooks. Teachers should select books for this purpose that are well written, accurate in terms of content and illustration, and appropriate to the age level of students. They should not simply be "baskets of facts," but should be written in an engaging and appealing way.

Teachers must carefully identify books that don't overwhelm students with difficult technical vocabulary and numerous complex concepts. The best informational books make even the most difficult terms and concepts comprehensible to students. Teachers also need to select books that clearly illustrate the text structure being taught. In many informational trade books, signal words are implied rather than explicitly stated. If this is the case, teachers should choose books with page layouts, headings, and tables of contents that provide students with important clues about the pattern used (Moss, 2004). Table 8.2 provides titles of books that are reflective of the various text structures. When reading informational trade books, teachers can follow three steps.

Step 1: Before reading. Develop links between students' experiences and the text itself. Use prereading activities that activate prior knowledge and stimulate thinking about the content of the book, such as K-W-L (what I **know**; what I **want** to learn; what I **have** learned) (Ogle, 1986), brainstorming, and problem solving. Make book concepts more concrete by using props, pictures, or actual examples of things mentioned in the book.

Step 2: During reading. Point out specific text features that can alert students to the text structure, such as signal words, table of contents, headings, and font size. Instruct students to read or listen carefully in order to remember as much as they can about the text.

Step 3: After reading. After students have listened to the book, encourage them to retell the text as a group. Record their responses on chart paper using the language experience approach, emphasizing for students the use of signal words as a means of identifying text organization.

Graphic Organizers

For students who have developed greater facility with English, graphic organizers are an excellent, visual way to increase understanding of text structures. Students can use graphic organizers while listening to a book being read aloud or while reading silently. Completing organizers during reading can provide a focus for reading and at the same time sensitize students to the patterns of exposition. As Vacca and Vacca (2005) note,

> when students learn how to use and construct graphic representations, they are in control of a study strategy that allows them to identify what parts of a text are important, how the ideas and concepts encountered in the text are related, and where they can find specific information to support more important ideas. (p. 399)

Furthermore, graphic organizers can serve as a prewriting tool for writing experiences requiring the use of the five common text structures.

As noted in Table 8.2, specific types of graphic organizers are associated with each text structure. Semantic maps can be used to illustrate descriptive texts, series-of-events chains show sequential structure, Venn diagrams illustrate compare/contrast, cause/effect maps portray the cause/effect structure, and problem/solution outlines show students how the problem/solution structure works.

Teachers can follow nine steps when teaching students about text structures using graphic organizers (Tompkins, 2002; cf. Moss, 2004):

1. Introduce the organizational structure.
2. Explain the structure and when authors use it. Point out the signal words associated with the structure and share an example.
3. Model ways students can determine text structures when signal words are not used. The table of contents and headings can help in this area.
4. Introduce the graphic organizer for the structure.
5. Read aloud a trade book or a section of a book that illustrates the appropriate text structure. Ask students to listen for signal words that can help them identify the structure.

6. Using the overhead projector, involve the group in completing a graphic organizer that illustrates the text structure.

7. Ask students to work in pairs to locate examples of the structure in informational trade books. They can search for examples of signal words, as well as use headings and other text features.

8. Involve students in diagramming the text structure using a graphic organizer.

9. Follow up with writing activities, if appropriate.

As students become increasingly familiar with using graphic organizers, they can complete them individually or in pairs during or after silent reading of a passage. For struggling students, teachers can provide partially completed organizers to help scaffold understanding. Eventually, after much modeling and experiences with organizers, students should be able to construct their own semantic maps, Venn diagrams, and so on.

Teacher Maria Alvarez's fifth graders were studying the California gold rush. As part of this study, Maria read aloud Rhoda Blumberg's (1989) *The Great American Goldrush*. After developing student understanding of the problem/solution structure and its signal words, she read aloud a section of the book about some of the problems that plagued an early city. After listening, students completed the problem/solution outline found in Figure 8.1.

FIGURE 8.1
Problem/Solution Outline for The Great American Goldrush

Problem
<u>Who</u> has the problem? The city of San Francisco.
<u>What</u> was the problem? Fires were commonplace.
<u>Why</u> was it a problem? Most buildings were made of wood and burned easily.

Solutions	**Outcomes**
City dwellers and businessmen started to build buildings out of bricks.	Buildings were more resistant to fire.

End Result
Rebuilding was no longer necessary after every fire because the new buildings were fire-resistant.

Reprinted with permission from Moss, B. (2003a). *25 strategies for guiding readers through informational texts* (p. 62). San Diego, CA: Academic Professional Development.

Writing

Writing activities are an excellent way to reinforce student understanding of text structures and are a natural extension to graphic organizers. Graphic organizers can become prewriting activities that help students organize their thoughts before they write. For example, if students are to write a compare/contrast paragraph about two cultures, they can first create and complete a Venn diagram. They can then develop the ideas for their paragraph from the organizer.

Written retellings let students play an active role in reconstructing expository text. After listening to or reading a book reflective of a particular text structure, students can complete graphic organizers and then use them to guide their written retellings. Retellings, which are not summaries, require students to recall as many details as they can. They allow students to recast materials they have read into their own form, a process requiring clear understanding of text content. Written retellings provide evidence of *how* as well as *how much* information students retain after reading or listening to a text. They also illustrate students' sensitivity to genre and their ability to organize information.

Paragraph writing frames can be used with students of all ages. Writing frames employ the cloze procedure, providing sentence starters that include signal words or phrases. When these are completed, students will have created a paragraph reflective of a particular text structure. The following steps can guide teachers' uses of paragraph frames:

1. Introduce the particular frame reflective of a text structure.

2. Share a textbook example of the text structure and review its characteristics with students.

3. With the entire group, model the writing of a sample paragraph that illustrates the text structure. Be sure to use appropriate signal words.

4. Give students their own paragraph frames to complete.

For example, teacher Jane Hammond wanted to teach her English learners about writing a contrast paragraph. After following the steps outlined above, she gave her students the contrast frame featured in Figure 8.2. Students completed their frames by

FIGURE 8.2
Contrast Frame

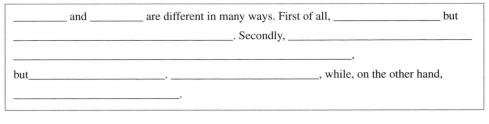

contrasting animals, types of cars, kinds of food, and other common features of everyday life. Later they progressed to contrasting more abstract ideas from their content area materials, such as democracy versus monarchy and mitosis versus meiosis.

Conclusion

Teaching English learners about expository text structures provides them with knowledge that not only enhances their understanding of expository texts but also contributes to their understanding of content. Through carefully designed learning experiences matched to students' levels of English acquisition, teachers can acquaint even young students with the five most common expository text structures. By providing English learners with the tools they need to understand expository text structures, teachers ensure students' success in developing the academic literacy skills essential to their future not only as students but also as citizens of the United States.

REFERENCES

Asher, J. (1982). *Learn another language through actions: The complete teachers' guidebook.* Los Gatos, CA: Sky Oaks.

Baumann, J.F. (2000). The first R yesterday and today: U.S. elementary reading instruction practices reported by teachers and administrators. *Reading Research Quarterly, 35,* 338–377.

Block, C.C. (1993). Strategy instruction in a student-centered classroom. *The Elementary School Journal, 94,* 137–153.

Carrell, P.L. (1984). The effect of rhetorical organization on ESL readers. *TESOL Quarterly, 18,* 441–469.

Chambliss, M. (1995). Text cues and strategies successful readers use to construct the gist of lengthy written arguments. *Reading Research Quarterly, 30,* 778–807.

Collier, V.P. (1989). How long? A synthesis of research on academic achievement in a second language. *TESOL Quarterly, 23,* 509–531.

Daniels, H. (2002). Expository text in literature circles. *Voices From the Middle, 9,* 7–14.

Duke, N.K. (2000). 3.6 minutes per day: The scarcity of informational texts in first grade. *Reading Research Quarterly, 35,* 202–224.

Fisher, C.W., & Hiebert, E.H. (1990, April). *Shifts in reading and writing tasks: Do they extend to social studies, science, and mathematics?* Paper presented at the American Educational Research Association, Boston, MA.

Flood, J., & Lapp, D. (1986). Types of texts: The match between what students read in basals and what they encounter in tests. *Reading Research Quarterly, 21,* 284–297.

Goldman, S.R. (1997). Learning from text: Reflections on the past and suggestions for the future. *Discourse Processes, 23,* 357–398.

Goldman, S.R., & Rakestraw, J.A. (2000). Structural aspects of constructing meaning from text. In M. Kamil, P.B. Mosenthal, P.D. Pearson, & R. Barr (Eds.), *Handbook of reading research* (Vol. 3, pp. 311–336). Mahwah, NJ: Erlbaum.

Grigg, W.S., Daane, M.C., Jin, Y., & Campbell, J.R. (2003). *National Assessment of Educational Progress: The Nation's Report Card: Reading 2002.* Washington, DC: U.S. Department of Education.

Hadaway, N.L., Vardell, S.M., & Young, T.A. (2002). *Literature-based instruction with English language learners, K–12.* Boston: Allyn & Bacon.

Hirsch, E.D. (2003). Reading comprehension requires knowledge—of words and the world. *American Educator, 27*(1), 10–29, 44, 45.

Hoffman, J.V., McCarthey, S.J., Abbott, J., Christina, C., Corman, L., Curry, C., et al. (1994). So what's new in the new basals? A focus on first grade. *Journal of Literacy Behavior, 26,* 47–73.

Kamil, M., & Lane, D. (1997, December). *Using information text for first-grade reading instruction: Theory and practice.* Paper presented at the National Reading Conference, Scottsdale, AZ.

Langer, J.A. (1985). Children's sense of genre: A study of performance on parallel reading and writing tasks. *Written Communication, 2*, 157–187.

McGee, L., & Richgels, D. (1985). Teaching expository text structure to elementary students. *The Reading Teacher, 38*, 739–748.

Meyer, B.J.F. (1985). Prose analysis: Purposes, procedures, and problems. In B.K. Britton & J.B. Black (Eds.), *Understanding expository text* (pp. 11–64). Hillsdale, NJ: Erlbaum.

Moss, B. (2003a). *25 strategies for guiding readers through informational texts*. San Diego, CA: Academic Professional Development.

Moss, B. (2003b). *Exploring the literature of fact: Children's nonfiction trade books in the elementary classroom*. New York: Guilford.

Moss, B. (2004). Teaching expository text structures through information trade book retellings. *The Reading Teacher, 57*, 710–718.

Moss, B., & Newton, E. (2002). An examination of information literature in recent basal readers. *Reading Psychology, 23*, 1–13.

No Child Left Behind Act of 2001, Pub. L. No. 107–110, 115 Stat. 1425 (2002).

Ogle, D. (1986). K-W-L: A teaching model that develops active reading of expository text. *The Reading Teacher, 39*, 564-570.

Pearson, P.D., & Duke, N.K. (2002). Comprehension instruction in the primary grades. In C.C. Block & M. Pressley (Eds.), *Comprehension instruction: Research-based best practice* (pp. 247–258). New York: Guilford.

Pearson, P.D., & Fielding, L. (1991). Comprehension instruction. In R. Barr, M.L. Kamil, P. Mosenthal, & P.D. Pearson (Eds.), *Handbook of reading research* (Vol. 2, pp. 815–860). White Plains, NY: Longman.

Peregoy, S.F., & Boyle, O.F. (2000). English learners reading English: What we know, what we need to know. *Theory Into Practice, 39*, 237–247.

Peregoy, S.F., & Boyle, O.F. (2001). *Reading, writing and learning in ESL: A resource book for K–12 teachers* (3rd ed.). White Plains, NY: Longman.

Raphael, T.E., Kirschner, B.W., & Englert, C.S. (1988). Expository writing programs: Making connections between reading and writing. *The Reading Teacher, 41*, 790–795.

Schmar-Dobler, E. (2003). Reading on the Internet: The link between literacy and technology. *Journal of Adolescent and Adult Literacy, 47*, 80–85.

Thomas, W.P., & Collier, V.P. (1995). Language minority student achievement and program effectiveness. *California Association for Bilingual Education Newsletter, 17*(5), 19, 24.

Tompkins, G. (2002). *Language arts: Content and teaching strategies*. Saddle River, NJ: Merrill Prentice Hall.

Vacca, R., & Vacca, J. (2005). *Content area reading* (8th ed.). Boston: Allyn & Bacon.

Venezky, R.L. (1982). The origins of the present-day chasm between adult literacy needs and school literacy instruction. *Visible Language, 16*, 113–136.

CHILDREN'S BOOKS CITED

Auch, A. (2002). *Tame and wild*. Minneapolis, MN: Compass Point Books.

Blumberg, R. (1989). *The great American goldrush*. New York: Simon & Schuster.

Branley, F. (1986). *What makes day and night?* New York: Crowell.

Cherry, L. (1992). *A river ran wild: An environmental history*. San Diego, CA: Harcourt Brace.

Cole, J. (1983). *Cars and how they go*. New York: Crowell.

Cole, J. (1991). *My puppy is born*. New York: Morrow.

Dorros, A. (1988). *Ant cities*. New York: Harper & Row.

Fowler, A. (1996). *Gator or croc?* Danbury, CT: Children's Press.

Gibbons, G. (1984). *Fire, fire*. New York: Crowell.

Gibbons, G. (1999). *Bats*. New York: Holiday House.

Levine, E. (1988). *If you traveled on the underground railroad*. New York: Scholastic.

Maestro, B. (1992). *What makes apples grow?* New York: HarperCollins.

Markle, S. (1991). *Outside and inside you*. New York: Bradbury Press.

Parsons, A. (1990). *Amazing snakes* (Eyewitness Juniors series). New York: Knopf.

Provensen, A. (1990). *The buck stops here: Presidents of the United States*. New York: Harper and Row.

Selsam, M.E., & Bubley, E. (1973). *How kittens grow*. New York: Scholastic.

Showers, P. (1985). *What happens to a hamburger?* New York: HarperCollins.

ORAL AND WRITTEN LANGUAGE

CHAPTER 9

Negotiating Meaning
Through Writing

Nancy L. Hadaway and Terrell A. Young

We all know there are no children with nothing to say. There are, however, many children who have, within the context of traditional schooling, decided that it is not worth writing...thoughtfully because they do not believe that they will be heard through the barriers. Collaborative projects in which students have a guaranteed place in the discussion make it possible for us to begin to understand and shift those barriers. (Fine, 1989, p. 507)

Teachers hear much about the implementation of process writing and writing workshops as a means of involving students in meaningful composing activity. Yet the recent national focus on reading instruction has lessened the emphasis on writing, especially with English learners and struggling readers. An overview of instructional practices used with English learners shows an avoidance of writing with students until they have mastered oral language and begun to read. Further, when writing is incorporated into the classroom, English learners rarely have a chance for authentic, communicative writing experiences designed to foster understanding of the complexities of the composing process (Heath, 1983; Leki, 1992). Instead, students generally encounter skills-based practice. "In an attempt to make parts of the whole learnable, writing [instruction] runs the risk of focusing excessively on practice instead of experience. Experience is holistic, encompassing the whole enterprise and entailing a purpose beyond practicing writing in...class" (Leki, 2003, p. 4).

Although the press for accountability and improved test scores has led to an increased focus on reading via oral-language instruction that targets phonemic awareness abilities, according to the International Reading Association (IRA; 1998), "Some research suggests that student engagement in writing activities that encourage invented spelling of words can promote the development of phonemic awareness" (n.p.). A more balanced approach is clearly indicated. So how do teachers encourage the overall language development, including writing, of English learners? IRA offers the following recommendations for all learners:

- Offer students a print-rich environment within which to interact.
- Engage students with surrounding print as both readers and writers.
- Engage students in language activities that focus on both the form and the content of spoken and written language.
- Provide explicit explanations in support of students' discovery of the alphabetic principle.
- Provide opportunities for students to practice reading and writing for real reasons in a variety of contexts to promote fluency and independence.

To this end, this chapter highlights some basic considerations in the writing development and instruction of English learners from primary grades through high school. More specifically, it examines two complementary instructional techniques of writing for real reasons—letter writing and dialogue journals—and offers excerpts of work by English learners trying these techniques for the first time.

Writing in a New Language

Research indicates that the development of writing for both first- and second-language learners is similar (Hudelson, 1984). For instance, with young English learners, teachers see many of the same developmental stages as with other students—from scribbling and making random marks to using one letter to stand for an entire word or thought, and on to phonetic spelling and eventually more traditional spelling. All young students go through these developmental stages.

Older English learners without previous school experience or literacy models in the home environment must progress through these stages as well, despite their age. Conversely, English learners who have previous schooling in their first language and have experienced the process of writing will probably present later developmental stages in their attempts at English writing.

There are differences in first- and second-language writing, however. Obviously, proficiency in English influences student writing. For instance, learners' oral-language errors in English syntax and grammar also occur in writing, and students' writing may lag behind their oral communication skills in English (Mora, 1998). Some of the errors are developmental, reflecting the "natural order" of language acquisition and resembling first-language learning (Krashen, 1982); other errors indicate incomplete English-language acquisition and a return to first-language competence.

In the initial stages of English acquisition, students may rely on first-language knowledge to help them in uncertain situations (Brown, 1994). In particular, English learners' early spelling reflects first-language letter–sound correspondence. Thus, teachers can use student writing to monitor English learners' emerging phonemic awareness in English and provide targeted instruction on problem phoneme areas between English and the first language (Helman, 2004). Awareness of these phases and issues in English learners' writing development moves teachers to the next phase, incorporating instructional methods to support student growth.

Finding a Starting Point for Writing in English

Learning to write well, especially for academic purposes, is difficult in a first language. For English learners, the process is even more complex. Writing instruction presents several interrelated challenges, including a cognitive load, a cultural load, and a language load (Meyer, 2000). As learners struggle with the syntax and vocabulary of English (language load), they also must consider the process of writing—how to generate ideas, to plan for audience, to revise (cognitive load). All of this takes place within the context of the classroom, with activities, processes, and curriculum that may be foreign to the English learner (cultural load).

Teachers can help to lessen the cultural and language loads by choosing activities and assignments, especially in the initial stages of language acquisition, that allow students to draw on prior knowledge and life experiences. Clark (1995) stresses that young writers overcome many initial writing struggles when they draw from three circles of ideas—the classroom, the school, and the family. And, rather than focusing on the forms and structures of a language, teachers can reduce the cognitive load by actively engaging students in what people *do* with language (Cooper, 1993). Interaction and collaboration are the "doing" tasks of language through which English learners gain linguistic proficiency and functional expertise (Burton & Carroll, 2001; Green & Green, 1993).

Dialogue journals and letters are two instructional techniques that engage students in the more personal process of collaboration and negotiating meaning, a process that is crucial to the development of language proficiency (Dolly, 1990). For instance, letter writing is a familiar, real-world process. At the most basic level, students see the daily mail arrive and understand that there is interaction required for some forms of correspondence. Because letter writing is transactional, teachers can draw parallels between the process of written and oral communication (Hennings, 1990).

Letters also help to lower the anxiety associated with writing because the normal format of a letter eases "blank page syndrome" (Schwartz, 1984). Writers automatically have the opening/greeting and sometimes more, if formulaic or ritualized phrases (e.g., *How are you? I'm fine*) are utilized. Plus, letter exchanges are versatile; they can be arranged within the same school, age group, or grade level as well as across school districts or geographical locations; e-mail exchanges extend instructional possibilities even further. In short, letters provide an opportunity to develop control of writing in a realistic, functional manner (Cambourne, 1988).

Dialogue journals easily fit into the category of transactional writing also. They are, in effect, a written conversation between two individuals—teacher (or other interested adult) and student, or two fellow students (e.g., peers or cross-age partners). Uncomplicated in structure, dialogue journals provide a purposeful writing task. Yet, despite their less structured nature, journal entries are a rich source of teaching material and a compact means of charting the development of student writing over time (Garcia, Berry, & Garcia, 1990; Reyes, 1991). In addition, journals can provide an outlet for self-expression, for sharing the lives young people live outside the walls of the school, and even for exchanging thoughts about school, if the climate is open. Journal writing can provide a personal outlet that is therapeutic, one in which students discover themselves through writing.

Thus, informal writing (e.g., letters and dialogue journals) is the ideal starting point for English learners. Although teachers cannot assume that students know how to write informally, it may be that students engage in informal writing as much as they engage in the more familiar face-to-face interaction (Hennings, 1990). In addition, the beginning level of language acquisition, like the work of beginning writers, is highly egocentric (Bizzell, 1992). Developing writers need a gradual transition from the egocentric stage of initial writing, which closely resembles their spoken interactions, to more formal writing assignments that challenge them with academic language and contexts foreign to their experiences. Letters and dialogue journals afford an excellent transitional activity to help students "experiment with the literate register" but in a familiar context (Blumenthal & Hildenbrand, 1993, p. 2).

Writing in a Supportive Environment

Convinced that "writing takes shape best not in the vacuum of freestanding writing [instruction] but when used for the real purposes it is intended to fill" (Leki, 2003, p. 3), the authors worked in a number of classrooms to encourage the implementation of dialogue journals and letters with English learners. Over the course of one year, they worked in both bilingual and English as a second language (ESL) classrooms in grades K–8. Young teamed with teachers in Washington schools to encourage their written interactions with English learners through dialogue journals. Hadaway initiated a letter exchange between English learners in several Texas classrooms and preservice teachers at a large state university.

The objective of the interactive writing project was to work with teachers to incorporate more authentic writing opportunities in their classrooms with English learners. Prior to the initiation of the project, writing emphasis was minimal and generally focused on story retellings and informative writing linked to content lessons. Work in these classrooms confirmed that interactive writing techniques, such as letters and dialogue journals, offer several key components of a supportive writing environment, including the following (Hadaway, Vardell, & Young, 2002):

- time and opportunity to write
- writing role models
- authentic communicative tasks
- freedom to take risks
- meaningful feedback
- a sense of community

The following sections explore these six components of writing as well as related personal/informal letter-writing and dialogue-journal excerpts of English learners. These excerpts are by English learners in bilingual and ESL classrooms in the elementary and middle schools that were part of the project.

Time and Opportunity to Write

A study of English learners conducted by Leki (2003) reports that the first condition that allows participants to become successful writers is time—time to develop a knowledge base about what they write and time to use writing as a tool for real purposes. However, the time intensity of the writing process is one reason teachers avoid writing with English learners, who may take up to three times longer to produce a page of text than fluent English-speaking students. Teachers often feel that English learners can move to writing only after they have a more developed oral-language foundation. Yet Leki argues, "the only way they can achieve a faster pace of producing text is through more experience" (p. 3).

Dialogue journals and letters provide a structured occasion to develop control of writing in a realistic, functional manner (Peyton & Reed, 1990; Peyton & Staton, 1993). With dialogue journals there is a set time to write and a set time to read a partner's response. With letter exchanges, the arrival of correspondence sets the cycle of reading and writing in motion. Moreover, the personal and informal nature of these interactive writing techniques allows students to use their existing knowledge base to participate in the exchange and to build knowledge with their pen pals and journal buddies along the way.

Working in collaboration with teachers in the project, the authors were able to observe how eagerly students anticipate writing when they know there will be a personal response to their composing efforts. As one middle school English learner in the project shared, "I was so glad to get your letter. I asked Miss Davis every day, 'Have the letters come yet?'"

When the project first began, however, teachers were reluctant to incorporate writing until the English learners had more control over their use of English. When students were provided the time and opportunity to write through the personal medium of letters and dialogue journals, they were allowed to use either their first language or English. The acceptance of writing in the first language allowed even students at the beginning level of proficiency in English to participate in writing, as the early dialogue journal entry of Alberto (grade 5) shows:

Maestra si estoi mui ocupado jugando kickball con mis amigos Jugamos kickball co los ninos i con mi ermano Chui i con mi sovrino David i con mi amigo Omar

[Teacher, yes, I am very busy playing kickball with my friends. We play kickball with the boys and with my brother, Chuy, and with my nephew, David, and with my friend, Omar.]

With such examples of authentic language, teachers began to see the benefits of assessing students' general language knowledge and background, whether first language or English. Indeed, using the first language enabled some students to demonstrate that they knew more about writing and language structure in general than their oral English proficiency indicated. In addition, teachers acquired valuable compare/contrast snapshots throughout the year as students gained greater knowledge of English vocabulary and syntax, their comfort level increased, and they began to transition into English. For instance, later in the year Alberto shared the following writing:

And I going to miss you wine I'n be in 6 grad if you can go to tiche in the Stivins and I goin to be there

[I am going to miss you when I'm in sixth grade. If you go to teach at Stevens, I'm going to be there.]

Depending on the proficiency levels and previous exposure to English, some students began writing in their first language while others started with limited text using simplified oral-language structures and familiar text forms (Mora, 1998). Many students combined illustrations and text to connect with their pen pals and journal buddies. Over time, teachers saw developing language (see Figure 9.1).

FIGURE 9.1
Student Writing: Developing English and Writing

Letter 1: Alma (grade 2) shares her excitement over having a pen pal.
I love you and I like a picture from you

Letter 2: With time and opportunity to write, Alma demonstrates her knowledge of the format of letters and some basic conventions of written interaction.
Dear Rhonda
Thank you for the letter I read the letter and Im glad off the letter.

Letter 3: By the end of the semester, Alma begins to recount events.
Dear Rhonda
I went to a party I eat some eggs and candy I don't like to mush candy My mom hat a bady her name is Cristina ant the bady is one month
[I went to a party. I ate some eggs and candy. I don't like candy too much. My mom had a baby. Her name is Cristina and the baby is one month old.]

Writing Role Models

Letter writing and journals are examples of real writing that many English learners have observed at home, whatever the level of English proficiency of the family. As students see family members write and receive letters, the idea that writing is important and useful is emphasized. Teacher and peer involvement, in the case of dialogue journals and letter exchanges, simply lends more credibility to the process. Moreover, when English learners form a bond with a pen pal or journal buddy, the negotiation of meaning between the correspondents becomes increasingly important.

The modeling effect of letters is particularly powerful when English learners are paired with proficient-English partners. In the project, pen pals demonstrated the way letters open and close as well as how to move correspondence along via questions and responses to students' inquiries. In short, they illustrated what a letter (and written English) looks and sounds like. Although students' letters and dialogue journal entries were not corrected, the learner had a model of correct syntax, wording, etc. Mora (1998) notes that English learners' editing skills develop as they compare their own forms to models and conventions. Further, writing is fixed, not passing, as in oral communication, so students are able to return to the models of writing, reread them, and develop their ability to self-correct based on feedback or responses over time (Garcia et al., 1990). Emilia, a second grader in a bilingual classroom, appreciated her new writing role model, sharing, "I'm so happy that you sint me a letter I like hao you right" (I'm so happy that you sent me a letter. I like how you write.).

Beyond modeling literacy, letters and journal entries also model attitudes about school and provide encouragement. By reviewing letters and journal entries, teachers clearly saw issues and perspectives about school, study, tests, and language learning. Ernesto's teacher even discovered a specific frustration in his writing that she was able to channel into an instructional opportunity—spelling:

> Well something made me mad boys and grils made a spelling contest and grils win the contest I'am going to stedid my words so next time boys win

In another dialogue journal, a student who was struggling with reading asked his teacher, "Le gusta leer istorias?" (Do you like to read stories?). She replied that she enjoyed reading very much. Through their continued interaction, the positive value placed on reading as a form of entertainment, not just as an academic task, was clearly communicated.

Pen pals also shared their experiences of learning another language and extended encouragement to students as they studied English. In a dialogue journal entry to her teacher, one English learner wrote, "Mrs. Clark can you help me to speak more inglish and to read better in the book." In addition, praise was offered for accomplishments. For example, Emilia's pen pal wrote, "You are very talented, Emilia. I like the letters and drawings you have sent me. They are hanging on the wall in my room."

Authentic Communicative Tasks

Writing proficiency is a "consequence of not only the time spent on the task, but also on the significance of the task" (Farnan, Lapp, & Flood, 1992, p. 551). Dialogue journals and letters underscore the idea that composing is a purposeful activity that is used to communicate thoughts and ideas. Through dialogue journals and letters, students privately shared their reactions, questions, and concerns about school and personal matters with teachers. Alberto, for example, in reference to his move to middle school, wrote "I'am goint to be ther if you dont go I'll miss you and I'll never se you agan" (I am going to be there. If you don't go, I'll miss you and I'll never see you again.).

Perhaps because topics are self-selected and deal with relevant concerns, interests, experiences, and questions, the quantity and quality of writing during interactive tasks (such as dialogue journal and letter writing) often exceeds writing of other assigned tasks (Garcia et al., 1990; Peyton, Staton, Richardson, & Wolfram, 1990). During the project, dialogue journals and letter exchanges definitely spurred communication. Some students, who had never written for teacher-assigned tasks, suddenly produced mountains of text. One young English learner found a new voice and illustrated and composed a poem, "Don't You Be Sad," to send to her pen pal.

The use of a familiar context offers writers an opportunity to share known topics from their own environment, thus encouraging language growth and validating students' cultural background. Letter exchanges are wonderful opportunities for pen pals from diverse backgrounds to compare and contrast their families, hometowns, interests, etc. For instance, students moved into the role of "teacher" as they shared words and phrases from their first language as a way of connecting with their pen pals and sharing their culture. In addition, in one elementary classroom, students were from Argentina, Bulgaria, Columbia, Mexico, Poland, Taiwan, and Venezuela. During the correspondence with elementary-teacher certification students at a local university, Alija, an English learner from Poland, shared that in her country "there are not as many cars," and they "stay at school only five hours." But, despite the differences, there is common ground, as Cathy (from Texas) and Alija discover when discussing their spring vacations. They both love to go to the beach and explore the seashore.

Freedom to Take Risks

The give-and-take process of conveying meaning through dialogue journals and letter writing serves as nonconfrontational feedback. This differs greatly from writing on demand for the teacher as sole audience. Assigned writing tasks may foster fear of failure that constrains meaningful communicative efforts. In contrast, with letters and dialogue journals, students are free to initiate their own topics, change topics as often as they wish, and utilize original formats (e.g., poetry or text with illustrations). In short, there is no "correct" way to write. This freedom helps students grow as writers. Miguel, a second grader, had never written for the teacher, but, given a pen pal and some time on a computer, he composed a short letter:

> Dear Heidi,
>
> Hello pen pal How are you I am fine
>
> I liked your letter. School is fine. We have to go this Saturday. I have a spelling test did very well. I will try my very best. I want to be a soldier. Love, Miguel

Although the ideas are not developed and appear disjointed, Miguel was beginning to risk.

Meaningful Feedback

On both ends of the exchange of letters or journals, responses are anxiously awaited. Correspondents read and try to answer important questions so that they can get to know each other. Students use feedback to modify their language output, to clarify and elaborate for comprehension, and to prevent and repair communication breakdowns (Dolly, 1990). As Leki (2003) points out:

> Writers improve only through writing they are doing, through their intellectual and emotional engagement with it. A teacher's effect on the writer can only be indirect; the teacher offers the opportunity to improve a text, thereby allowing the student to improve as a writer. In other words, improving writing proficiency is an internal process that only the writer can access directly; teachers cannot. (p. 4)

Responses need to encourage and stimulate a continued dialogue. Elaborative responses from pen pals and journal buddies can lead to increased written output by students, coupled with rich linguistic and communicative responses (Garcia et al., 1990). Elaborative responses deal with process-related requests (*how, why, what if,* etc.) as opposed to affirmative/evaluative responses (*OK, great, I agree,* etc.), which request minimal communicative requirements from students. This process of extending text and elaborating more fully is shown in Figure 9.2. Not only do responses extend student dialogue and provide correct models, but they also provide the support necessary to help students accomplish writings that they might not achieve on their own. Thus, English learners are helped in the beginning, but that assistance is gradually reduced until they can function on their own.

A Sense of Community

Leki (2003) notes,

> A more subtle feature of this [writing] process is that it is necessarily embedded within a context of how the writer's work is received (accepted or not accepted, for example), how the writer is received as an individual in a particular social setting (with high or low expectations, for example), and how the writer wants to be received within that socioacademic context, including the writer's self-image, desire for affiliation, and interest in joining that community. (p. 4)

FIGURE 9.2
Student Writing: Elaborative Responses

In answer to initial questions from his pen pal, Mario (fifth grade) furnished the following information:
I like to come to school because I want to learn how to speak more English. I enjoy playing baseball. I also like my bike and being with my friends. I have a big family. When I am out of school, I would like to go to Mexico and visit my cousins.

Because Mario's ideas are not fully developed, in the next letter, Mario's pen pal used elaborative responses to encourage him to relate more about his baseball interests. His reply shows the impact of such prompts.
You asked me if I played baseball on a team, but I don't. I just play it for fun. I play baseball with my friends and my cousins, too. When they come to my house we always go to the baseball field and play baseball. I would like to be in a baseball team when I am in high school.

Interactive writing involves students with pen pals and journal buddies who share something of themselves. When the whole class is involved in this type of writing activity, students feel linked within a community of meaning, exercising both reading and writing. Students are actively involved in literacy as individuals and as a group. As they write their own journal entries and letters and read the ones from their partners, students assist one another in the reading and writing task. They share letters and journal entries from their writing partners, help classmates brainstorm for ideas, put their ideas down on paper, and correct vocabulary and spelling in English. For instance, during the project, when letters arrived for Guadalupe, a second grader who was a recent immigrant and spoke only Spanish, classmates helped her by translating. They discussed and offered ideas for ways to respond to her pen pal's questions. In such communities, students learn to value other students' accomplishments as well as their own (Hansen, 1987). This warm, responsive environment and cooperative network fosters language acquisition (Peyton & Staten, 1993). In short, students involved in the project communicated—by their enthusiasm and hard work on responses—that they wanted to join the writing community.

Reflecting on the Interactive Writing Project: Some Recommendations

The impact of the interactive writing project was valuable but for the most part indirect. Students learned about writing through writing and through reading letters and their teachers' journal entries. This was an important beginning to involve students in the act of writing. However, increasing attention is being focused on the critical need for English learners to "develop competence in the highly abstract, often decontextualized language of academic discourse, which is a central purpose of schooling" (Gersten & Baker, 2000, n.p.). This is an expectation even for students at the beginning proficiency level, who are in a race to catch up to their fluent English-speaking peers. This means that teachers need to move students beyond the personal, social language and process of collaborative writing and incorporate some direct instruction. Such instruction can be addressed in a relevant manner by merging the authentic process of letter/journal exchanges with specific direct-instruction strategies.

The authentic language of letters/journal entries serves as a rich source of techniques for communicating across barriers and keeping correspondence going. It also offers a database of examples for the teaching of mechanics and grammar in context. Teachers must draw English learners' attention to these examples and strategically utilize them to engage students in academic discussions about writing. For instance, teachers can use letters and journal entries to assist students through the following nine instructional techniques:

1. Structured writing activities. Mora (1998) suggests leading English learners through a structured writing process with extended prewriting oral-language development and practice and by making "vocabulary and content explicit and visible for referencing through wall charts and other materials" (n.p.). Further, she encourages leading students through several steps, including modeled writing, shared writing, guided writing, and, finally, independent writing.

Using letters or journals as examples, in modeled writing, the teacher utilizes thinking aloud about writing with students and models the process and content of letters or journal entries. Next, during shared writing, the class creates a joint letter/journal entry, with students contributing ideas and the teacher scribing and providing help with organization. In guided writing, the teacher offers a framework for writing, prompting students and promoting critical thinking. Finally, in independent writing, students use the ideas from shared writing to produce a draft.

2. Instruction and targeted academic discussion of the process of writing letters and journal entries. Teachers can begin by sharing their own letters or journal entries on an overhead transparency, thinking aloud about their own writing processes, and working through the stages of the process. This serves as an introduction to the writing process and purposes of writing as well as to the academic language involved (such as prewriting, drafting, revising, editing, etc.). Students can join in this process by sharing their work when they are comfortable. For instance, several times a week, students might read aloud either pen pals' responses or the student's own letter and brainstorm writing ideas.

3. One-to-one writing conferences. Letters and journal entries can be used for writing conferences just as other types of academic writing. Each writing example allows the teacher to gain a better understanding of each individual student's strengths and weaknesses. A letter/journal exchange with consistent writing partners over the course of a year affords tremendous potential for teachers to see the specific areas of learners' growth and the continuing difficulties that they experience.

4. A focus on mechanics, grammar, and spelling in the context of students' actual work. Rather than using a whole-class approach with worksheets and drills, teachers can use letters and journal entries to pinpoint areas of student need for targeted, direct instruction. This might be the most effective process, given the range of English proficiency and knowledge of language processes among English learners in many classrooms. In addition, different language backgrounds present different challenges in terms of English alphabet, phonemes, and syntax.

5. Personalized word study. Students can create their personal spelling and vocabulary word lists from their letters and journals; these would then include words that they are trying to use in authentic contexts. Students' personal word lists can even be shared with the class as part of a word wall that can grow as the collaborative exchange continues. For instance, students' pen pals may share new words that the student could then share with the class.

6. Focused minilessons for groups of students. Once specific needs have been pinpointed, working in small groups with focused minilessons on those needs is an effective technique. Such small-group work provides a comfort zone for English learners to ask questions and respond to the teacher.

7. Voluntary sharing with peers or partners throughout the writing process. Reading letters or journal entries aloud to the class, discussing writing with peers, coaching one another through the writing process—all of these interactions provide opportunities to practice English and to focus on more complex language. Students might use peer editing groups to get their letters/journal entries ready to mail or exchange. Research documents the limited nature of oral-language opportunities in classrooms for English learners, especially ones focused on more complex language (Gersten, 1996a, 1996b). The need for involvement at a meaningful oral-language level is great.

8. Extension of the writing process to its ultimate conclusion: publication. The class can work together to publish a volume of favorite letters from the semester-long or yearlong letter exchange. This process engages students in reading and rereading their partners' and their own work and making choices about what to include and why. Going back to reflect on earlier work also allows students to see their own progress over time. The volume can even include a foreword that introduces and provides some background about the exchange and a conclusion, with lessons learned from the experience.

9. Use of letters to teach a mode of writing. Mora (1998) recommends providing frameworks for different genres of writing that help students with expressions, phrases, transitions, and grammatical structures. For instance, students can compare/contrast profiles of their pen pals in class and in small-group discussions, charting the similarities and differences. They can use this experience as a scaffold for a compare/contrast paper. The class might also compare/contrast letter writing with journal writing as a powerful introduction to the many types of text that they may encounter.

Other recommendations include incorporating e-mail connections to assist in the logistics of such a project and to engage students in the use of technology. E-mail correspondence between teacher and students and students and pen pals provides direct and timely access and the possibility of immediate feedback. With increased ease of contact, pen pals and journal buddies might interact more, extending the collaborative discussion to include content topics, literature, etc.

Finally, teachers can use letters and journal entries for assessment purposes to determine where students are in their writing development. They can then make decisions about how to help students grow as writers. Mora (1998) defines four phases of developmental writing: (1) experimental writing, (2) early writing, (3) conventional writing, and (4) proficient writing.

Phase 1: Experimental Writing. Students write using simplified oral structures, but they have a sense of sentence conventions and some written conventions. At this stage, writing is very limited and may consist of main words, phrases, and memorized language routines, such as "how are you?" Alma's initial letter in Figure 9.1 displays this pattern, with her formulaic use of "I love you and like a picture from you." At this stage, classroom instruction should focus on oral-language development and extensive prewriting vocabulary generation.

Phase 2: Early Writing. At this point, students limit their writing to personal topics using a small range of familiar forms. In the project, teachers observed many letters and journal entries at this level. Students generate very short, simple sentences with the same format over and over again. Juan, for instance, wrote, "I am Juan. I am 11 years old. I have two brother and one sister. I like school always." Targeted minilessons with practice on different sentence formats and sentence combining is called for during this phase.

Phase 3: Conventional Writing. As students move into the conventional writing phase, they have a developing sense of audience and purpose. With continued contact during the project, teachers noticed more two-way communication attempts. Students struggled to make contact with their pen pals by reading their letters and asking questions, as in Figure 9.2. This questioning strategy to foster more interchange was seen when Esmeralda asked her pen pal, "Do you enjoy college? I hope you do! Where did you come from before you came to Texas?" Esmeralda's questions allowed her pen pal to target responses that they both continued to discuss over the course of their correspondence.

Phase 4: Proficient Writing. Students plan and organize their ideas, utilize simple and compound sentences, develop their topics, and seek precision in word use. During the project, teachers saw writers at the first three developmental phases, but none had moved into proficient writing.

Taking It Further: Letter and Journal Writing Across the Curriculum

Once students are on the road with a letter/journal exchange, it isn't a big step for teachers to build from the format and transactional processes involved to incorporate activities across the curriculum. Indeed, letters or journals can provide a framework for a thematic or interdisciplinary unit. Such reinforcement of content, language, and format is particularly helpful to the English learner.

As a beginning, teachers can introduce the literature of letters and journals. There are many trade books that feature letters, letter writing, and journals (see Table 9.1 for examples with appropriate grade ranges noted). These books can provide a powerful model for the writing format of letters and journals, and teachers can draw attention to

TABLE 9.1
Literature That Features Letters and Journals

Books Written in Letter Format

Dear Alexandra: A Story of Switzerland, Helen Gudel (1999), Grades P–8
Dear Levi: Letters From the Overland Trail, Elvira Woodruff (1994), Grades 3–12
Dear Mr. Henshaw, Beverly Cleary (1983), Grades 3–9
Kate Heads West, Pat Brisson (1990), Grades P–6
Letters From Rifka, Karen Hesse (1992), Grades 3–12
Postcards From Pluto, Loreen Leedy (1993), Grades 1–8
Regarding the Fountain: A Tale, in Letters, of Liars and Leaks, Kate Klise (1998), Grades 4–12

Books Written in Journal Format

A Coal Miner's Bride: The Diary of Anetka Kaminska, Lattimer, Pennsylvania, 1896, Susan Bartoletti (2000), Grades 4–12
Across the Wide and Lonesome Prairie: The Oregon Trail Diary of Hattie Campbell, 1847, Kristiana Gregory (1997), Grades 4–12
A Gathering of Days: A New England Girl's Journal (1830–1832), Joan Blos (1979), Grades 4–12
A Journey to the New World: The Diary of Remember Patience Whipple, Mayflower/Plymouth Colony, 1620, Kathryn Lasky (1996), Grades 4–12
Amazon Diary: Property of Alex Winters, Hudson Talbot and Mark Greenberg (1996), Grades 3–12
Harriet the Spy, Louise Fitzhugh (1964), Grades 3–8
The Island, Gary Paulsen (1988), Grades 9–12
The Ledgerbook of Thomas Blue Eagle, Gay Matthaei and Jewel Grutman (1994), Grades 3–12
Patches Lost and Found, Steven Kroll (2001), Grades P–5
Rachel's Journal: The Story of a Pioneer Girl, Marissa Moss (1998), Grades 3–12
Thura's Diary: My Life in Wartime Iraq, Thura Al-Windawi (2004), Grades 5–12
Zlata's Diary: A Student's Life in Sarajevo, Zlata Filipovic (1994), Grades 5–12

For more outstanding examples, see the Dear America and The Royal Diary series (both Scholastic) and the Dear Mr. President series (Winslow Press).

the details that make good letters and journal entries. One note about Table 9.1, however: The journal format highlighted in this chapter, the dialogue journal, is only one journal format. The majority of journal book examples in the table fall into the category of fictionalized personal journal.

A study of journals is an excellent interdisciplinary focus, however, because journals are primary-source documents that provide much historical knowledge. Once students are familiar with the format and possibilities of letters and journals, the study can stretch across the whole curriculum. Table 9.2 offers just a few ideas to fuel student interest in letters and journals. Many of these examples could have been utilized to extend learning during the interactive writing project.

TABLE 9.2
Cross-Curricular Activities With Letters and Dialogue Journals

Language Arts	• Use the exchange to introduce the study of letters (e.g., friendly, business, complaint) and the many types of journals (e.g., learning logs, dialogue journals, personal journals).
	• Bring examples of real-world letters (junk mail, etc.) to post in the classroom. Look for similarities and differences. Label the parts of business letters (e.g., greeting).
	• Have students write to their favorite authors, poets, or illustrators.
	• Have students write a letter or journal entry to a favorite book character or from a character's point of view.
	• Have students write letters to a local newspaper editor about issues that are important to them.
	• Have students write different kinds of letters (e.g., friendly, business, consumer) and mail them.
	• Have students attempt different formats for correspondence (e.g., postcards, invitations, greeting cards, thank-you notes).
	• Connect students with international pen pals.
Social Studies	• Create a bulletin board with a class map showing the birthplaces/hometowns/native countries of all those involved in the letter/journal exchange.
	• Discuss the first languages of all the students and their pen pals and journal buddies (e.g., discuss differences and similarities in terms of alphabet, syntax, and vocabulary).
	• Have students research the cities, states, and countries of origin of their pen pals.
	• Have students take on a new identity (e.g., a famous or historical figure) and then write a letter or journal entry.
Math	• Using the social studies class map (noted above), ask students to compute the distance between writing partners' birthplaces/hometowns/home countries.

(continued)

TABLE 9.2
Cross-Curricular Activities With Letters and Dialogue Journals *(continued)*

	• Ask students to tabulate statistics (e.g., number of brothers/sisters, favorite foods, types of pets) from letters and journal entries. • Have students graph data from letters and journals using bar, line, and/or pie graphs.
Science	• As a class, share information about differences in geography, climate, weather, and plant/animal life among the various places where pen pals and journal buddies live.
Art	• Suggest that students draw "wordless" letters or cut pictures from magazines to "write" a letter or journal entry. • Have students use a combination of drawings, photos, and pictures with labeling to communicate with their pen pals and journal buddies. • Have students illustrate letters and journal entries with drawings of self, family, pets, and hobbies.
Music	• As a class, share information and even tapes of favorite music. • Have students write out the words to a favorite song in their native language and provide a translation with words, pictures, and/or drawings.
Cooking	• Ask students to share favorite recipes with their pen pals and journal buddies. • Hold a class discussion about the differences and similarities among pen pals in diet, foods, and food preparation.
Dramatics	• Role-play a meeting between student and pen pal based on information in letters or journal entries.

Conclusion

"Real writing has real consequences. It is purposeful, with content and context which are meaningful to the writer" (Farnan et al., 1992, p. 555). The interactive writing project afforded real writing tasks with authentic audiences. Students had to consider their pen pals' interests and tailor their responses, utilizing such strategies as elaborative response, to move the communication forward. This chapter shares just a few examples of the impact of transactional writing on English learners and offers some recommendations about how teachers can extend the study of letters and journals across the curriculum (with some direct instruction and academic-language focus). Given the total literacy workout that interactive tasks involve and their potential for assessing language development (Tannenbaum, 1996), they are certainly worth considering for linguistically diverse classrooms. Interactive writing, after all, provides English learners with personal experience and a well-deserved active audience "who recognizes the voice of the writer" (Jochum, 1989, p. 1).

REFERENCES

Bizzell, P. (1992). *Academic discourse and critical consciousness*. Pittsburgh, PA: University of Pittsburgh Press.

Blumenthal, A., & Hildenbrand, J. (1993, December). *Tone and role: From "participant" stance to the "spectator" stance in the writing of African American college composition students*. Paper presented at the Annual Meeting of the Modern Language Association, Toronto, ON.

Brown, H.D. (1994). *Principles of language learning and teaching* (3rd ed.). Englewood Cliffs, NJ: Prentice Hall.

Burton, J., & Carroll, M. (2001). *Journal writing*. Alexandria, VA: Teachers to Speakers of Other Languages.

Cambourne, B. (1988). *The whole story: Natural learning and acquisition of literacy in the classroom*. Auckland, New Zealand: Ashton Scholastic.

Clark, R. (1995). *Free to write: A journalist teaches young writers*. Portsmouth, NH: Heinemann.

Cooper, J.D. (1993, Winter). Helping children construct meaning: A changing view of literacy learning. *Educators' Forum*, pp. 1–2.

Dolly, M.R. (1990). Integrating ESL reading and writing through authentic discourse. *Journal of Reading, 33*, 360–365.

Farnan, N., Lapp, D., & Flood, J. (1992). Changing perspectives in writing instruction. *Journal of Reading, 35*, 550–556.

Fine, E.S. (1989). Collaborative writing: Key to unlocking the silences of students. *Language Arts, 66*, 501–508.

Garcia, G.E., Berry, C., & Garcia, E.E. (1990). The effect of teacher reaction on students' interactive journal entries. *Early Student Development and Care, 56*, 35–47.

Gersten, R. (1996a). The double demands of teaching English learners. *Educational Leadership, 53*(5), 18–22.

Gersten, R. (1996b). Literacy instruction for language-minority students: The transition years. *The Elementary School Journal, 96*, 227–244.

Gersten, R., & Baker, S. (2000). *An overview of instructional practices for English-language learners: Prominent themes and future directions* (Topical Summary: Practices for English-Language Learners). Denver, CO: National Institute for Urban School Improvement. Retrieved September 12, 2004, from http://www.inclusiveschools.org/ts_eng.htm

Green, C., & Green, J.M. (1993). Secret friend journals. *TESOL Journal, 2*, 20–23.

Hadaway, N.L., Vardell, S.M., & Young, T.A. (2002). *Literature-based instruction with English learners, K–12*. Boston: Allyn & Bacon/Longman.

Hansen, J. (1987). *When writers read*. Portsmouth, NH: Heinemann.

Heath, S.B. (1983). *Ways with words: Language, life, and work in communities and classrooms*. New York: Cambridge University Press.

Helman, L.A. (2004). Building on the sound system of Spanish: Insights from the alphabetic spellings of English-language learners. *The Reading Teacher, 57*, 452–460.

Hennings, D.G. (1990). *Communication in action: Teaching the language arts* (4th ed.). Boston: Houghton Mifflin.

Hudelson, S. (1984). Kan yu ret an rayt en ingles: Students become literate in English as a second language. *TESOL Quarterly, 18*, 221–238.

International Reading Association. (1998). *Phonemic awareness and the teaching of reading* (Position statement). Newark, DE: Author. Retrieved June 13, 2005, from http://www.reading.org/downloads/positions/ps1025_phonemic.pdf

Jochum, J. (1989). Writing: The critical response. *Texas Reading Report, 12*, 1, 10.

Krashen, S. (1982). *Principles and practices in second language acquisition*. Oxford, England: Pergamon Press.

Leki, I. (1992). *Understanding ESL writers: A guide for teachers*. Portsmouth, NH: Boynton/Cook.

Leki, I. (2003). Research insights on second language writing instruction. *CAL Digest*. Retrieved July 10, 2005, from http://www.cal.org/resources/digest/0306leki.html

Meyer, L. (2000). Barriers to meaningful instruction for English learners. *Theory Into Practice, 4*, 228–236.

Mora, J.K. (1998). *Development of second-language writing*. Retrieved July 28, 2004, from http://coe.sdsu.edu/people/jmora/L2WritingMMdl

Peyton, J.K., & Reed, L. (1990). *Dialogue journal writing with nonnative English speakers: A handbook for teachers*. Alexandria, VA: Teachers to Speakers of Other Languages.

Peyton, J.K., & Staton, J. (1993). *Dialogue journals in the multilingual classroom: Building language fluency and writing skills through written interaction*. Norwood, NJ: Ablex.

Peyton, J.K., Staton, J., Richardson, G., & Wolfram, W. (1990). The influence of writing task on ESL students' written production. *Research in the Teaching of English, 24,* 142–171.

Reyes, M.L. (1991). A process approach to literacy using dialogue journals and literature logs with second language learners. *Research in the Teaching of English, 21,* 291–313.

Schwartz, M. (1984). Defining voice through letter writing. *The English Record, 35,* 10–12.

Tannenbaum, J. (1996). *Practical ideas on alternative assessment for ESL students.* (ERIC Document Reproduction Service No. ED395500)

CHILDREN'S BOOKS CITED

Al-Windawi, T. (2004). *Thura's diary: My life in wartime Iraq.* New York: Viking.

Bartoletti, S.C. (2000). *A coal miner's bride: The diary of Anetka Kaminska, Lattimer, Pennsylvania, 1896.* New York: Scholastic.

Blos, J. (1979). *A gathering of days: A New England girl's journal (1830–1832).* New York: Scribner.

Brisson, P. (1990). *Kate heads west.* New York: Bradbury Press.

Cleary, B. (1983). *Dear Mr. Henshaw.* New York: Morrow.

Filipovic, Z. (1994). *Zlata's diary: A student's life in Sarajevo.* New York: Viking.

Fitzhugh, L. (1964). *Harriet the spy.* New York: Harper & Row.

Gregory, K. (1997). *Across the wide and lonesome prairie: The Oregon Trail diary of Hattie Campbell, 1847.* New York: Scholastic.

Gudel, H. (1999). *Dear Alexandra: A story of Switzerland.* Norwalk, CT: Sound Prints.

Hesse, K. (1992). *Letters from Rifka.* New York: Puffin.

Klise, K. (1998). *Regarding the fountain: A tale, in letters, of liars and leaks.* New York: Avon.

Kroll, S. (2001). *Patches lost and found.* Delray Beach, FL: Winslow Press.

Lasky, K. (1996). *A journey to the New World: The diary of Remember Patience Whipple, Mayflower/Plymouth Colony, 1620.* New York: Scholastic.

Leedy, L. (1993). *Postcards from Pluto.* New York: Holiday House.

Matthaei, G., & Grutman, J. (1994). *The ledgerbook of Thomas Blue Eagle.* Charlottesville, VA: Thomasson-Grant.

Moss, M. (1998). *Rachel's journey: The story of a pioneer girl.* San Diego, CA: Harcourt Brace.

Paulsen, G. (1988). *The island.* New York: Orchard.

Talbot, H., & Greenberg, M. (1996). *Amazon diary: Property of Alex Winters.* New York: Scholastic.

Woodruff, E. (1994). *Dear Levi: Letters from the Overland Trail.* New York: Alfred A. Knopf.

CHAPTER 10

Language Play, Language Work: Using Poetry to Develop Oral Language

Nancy L. Hadaway, Sylvia M. Vardell, and Terrell A. Young

Oral language plays a powerful role in acquiring a language and laying the groundwork for reading and writing. Research shows that oral-language development affords a foundation in phonological awareness and allows for subsequent learning about the alphabetic structure of English that is so important to later reading and writing efforts (Snow, Burns, & Griffin, 1998). Unfortunately, oral-language activities with English learners too often focus on basic communication skills or phonemic awareness drills. The lack of opportunity to play with oral language and become involved in abstract and academically oriented oral language deprives students of a natural transition to reading and writing.

This chapter discusses the importance of ongoing oral-language development, the particular needs of English learners, and the appropriateness of poetry as a vehicle for providing practice and pleasure in oral-language skill development. Speaking in front of an audience, participating in a group oral presentation, and mastering the pronunciation of progressively more challenging vocabulary are important skills. Our experiences sharing poetry chorally in diverse classrooms from elementary through high school have shown that students need practice developing their oral fluency and that they find poetry a particularly less intimidating and fun way to do so.

Supporting Oral-Language Development

How do teachers best support oral-language development among students in their classrooms? Gibbons (1993) offers a description of a supportive classroom for English learners. These classroom characteristics especially address the elements needed to foster oral-language development among English learners including

- a comfortable, supportive environment,

Supporting the Literacy Development of English Learners: Increasing Success in All Classrooms, edited by Terrell A. Young and Nancy L. Hadaway. Copyright © 2006 by the International Reading Association.

- opportunities for meaningful interaction,

- assistance to help learners understand the content, and

- encouragement to function as active learners rather than as passive information receivers.

The first and most important element is a comfortable learning environment. English learners need to feel secure as they experiment with speaking a new language; comfort level can influence how accurately students hear the English used by the teacher and classmates. When students feel anxious or frightened, a barrier to communication is created and less input gets through to the learner (Krashen & Terrell, 1983).

The second characteristic of a supportive language-learning environment is planned opportunities for meaningful interaction. Too often, English learners find themselves in special language classrooms without fluent English-speaking classmates (and thus few models of proficient English use) or in content classes in which the pace of oral language is beyond their comprehension level. Collaborative learning through paired and small-group activities provides authentic listening and speaking opportunities (Scarcella & Oxford, 1992). For greatest impact on language learning, Mora (n.d.) recommends that English learners be flexibly grouped according to their growing language proficiencies and provided with numerous occasions each day for interaction in large- and small-group activities. The range of language utilized must be understandable while also encouraging new ways of expressing meaning. Students need to hear models of spoken language that promote increased proficiency and understanding. A variety of input options (e.g., pairs/small-group discussions, read-alouds by the teacher or guests, taped readings, videos, and guest speakers) may be utilized.

Further, when English is used, the teacher and fellow classmates must make special efforts to help English learners understand the content. Mora (n.d) offers the following suggestions for accomplishing the goal of comprehensibility:

Listening Activities

- Provide repetition and regular patterns.

- Focus student attention on a few new words or structures.

- Make sure activities are purposeful and authentic.

- Adjust activity in pace and rhythm.

Speaking Activities

- Reinforce formulas and common expressions.

- Structure the activity initially but allow for creativity as levels progress.

- Provide rehearsal and practice in nonthreatening ways.

Reading Activities

- Focus on meaning as well as decoding.
- Create literature-based activities with integrated skills.
- Accommodate activities to both home language and English literacy levels and strategies.
- Relate to oral-language level and skills.

(See the following section titled "Reading Poetry With English Learners" for how poetry fits with these strategies.)

Finally, as English learners engage in collaborative learning and meaningful interactions with the teacher and peers, they need to be encouraged to function as problem solvers rather than as information receivers. Although English learners initially spend some time in a silent period of language acquisition, and are thus information receivers, they must move beyond this stage to learn English. Yet recent research cites inadequate time for English-language development as a major problem with current practice. A low level of student oral-language use in English-language development classes, only 21% of the time, is noted in a study by Arreaga-Mayer and Perdomo-Rivera (1996). Likewise, Ramírez (1992) notes, "consistently, across grade levels within and between...programs, students are limited in their opportunities to produce language and in their opportunities to produce more complex language" (p. 9).

Reading Poetry With English Learners

Poetry is an ideal *entry point* into language learning. The range of poetry options—from humorous to serious, content-related to multicultural, brief to long, informal to formal language—affords an opportunity to meet almost any instructional and proficiency level, so teachers need not limit their choices to volumes specifically labeled *poetry*. Beyond the traditional narrative, lyric, free verse, limerick, ballad, concrete, and haiku poetry books, poetry comes in a variety of rhyming and patterned books that don't necessarily look like poetry (see Table 10.1 for examples). This rich diversity of poems, poetic picture books, poetry collections, and such is ideally suited for English learners. They meet varying language proficiency needs and backgrounds and can help to increase word knowledge, familiarity with English syntax patterns, and even conceptual background knowledge.

In addition to providing a range of options, poetry provides many instructional advantages. First, poetry is "packaged" in very few words, relatively speaking (Cullinan, Scala, & Schroder, 1995). Poems can be read and reread in very little time. The length is less intimidating to English learners and, although poetry also may present new words and concepts, its shorter appearance provides a motivating advantage. Further, because of its brevity, poetry serves as a brief but powerful anticipatory set for longer literary works

TABLE 10.1
Rhyming and Pattern Books

Alphabet Book: *It Begins With A*, Stephanie Calmenson (1993)
Clapping Games, Chants, Cheers: *Street Rhymes Around the World*, Jane Yolen (1992)
Counting Book: *An Invitation to the Butterfly Ball*, Jane Yolen (1976)
Easy-to-Read Book: *"Not Now!" Said the Cow*, Joanne Oppenheim (1989)
Folk Song: *Arroz Con Leche*, Lulu Delacre (1989)
Jump-Rope and Ball-Bouncing Rhyme: *Anna Banana*, Joanna Cole (1989)
Predictable Book: *Is Your Mama a Llama?*, Deborah Guarino (1989)
Rhyming Picture Book: *Sheep in a Jeep*, Nancy Shaw (1986)
Rhythmic Picture Book: *Goodnight, Moon*, Margaret Wise Brown (1947)
Riddles, Tongue Twisters, Counting Games, Nonsense Verse: *And the Green Grass Grew All Around*, Alvin Schwartz (1992)
Song Picture Book: *Mary Had a Little Lamb*, Bruce McMillan (1990)
Story in Rhyme: *Green Eggs and Ham*, Dr. Seuss (1960)
Street Songs and Raps: *Night on Neighborhood Street*, Eloise Greenfield (1978)

and for the introduction of concepts and content across the curriculum (Chatton, 1993; Cullinan et al., 1995). Teachers can set the stage for a new topic, unit, etc., with a quick look at a poem. What is more, poetry is a source of brief character sketches, scenes, and stories that can prompt writing from students (Vogel & Tilley, 1993). For example, *Gracie Graves and the Kids from Room 402* (Paraskevas, 1995) offers readers a series of brief character sketches of a variety of children in an elementary school, and *My Name is Jorge: On Both Sides of the River* (Medina, 1999) is a collection of poems describing Jorge's adjustment to school and life in the United States after moving from Mexico.

The strong oral quality of poetry is another powerful pedagogical plus. Poetry is meant to be read aloud. The poem's meaning is communicated more clearly when both read and heard. Read-alouds help language learners acquire correct word pronunciations. They incorporate listening vocabulary, aiding students' overall comprehension. In addition, the rhythm and rhyme of poetry helps English learners get a sense of the sound of English words and phrases. Using artful, yet natural, language, poetry contains "elements of predictability such as rhyme, rhythm and repetition which make reading easier" (Gill, 1996, p. 28). When English learners participate in choral reading, they have the opportunity to develop their own oral fluency. As English learners gain practice reading aloud poems of various formats, they become more fluent in their delivery, and that builds confidence in their performance. Moreover, recent research (Center for the Improvement of Early Reading Achievement [CIERA], 2003) indicates that "repeated oral reading substantially improves word recognition, speed, and accuracy as well as fluency. To a lesser but still considerable extent, repeated oral reading also improves reading comprehension" (p. 24).

Another benefit of poems is that they tend to be about one topic. This crystallized focus of poetry can aid English learners as they use their word knowledge to make sense of new content. A poem's context can help English learners incorporate new vocabulary. For instance, in *A Light in the Attic* (Silverstein, 1981), the poem "Ations" offers a list of words (e.g., *communication*, *negotiation*, *reconciliation*) that end in the sometimes troublesome *-tion*. In a couplet, the poet playfully defines the words, providing a format that students can use to consider additional words with the same ending. Another example of context helping students gain new vocabulary is the Thanksgiving poem "Leftovers" in *It's Thanksgiving* (Prelutsky, 1982), which is very clearly about one subject. Although words such as *bisque* and *fritters* may be unfamiliar, the poem's context provides a framework to clarify meaning. When English learners read the poem, hear the poem, read it aloud, and participate in choral reading of the poem, they are given multiple modes of reinforcement for meaningful language learning.

Focusing on the need to build academic language, teachers can find poems that extend across the curriculum, engaging students and breaking the monotony of textbooks. For example, poetry can reinforce concepts that students need to remember and can provide sensory experiences, giving students the sense of touching, feeling, smelling, and seeing. Poems help to make a topic memorable through the use of highly charged words and vivid images. Many recent poetry anthologies focus on specific content areas or concepts. Lee Bennett Hopkins has written several collections of poems ideal for English learners with beginning language proficiency. His books of poems, such as *Blast Off! Poems About Space* (1995), *Dino-Roars* (1999a), and *Sports! Sports! Sports!* (1999b), provide simple poems with strong rhyme and imagery that are ideal for English learners.

Teachers can use poetry to introduce a unit or lesson and its concepts or weave poetry throughout a thematic or interdisciplinary study. For a thematic unit on weather, teachers can choose from countless poetry collections, such as *Just Around the Corner: Poems About the Seasons* (Jacobs, 1993), *Voices on the Wind: Poems for All Seasons* (Booth, 1990), *A Circle of Seasons* (Livingston, 1982), and *Snow, Snow: Winter Poems for Children* (Yolen, 1998).

Finally, various poetry formats (such as list poems, biopoems, diamantes, and found poems) are great initial formats that can help students talk about the concepts and ideas they are learning and lead them to written reporting of content and concepts. Collections of poems with similar form can help teachers provide multiple models of one kind of poem. *Splish Splash* (Graham, 1994), for example, a poetry book of only concrete (or shape) poems, allows English learners to look at several examples of the same form all in one place. Highlighting poems with a common format through choral reading naturally leads English learners to try writing poetry.

Strategies for Sharing Poetry

Once teachers understand the many benefits of poetry, they must next turn their attention to inviting English learners into the world of poetry. Following are several strategies for sharing poetry with attention to the special needs of English learners. These strategies will work across grade levels from early childhood through high school. Teachers will only need to adjust the poems that are used with the class.

Teacher Modeling

Teacher modeling is the best place to start introducing English learners to poetry; simply read poems aloud to the class. Cullinan and colleagues (1995), in fact, recommend that teachers read a poem at least twice, paying attention to the line breaks for read-aloud cues. Reading poems out loud helps students attend to both the sounds of the words and the lines, as well as to meaning. For English learners, this modeling step cannot be skipped. It familiarizes students with the sounds of the poem's words and engages their listening comprehension in making sense of the poem. As Blau (2001) notes, "to read fluently, students must first hear and understand what fluent reading sounds like. From there, they will be more likely to transfer those experiences into their own reading" (n.p.). Teachers should also follow up, asking students how their reading was like what good readers do, so that students begin to focus on the elements of fluent reading.

Teachers can begin the modeling process by choosing poems they enjoy personally. Then they can read the poem with expression and enthusiasm without rushing the lines. Teachers can display the words of the poem on the board or with an overhead projector. This is essential for English learners at the beginning and intermediate levels of language proficiency. Seeing the words while hearing them is additional reinforcement for students learning to read. Blau (2001) offers the following poetry-sharing routine for modeling fluent oral reading:

1. Choose a short poem, preferably one that fits into the current unit of study.
2. Copy it to an overhead transparency.
3. Make a copy of the poem for each student.
4. Read the poem aloud several times while students listen and follow along.
5. Take a moment to discuss reading behaviors such as *phrasing* (ability to read several words together in one breath), *rate* (speed of reading), and *intonation* (emphasis given to particular words or phrases).
6. Ask students to engage in *echo reading* (teacher reads a line and all students repeat the line).
7. Have students choral read the entire poem together.

From the beginning, teachers should call attention to text features, such as italics and boldface print, to provide clues about how to read certain words, phrases, or lines. This is an excellent opportunity to have an academic discussion about text features. As proficiency improves and students become accustomed to the poetry sharing/modeling routine, teachers can mention literary techniques, such as alliteration and personification, and the effect they create. Teachers shouldn't overdo this, but the opportunity to help English learners with academic vocabulary and concepts should not be overlooked.

A second-grade teacher shared the list poem "What the Wind Swept Away Today" from *Bing Bang Boing* (Florian, 1994). The poet simply weaves together a list of items that the wind has blown away. In order to help English learners comprehend each of the items, the teacher had each student create a picture from one line of the poem (e.g., "a purple leaf [off a tree]"; "Someone's homework [graded D]"). After reading the poem and sharing the illustrations, the class discussed the humor found in the last line of the poem ("And my little sister Claire"). The teacher asked, "Could this really happen?" Sharing a poem out loud every day should be a regular part of the daily routine:

> Hearing a model of fluent reading is not the only benefit of reading aloud to children. Reading to children also increases their knowledge of the world, their vocabulary, their familiarity with written language ("book language"), and their interest in reading. (Blau, 2001, n.p.)

One elementary teacher noted that, although she was using one poem per day for choral response, she planned to include more because students really look forward to the poems and always ask for more. Bagert (1992) recommends a sequence of choral sharing that begins with teacher performance (modeling), moves to group performance, then to short individual performances, and finally to individual performance as a poetry troupe. When invited to participate, English learners can be creative in inventing their own methods of choral presentation. Experimenting with this idea, a middle school teacher noted,

> The appreciation for choral reading was a complete surprise. I thought that sixth-grade boys would not want to read poetry together in a group, but I was mistaken. They thoroughly enjoyed it and experienced a great deal of success. I will continue to offer this...to my ESL students.

Reading in Unison

Once the stage has been set for hearing poems read aloud, invite students to join in for unison read-alouds—if they haven't already jumped in! Choose shorter poems with a strong rhythm or repetitive language, and read the poems aloud first as a model. Even reluctant readers can participate in reading aloud poems when their voices needn't carry the whole poem.

Joining in on Refrain

This third strategy for choral reading requires that students learn about timing, and they jump in only when their lines come up. However, they still participate as a whole class for their given line or lines, with no pressure to perform individually. As always, the teacher reads the entire poem aloud first. Then, in repeated readings, students join in on a line or refrain that pops up repeatedly in the poem. Many poems are particularly effective for this performance strategy. In "Louder" from *The New Kid on the Block* (Prelutsky, 1984), students read aloud the word *louder* whenever it appears. When reading "Things" in *Honey, I Love* (Greenfield, 1978), students say the line "ain't got it no more" each time it occurs. For English learners, this is a way to participate as a group with all of the other students. It is low pressure because all of the voices blend together. It can be helpful to write the word or phrase on a strip of paper and lift it high when students take their turn, as a visual cue.

Call and Response

Once students are familiar with poems read aloud in parts, the teacher can divide the class in half to read poems in a call-and-response method. The best poems for this poetry performance strategy are those with lines structured in a kind of back-and-forth way. In "Copycat," from *Which Way to the Dragon* (Holbrook, 1997), for example, the lines of the poem sound just like two groups of children mimicking each other, repeating what the others say.

Multiple Groups, Multiple Stanzas

Once the teacher has tried all these strategies, the students probably are ready for more challenging choral reading. Using multiple small groups is the next step in bringing poems to life with oral presentation. This puts the focus on fewer students; thus, it may take more practice. But when English learners have participated in unison and large-group read-alouds, small groups are not usually a problem. Small groups may try "Face It," for example, from *A Suitcase of Seaweed* (Wong, 1996). This poem has three stanzas that reflect the writer's musings on her nose, her eyes, and her mouth and how each represents a different part of her identity. Three groups could each read a different stanza, using motions to point to each body part in turn. Or students may try "The Question" in *Dogs and Dragons, Trees and Dreams* (Kuskin, 1980), a poem that poses multiple answers to the question "What do you want to be when you grow up?" Each student group can pipe in with a different answer; for example, "I think I'd like to be the sky," "Or be a plane or train or mouse," "Or maybe a haunted house," "Or something furry, rough and wild...," "Or maybe I will stay a child." If English learners participate with a small group or a partner, they generally feel more secure in joining in this oral exercise.

Solo Lines

Some poems are list-like in structure and work well for what sometimes is called "line-around" choral reading. In line-arounds, individual voices read single lines. After English learners have participated in group variations, most usually are eager to volunteer to read a line solo. However, be sure the poem is familiar to students before they volunteer for individual lines. Language learners can feel especially vulnerable about mispronouncing words or messing up timing. With practice, this interplay of group and individual voices can be very powerful for bringing a poem to life.

Bagert (1992) advises students to think about "What face should I make when I say these words?" to help them create appropriate facial expressions, voice inflection, and even body movement. Students might turn to a partner to practice their line and discuss these decisions as well. As a beginning line-around poem, teachers might try "What If?" (Silverstein, 1981) with each "what-if worry" read by a different student. One kindergarten teacher used "Delicious Wishes" from *Bing, Bang, Boing* (Florian, 1994), with each student taking a different wish (e.g., "I wish I could whistle") to read and act out. As an informal evaluation, the teacher watched to see if students were able to act out the new vocabulary as they recited their lines. This poem also allowed Spanish speakers to practice the difficult /sh/ sound, which can prove to be problematic for them.

Creative Dramatics

Poetry affords an easy avenue into drama—through choral reading, Readers Theatre, and role-playing (Gasparro & Falletta, 1994; Kelly, 1992; McCauley & McCauley, 1992). Readers Theatre, an oral performance of a script, is particularly effective in promoting fluency. Blau (2001) offers some basic steps for getting started with Readers Theatre in the classroom:

- Give each student a copy of the script or poem, and read it aloud.
- After the read-aloud, lead the class in an echo reading and a choral reading of the script in order to involve the entire class.
- Divide the class into groups. Each group discusses the poem and comes up with an interpretation.
- Once the class has enough practice, choose students to read the various parts and perform a Readers Theatre of the poem.
- Put together a few simple props and costumes, and invite other classes to attend the performance.

This exposes the class numerous times to the literary selection, resulting in far more readings than a regular class situation affords. Such natural repetition of language is suited ideally for English learners and fosters the development of oral-language and reading fluency (Cullinan et al., 1995; Richard-Amato, 1996).

Other Creative Strategies

Once the invitation to share poems chorally has been extended, students can generate their own creative alternatives. Chatton (1993) challenges teachers to consider pantomime, sound effects, and background music and to consider inviting English learners to translate their favorite poems from English into their native languages or American Sign Language. English learners may want to adapt their favorite poems to rap, chants, or yells, and use puppets, props, gestures, or clapping.

For beginning English learners, "frame" sentences provide a syntax structure in which to plug new vocabulary. Frame sentences can be used to create list poems that can be read as chants. One pattern that works well is the frame "I like _____ but I don't like _____." In a first-grade ESL class, students came up with the following completions that they then performed as a chant:

> We all like pizza but we do not like speng [spinach].
>
> We all like brown bins [brown beans] but we do not like green bins [green beans].
>
> We all like turckies [turkeys] but we do not like pig feet.

Ada, Harris, and Hopkins (1993), in their anthology *A Chorus of Cultures*, suggest that "physical involvement puts children at ease and encourages listening comprehension" and that "representing the actions of a poem, the feelings in the poem, allowing even for silent participation, especially for children acquiring English" (p. 32) is essential to language learning. Indeed, this linking of language and action is the foundation of the very popular ESL instructional method total physical response (TPR; Asher, 1982). Moreover, many poems lend themselves to acting out or highlighting vocabulary. The poem "Boa Constrictor" from *Where the Sidewalk Ends* (Silverstein, 1974) focuses on body parts, and "The Bully" from *Bing Bang Boing* (Florian, 1994) provides numerous action phrases.

A kindergarten teacher had students make monster masks out of paper plates to use as they acted out monster motions to accompany the oral reading of "A Monster's Day" (Florian, 1994). More creative teaching ideas can be found at the Potato Hill Poetry website (www.potatohill.com), which features a regular "poem of the week" and excellent teaching tips, and in the anthology *The Poetry Break* (Bauer, 1995).

For additional practice, Steinbergh (1994) recommends classrooms include a listening center to highlight poetry. Poems on tape, along with the corresponding books or poems, make an excellent addition to the listening center. They provide additional practice in listening/reading; models of effective read-aloud, pronunciation, and expression; and models of writing. Indeed, recent research supports tape-assisted reading, an activity in which students read along in their books as they listen to a fluent reader read the book on an audiotape. The steps for tape-assisted reading are as follows:

1. Find books at a students' independent reading levels and tape recordings of the books read by fluent readers.

2. Avoid tapes with sound effects or music.

3. For the first reading, have students follow along with the tape, pointing to each word in the book as the reader reads it.

4. Ask students to read aloud along with the tape.

5. Ask students to continue until they are able to read the book independently, without the support of the tape.

6. When students are comfortable with reading aloud favorite poems, have them record themselves reading the poems aloud, copy the poems in their best handwriting, illustrate the poems themselves, and place the poems and tapes in the listening center for other students to enjoy. (CIERA, 2003, p. 28)

An additional asset to a listening center poetry collection is bilingual poetry. There are many collections of poetry in both English and Spanish, including *Laughing Out Loud, I Fly* (Herrera, 1998) and *My Mexico~Mexico Mio* (Johnston, 1996). There are also poems that have examples of code switching—using Spanish words and phrases within English text, such as *Confetti* (Mora, 1999) and *Canto Familiar* (Soto, 1995).

English learners or their parents may also read poems in their native language and provide a written version as well. Such a focus on promoting other languages can foster a positive learning environment. This can be a source of pride as well as language practice. Finally, several websites offer audio versions of poems, including new kinds of experimental poetry. Check out the following resources:

- Electronic Poetry Center homepage offers all kinds of experimental poetry: www.wings.buffalo.edu/epc

- Poets & Writers offers audio files of some poems, and poem trivia: www.pw.org

- Digital Passions *Poetry Magazine* supplies audio clips of individual poems: www.poetrymagazine.com

Responding to Poetry

Teachers lay the foundation for understanding poetry by first providing enjoyment. They should emphasize the *oral* presentation of poetry. Sharing poetry orally is an important ingredient of providing access to this genre for English learners. An emphasis on the oral aspects of poetry acknowledges students' unique need to incorporate heard and spoken words into their vocabularies before attempting to read and write them. Read-alouds, choral readings, and creative dramatics offer fun, active ways to engage students with the literature and to practice oral language and build fluency. However, an additional focus on reading and responding to poetry is needed to move English learners into the academic-language domain.

To foster academic language, the next step is the follow-up response to poetry. However, Kucer (1995) notes, in a study with bilingual students, "at the beginning of the year, students were unwilling or unable to react to what was read and often appeared puzzled by requests to do so" (p. 25). As teachers invite English learners to dig deeper into poetry and examine the craft of the poet, they need to begin with oral discussion and small-group sharing to help students articulate what they see—before urging them to write their analyses or create original poetry.

How do teachers proceed without butchering a poem? Poet and teacher Georgia Heard (1999) helps students through what she calls three "layers" of poetry: inviting students into poetry, helping students connect with poetry, and guiding students toward analyzing the craft of poetry. In addition, McClure (1990) suggests using one or two of the following facilitating prompts:

- What did you think?
- What did you like about the poem?
- Does this remind you of anything you know about?
- What is the poet saying here?
- Any comments about that?
- Let's discuss what is going on.
- What is this about?

Furthermore, Lockward (1994) offers the following advice to teachers on what *not* to do with poetry:

- Do not explain the poem to students.
- Do not give tests on poetry.
- Do not be overly concerned with techniques.
- Do not approach a poem with historical matters.
- Do not impose the critics on students.

Instead, Lockward urges teachers to do the following:

- Expose students to beautiful, powerful language.
- Allow time for multiple oral readings of a poem.
- Lead discussions that encourage a personal relationship with a poem.
- Teach poems that are accessible to students.
- Allow students to sometimes choose their own poems.
- Provide opportunities for students to write poetry.

For English learners who are anxious about contributing to class discussions because their language skills may not yet be fluent, alternative grouping may be more helpful than asking the right questions. Ask English learners to turn to a partner and talk with her or him about "what the poet is saying here." English learners are often more comfortable sharing their opinions with one classmate rather than with the class as a whole. For digging deeper into a poem's meaning, small groups or poetry circles also function well.

Poetry circles, patterned along the line of literature circles (Harste, Short, & Burke, 1988), offer a wonderful, collaborative opportunity for students to share preferences, read aloud, and talk about poems. The small-group atmosphere establishes a safety level that encourages the sharing of more personal reactions, positive and negative. According to Christenbury (1992), group work with literature can be facilitated with the use of cooperative learning and assigned roles to question and guide the conversation, to highlight important vocabulary and help group members use context to decipher the meaning, and to focus on good examples of elements to discuss.

Creating a Classroom Collection of Poetry

In order to meet the variety of proficiency levels and interests of students, teachers need to build a list of poetry options; even better is to build their own classroom library so that students can browse through the books at leisure. Studies of children's preferences indicate that most children enjoy narrative, storytelling poems that have a regular, distinctive rhythm, strong sound patterns, plenty of humor, and not too much abstract and figurative language (see Kutiper & Wilson, 1993). However, children develop a taste for many different kinds of poems once they are introduced to them. Therefore, the following overview of a few trends in poetry books for young people considers how these trends might benefit English learners.

Anthologies

The format of the poetry anthology has been around since publishing began. It is a practical way to offer a multitude of poems on a variety of subjects by many different poets. These oversized books with hundreds of poems are generally not very inviting and have been replaced gradually by other kinds of more selective anthologies. Indeed, Hopkins (1993) makes a distinction between collections and anthologies. Using his nomenclature, there are two types of collections: "single author," in which all of the poems are by the same poet (e.g., *Who's Been Sleeping In My Porridge?*, McNaughton, 1990), and "single topic" collections, in which all of the poems address the same topic (e.g., *Halloween Poems*, Livingston, 1989). Hopkins defines anthologies as "books put together to highlight a variety of topics with multiple poets" (p. 202) (e.g., *Sing a Song of Popcorn*, de Regniers, Moore, White, & Carr, 1988). An example of a single-topic compilation is a collection of animal poems titled *The Beauty of the Beast* (Prelutsky, 1997). Its more narrow topic of animals makes it easy for teachers or librarians to connect it with the current curriculum. Teacher-friendly thematic collections are becoming very popular.

Practically speaking, it makes it even easier to open a science or social studies lesson with a poem. For English learners, content connections provide an enormous help for comprehension because poems are related to subject matter (Krashen & Terrell, 1983).

Multicultural Poetry

Multicultural poetry speaks to English learners in particular, with themes of biculturalism, cultural identity, and cultural heritage. Poets such as Janet Wong, Gary Soto, and Nikki Giovanni give voice to these and many other experiences. Giovanni, in works such as *Ego-Tripping and Other Poems for Young People* (1993), offers readers a view of the African American experience. And African American poet Eloise Greenfield, winner of the National Council of Teachers of English Poetry Award for lifetime contribution to poetry for children, is not to be missed (*Honey, I Love*, 1978, and *Night on Neighborhood Street*, 1991). In social studies, when reading about the Underground Railroad, share the spirited poem "Harriet Tubman" (Greenfield, 1978). Students enjoy the minibiography as well as the strong rhythm of the language.

There are more and more published collections of Hispanic poetry for children. Teachers can choose favorites to read aloud from the classroom collection; for example, "My Teacher in the Market Place" from *Canto Familiar* (Soto, 1995), and "Spanish," in which the writer paints a joyous picture of bilingualism, expressing that knowing two languages can actually enlarge one's world.

One outstanding Asian American poet is Janet Wong, an author whose early work explores her Korean-Chinese-American roots in a fresh and direct way that English learners find very relevant. Her poem "Speak Up" (*Good Luck Gold*, 1994) can be read chorally with many voices versus a lone voice. This reading can vividly bring home the point that people may look different, but they are still Americans.

Finally, teachers should not overlook Native American poetry, which includes a variety of forms (rhymes, free verse, chants, charms, prayers, blessings, lullabies, warnings, eulogies, wishes, prophecies, healings, war chants, night songs, magic songs, medicine songs, mother/child poems, and more). Joseph Bruchac has several collections: *Between Earth and Sky* (Bruchac & Locker, 1996), *Four Ancestors: Stories, Songs, and Poems from Native North America* (Bruchac, Burrus, Jacob, & Strait, 1996), *The Earth Under Sky Bear's Feet* (Bruchac & Locker, 1998), and *Thirteen Moons on Turtle's Back* (Bruchac & London, 1992).

Mother Goose Poems and Nursery Rhymes

There are Mother Goose traditions of simple songs and rhymes in every culture, and gradually many of these are making their way into book form, as in *Arroz Con Leche: Popular Songs and Rhymes From Latin American* (Delacre, 1989) and *Chinese Mother Goose Rhymes* (Wyndham, 1998).

Collections by Individual Poets

Poetry also comes in the form of works by individual poets. Krashen and Terrell (1983) note the benefits of using several works (or collections of poems) by one author. They argue that such "narrow reading" helps English learners because of the familiar authorial style. *Where the Sidewalk Ends* (Silverstein, 1974) is probably the most well-known example of a collection by an individual poet. Such "standards" by Silverstein, Prelutsky, and Viorst are readily available, and children often vote these poets as their favorite (Kutiper & Wilson, 1993). However, other writers are gaining in popularity, too, such as Kalli Dakos, Douglas Florian, and Naomi Shihab Nye. Florian's *Bing, Bang, Boing* (1994) is an excellent collection to have on hand; it is packed full of rhythmic, humorous, appealing poetry that works well with nearly all proficiency and grade levels.

Conclusion

The focus on poetry with English learners is ideal when one considers the unique qualities of the genre: brevity, strong rhythm, focused content, strong emotional connection, and powerful imagery. Plus, oral poetry sharing can provide the necessary language practice in a context that is relaxed and pleasurable, where all learners can participate as equals in enjoying the playfulness and power of language. For English learners, teacher-guided choral reading of poetry meets many of the conditions that are critical to fostering oral-language proficiency: teacher demonstration, encouragement of even approximate pronunciations, student immersion, practice, and student responsibility for their own participation (Hadaway, Vardell, & Young, 2001, 2002). Such approaches reinforce students' language development as well as expose English learners to a broad range of authors, topics, and poetic formats. Poetry offers a bridge from culture to culture, language to language.

REFERENCES

Ada, A.F., Harris, V., & Hopkins, L.B. (1993). *A chorus of cultures: Developing literacy through multicultural poetry*. Carmel, CA: Hampton-Brown.

Arreaga-Mayer, C., & Perdomo-Rivera, C. (1996). Ecobehavioral analysis of instruction for at-risk language-minority students. *The Elementary School Journal, 96*(3), 245–258.

Asher, J. (1982). *Learning another language through actions: The complete teachers' guidebook*. Los Gatos, CA: Sky Oaks.

Bagert, B. (1992). Act it out: Making poetry come alive. In B. Cullinan (Ed.), *Invitation to read: More children's literature in the reading program* (pp. 14–23). Newark, DE: International Reading Association.

Bauer, C.F. (1995). *The poetry break: An annotated anthology with ideas for introducing children to poetry*. New York: H.W. Wilson.

Blau, L. (2001). Five surefire strategies for developing reading fluency. *Instructor*. Retrieved September 12, 2001, from http://teacher.scholastic.com/professional/teachstrat/readingfluencystrategies.htm

Center for the Improvement of Early Reading Achievement (CIERA). (2003). *Put reading first: The building blocks of reading instruction, kindergarten through grade 3* (2nd ed.). Retrieved September 12, 2004, from http://www.nifl.gov/partnershipforreading/publications/Cierra.pdf

Chatton, B. (1993). *Using poetry across the curriculum: A whole language approach*. Phoenix, AZ: Oryx.

Christenbury, L. (1992). "The guy who wrote this poem seems to have the same feelings as you have": Reader-response methodology. In N.J. Karolides (Ed.), *Reader response in the classroom: Evoking and interpreting meaning in literature* (pp. 33–44).

Cullinan, B., Scala, M., & Schroder, V. (1995). *Three voices: An invitation to poetry across the curriculum*. York, ME: Stenhouse.

Gasparro, M., & Falletta, B. (1994, April). *Creating drama with poetry: Teaching English as a second language through dramatization and improvisation* (ERIC Document No. 368 214). Washington, DC: ERIC Clearinghouse on Languages and Linguistics.

Gibbons, P. (1993). *Learning to learn in a second language*. Portsmouth, NH: Heinemann.

Gill, S. (1996). Shared book experience with poetry. *The State of Reading, Journal of the Texas State Reading Association, 3,* 1, 27–30.

Hadaway, N.L., Vardell, S.M., & Young, T.A. (2001). Scaffolding oral language development through poetry for students learning English. *Reading Teacher, 54,* 796–809.

Hadaway, N.L., Vardell, S.M., & Young, T.A. (2002). *Literature-based instruction with English learners, K–12.* Boston: Allyn & Bacon/Longman.

Harste, J.C., Short, K.G., & Burke, C. (1988). *Creating classrooms for authors: The reading-writing connection.* Portsmouth, NH: Heinemann.

Heard, G. (1999). *Awakening the heart: Exploring poetry in elementary and middle school.* Portsmouth, NH: Heinemann.

Hopkins, L.B. (1993). Poetry—practically. In M.K. Rudman (Ed.), *Children's literature: Resource for the classroom* (pp. 201–210). Norwood, MA: Christopher-Gordon.

Kelly, P.P. (1992). Two reader-response classrooms: Using pre-reading activity and Readers Theatre approaches. In N.J. Karolides (Ed.), *Reader response in the classroom: Evoking and interpreting meaning in literature* (pp. 84–91). White Plains, NY: Longman.

Krashen, S.D., & Terrell, T.D. (1983). *The natural approach.* San Francisco: Alemany Press.

Kucer, S.B. (1995). Guiding bilingual students "through" the literacy process. *Language Arts, 72*(1), 20–29.

Kutiper, K., & Wilson, P. (1993). Updating poetry preferences: A look at the poetry children really like. *The Reading Teacher, 47,* 28–34.

Lockward, D. (1994). Poets on teaching poetry. *English Journal, 83*(5), 65–70.

McCauley, J., & McCauley, D. (1992). Using choral reading to promote language learning for ESL students. *The Reading Teacher, 45,* 526–533.

McClure, A. (1990). *Sunrises and songs: Reading and writing poetry in the classroom.* Portsmouth, NH: Heinemann.

Mora, J.K. (n.d.). *A road map for effective biliteracy instruction: A knowledge base and teaching strategies.* Retrieved July 8, 2005, from http://coe.sdsu.edu/people/jmora/MoraModules/BiliteracyRoadMap.htm

Mora, J.K. (1998). *Development of second-language writing.* Retrieved July 28, 2004, from http://coe.sdsu.edu/people/jmora/L2WritingMMdl

Ramírez, J.D. (1992). Executive summary. *Bilingual Research Journal, 16,* 1–62.

Richard-Amato, P. (1996). *Making it happen: Interaction in the second language classroom* (2nd ed.). New York: Longman.

Scarcella, R.C., & Oxford, R.L. (1992). *The tapestry of language learning: The individual in the communicative classroom.* Boston: Heinle & Heinle.

Snow, C., Burns, S., & Griffin, P. (Eds.). (1998). *Preventing reading difficulties in young children.* Washington, DC: National Academy Press.

Steinbergh, J. (1994). *Reading and writing poetry: A guide for teachers.* New York: Scholastic.

Vogel, M., & Tilley, J. (1993). Story poems and the stories we've been waiting to tell. *English Journal, 82,* 86–89.

CHILDREN'S BOOKS CITED

Booth, D. (1990). *Voices on the wind: Poems for all seasons.* New York: Morrow.

Brown, M.W. (1947). *Goodnight, moon.* New York: Harper & Row.

Bruchac, J., Burrus, S.S., Jacob, M., & Strait, D. (1996). *Four ancestors: Stories, songs, and poems from Native America.* Mahwah, NJ: Bridgewater Books.

Bruchac, J., & Locker, T. (1996). *Between earth and sky.* San Diego, CA: Harcourt Brace.

Bruchac, J., & Locker, T. (1998). *The earth under Sky Bear's feet: Native American poems of the land.* New York: PaperStar.

Bruchac, J., & London, J. (1992). *Thirteen moons on Turtle's back.* New York: Philomel Books.

Calmenson, S. (1993). *It begins with A.* New York: Hyperion Books.

Cole, J. (1989). *Anna Banana: 101 jump rope rhymes.* New York: Beech Tree Books.

Delacre, L. (1989). *Arroz con leche: Popular songs and rhymes from Latin America*. New York: Scholastic.

de Regniers, B.S., Moore, M., White, W., & Carr, J. (Eds.). (1988). *Sing a song of popcorn*. New York: Scholastic.

Florian, D. (1994). *Bing, bang, boing*. San Diego, CA: Harcourt Brace.

Giovanni, N. (1993). *Ego-tripping and other poems for young people*. New York: Lawrence Hill Books.

Graham, J.B. (1994). *Splish splash*. Boston: Houghton Mifflin.

Greenfield, E. (1978). *Honey, I love*. New York: HarperCollins.

Greenfield, E. (1991). *Night on neighborhood street*. New York: Dial.

Guarino, D. (1989). *Is your mama a llama?* New York: Scholastic.

Herrera, J.F. (1998). *Laughing out loud, I fly: Poems in English in Spanish*. New York: HarperCollins.

Holbrook, S. (1997). *Which way to the dragon*. Honesdale, PA: Boyds Mills Press.

Hopkins, L.B. (Ed.). (1995). *Blast off! Poems about space*. New York: HarperCollins.

Hopkins, L.B. (Ed.). (1999a). *Dino-roars*. New York: Golden Books.

Hopkins, L.B. (Ed.). (1999b). *Sports! Sports! Sports!* New York: HarperCollins.

Jacobs, L. (1993). *Just around the corner: Poems about the seasons*. New York: Henry Holt.

Johnston, T. (1996). *My Mexico~Mexico Mio*. New York: Penguin Putnam.

Kuskin, K. (1980). *Dogs and dragons, trees and dreams: A collection of poems*. New York: HarperCollins.

Livingtson, M.C. (1982). *A circle of seasons*. New York: Holiday House.

Livingston, M.C. (Ed.). (1989). *Halloween poems*. New York: Holiday House.

McMillan, B. (1990). *Mary had a little lamb*. New York: Scholastic.

McNaughton, C. (1990). *Who's been sleeping in my porridge?* Cambridge, MA: Candlewick.

Medina, J. (1999). *My Name is Jorge: On both sides of the river*. Honesdale, PA: Boyds Mills Press.

Mora, P. (1999). *Confetti: Poems for children*. New York: Lee & Low.

Oppenheim, J. (1989). *"Not now!" said the cow*. New York: Bantam.

Paraskevas, B. (1995). *Gracie Graves and the kids from room 402*. New York: Harcourt.

Prelutsky, J. (1982). *It's Thanksgiving*. New York: Scholastic.

Prelutsky, J. (1984). *The new kid on the block*. New York: Greenwillow.

Prelutsky, J. (1997). *The beauty of the beast: Poems from the animal kingdom*. New York: Knopf.

Schwartz, A. (1992). *And the green grass grew all around*. New York: HarperCollins.

Seuss, Dr. (1960). *Green eggs and ham*. New York: Beginners Books.

Shaw, N. (1986). *Sheep in a jeep*. Boston: Houghton Mifflin.

Silverstein, S. (1974). *Where the sidewalk ends*. New York: HarperCollins.

Silverstein, S. (1981). *A light in the attic*. New York: HarperCollins.

Soto, G. (1992). *Neighborhood odes*. San Diego, CA: Harcourt Brace Jovanovich.

Soto, G. (1995). *Canto familiar*. San Diego, CA: Harcourt Brace.

Wong, J.S. (1994). *Good luck gold*. New York: Margaret K. McElderry.

Wong, J.S. (1996). *A suitcase of seaweed*. New York: Margaret K. McElderry.

Wyndham, R. (1998). *Chinese Mother Goose rhymes*. New York: PaperStar Books.

Yolen, J. (1976). *An invitation to the butterfly ball*. New York: Parents Magazine Press.

Yolen, J. (1992). *Street rhymes around the world*. Honesdale, PA: Wordsong/Boyds Mill Press.

Yolen, J. (1998). *Snow, snow: Winter poems for children*. Honesdale, PA: Boyds Mills Press.

CHAPTER 11

Using Puppets With English Learners to Develop Language

Vida Zuljevic

Students:	Firefighter, Firefighter, what do you do?
Firefighter:	I put out fires, that's what I do.
Students:	Police Officer, Police Officer, what do you do?
Police Officer:	I take care of people's safety, that's what I do.
Students:	Doctor, Doctor, what do you do?
Doctor:	I take care of people's health, that's what I do.
Students:	Teacher, Teacher, what do you do?
Teacher:	I teach students, that's what I do.
Students:	Cook, Cook, what do you do?
Cook:	I cook food for people, that's what I do.

A teacher developed this puppet play to teach her kindergarten English learners about community helpers. Throughout the practice and presentation of the play, the students were highly engaged and enjoyed interacting with the puppets. In my own work with elementary-grade students in Bosnia-Herzegovina, Croatia, Germany, and the United States, I find that no matter what culture students belong to or what language they speak, they play with puppets openly, using their hands, thoughts, and feelings; developing friendships; and, most importantly, developing language.

What is the magic of puppets that has motivated people to create them and use them in different cultures for centuries? According to Dostyevsky, the magic power of puppets lies in the open, honest, and trustworthy communication of the puppeteer with the audience (see Pokrivka, 1991). In *The Hand: How Its Use Shapes the Brain, Language, and Human Culture*, Wilson (1998), a neurologist, examines the role of human hands

Supporting the Literacy Development of English Learners: Increasing Success in All Classrooms, edited by Terrell A. Young and Nancy L. Hadaway. Copyright © 2006 by the International Reading Association.

in human development in light of new research in anthropology, neuroscience, linguistics, and psychology. The conclusion is that using the human hand is directly connected with learning and that people use their hands to leave a personal mark on the world in which they live. Wilson's research includes experiences of musicians, surgeons, puppeteers, and mechanics. Given their many benefits, puppets can be used with great success with English learners. This chapter provides practical suggestions for elementary school teachers to consider when using puppets in their classrooms.

Current research on child development and language acquisition points to the benefits of puppetry. Vygotsky's (1934/1978) research and theories on child development, especially language and social development, form the foundation of the constructivist approach to teaching, underlining the importance of play to child development. The major theme of his theoretical framework is that social interaction in early childhood plays a fundamental role in cognitive development. Vygotsky argues that learning is frequently achieved through interactions supported by talk, and that language and talk often are associated with the development of higher order thinking. Play with puppets is well suited to foster social interactions supported by talk and the higher order learning that occurs as a natural consequence. Through puppetry, students are immersed in both social interaction and the use of language.

Krashen (1981) underscores the importance of interaction for English learners, noting that "acquisition requires meaningful interaction in the target language—natural communication—in which speakers are concerned not with the form of their utterances but with the messages they are conveying and understanding" (p. 1). Students who engage in puppet play production, whether a short dialogue or a complete play, are using meaningful, natural conversation in a nonthreatening and enjoyable interaction. Students' anxiety level is low because they don't worry so much about the correctness of their puppet's speech as they do about conveying the message they want understood. Thus, acquisition of the target language occurs more naturally and easily than with a drill approach.

A Personal Journey With Puppets

As a kindergarten teacher in Bosnia-Herzegovina, my native country, I used puppets as tools to introduce a piece of literature or a math concept, to talk about faraway places or music from different cultures, to introduce the seasons, and for countless other purposes. Through these activities, I tried to develop an appreciation for literature, creative thinking, and expressiveness in students. I hoped to give them a sense of the characters, places, and time, and to connect information learned in different subject areas. In addition to academic goals, I focused on helping students to become self-confident, to develop social skills, to deal with conflict issues that would occasionally arise, and to release their fears and frustrations in an appropriate manner (Zuljevic, 2005). These goals address the affective dimension of puppetry.

The affective power of puppetry emerged again when I was forced by war to flee my country and live in several refugee camps. Even though, as an adult, I was stronger and more aware of the situation, my puppetry work in the camps helped me handle my own war traumas. Knowing this, I involved the refugee children in puppetry, helping them to concentrate on something productive, to sort out their traumas, and to overcome the stress caused by war. The puppets proved to be a powerful tool.

My next step in this journey occurred when my family moved to the United States. Neither my husband, my young daughter, nor I knew English. After being coached by my two older children who had studied some English in schools in Europe, I embarked on a job search and was offered the position of preschool teacher. I entered the classroom armed only with my limited English and Ana, a puppet that I had made. Ana was my shield of protection from embarrassment and my ambassador to students' hearts and minds. She helped by borrowing my voice and singing songs to students in Serbo-Croatian, my native tongue. The 2- and 3-year-old toddlers gathered around me, and even though they could not understand a word Ana was saying, they would listen patiently, clap their hands, touch Ana, and soon ask if they could hold Ana on their own.

In these interactions, students shared popular children's favorites, such as "The ABC Song," "Rain, Rain, Go Away," "B-I-N-G-O," and "Mary Had a Little Lamb," and I started learning English very fast. Ana was a bridge between the students and me. In six months, I learned enough English to perform a puppet show called "Are You My Mother?" for the students at the preschool.

A Professional Journey With Puppets

A move to a new state (and obtaining my teaching certificate there) brought me an opportunity to implement my discovery about the power of puppets to help English learners in their language development. My new job was to help the new-to-school, mostly migrant, Spanish-speaking students to feel welcome, and to teach ESL as a part of the resource room curriculum. Although I knew absolutely no Spanish, my puppet Ana was there to help my students—just as she had helped me in the beginning. Ana pointed with her hand to herself when saying her name and toward students when asking about theirs, and used simple introductory sentences such as "Hello, my name is Ana. What is your name?" Students quickly understood and learned. Ana gained students' trust and became a member of the small group. Puppets, I quickly discovered, were the best teaching tool for English-language development.

The Potential of Puppetry: Two Examples

Two examples demonstrate the potential of puppetry to develop language and interaction in the classroom. The first is a collaborative experience with my colleague Bennette

Sanner, a teacher of a third- and fourth-grade class of Spanish-speaking English learners. The second experience is with my own kindergarten class of Russian-speaking English learners.

A Science Puppet Play

Bennette knew that her third- and fourth-grade students needed more English-language experiences, and that experiences that come through a fun activity, such as puppetry, are beneficial for students. We made a plan to perform a play about life under the ocean. To build content background knowledge about the different ocean species and their habitats, Bennette provided students with encyclopedias, dictionaries, magazines, and websites. I used art classes to coach students through the process of making stick puppets, simultaneously introducing art concepts. Bennette taught the vocabulary that students would need, so when I came to work on the puppets and teach the art concept of the week, students were always "ready to go."

When the puppets were finished, we practiced the play, first reading the script like a Readers Theatre script—paying attention to fluency, intonation, and voice expression (Young & Vardell, 1993)—and then practicing for the performance with a practical pipe stage I purchased online. In the beginning some of the English learners were hesitant to talk, but with encouragement and support they would try. A few students asked to say their lines in Spanish. "Yes," we said, "let us have the fisherman speak Spanish, why not?" This was one of the ice-breaking moments that assured students that we were there to support them and help them become better English speakers, better readers, and confident performers. The class practiced the play with the puppets, stage, and stage decorations made in art classes. Bennette's eagerness to explore and share ideas about the ocean habitat and particular fish depicted in the play—and just how she imagined a voice of a mother whale or father whale—was a resource and motivation for the class.

The culmination of the effort was a performance of the puppet play for the entire school and parents. The performance was a success. Students knew their lines, led the puppets skillfully at the stage, and played with their voices as they imagined all the sea creatures they were presenting. They were engaged in the puppet play production as well as in an unconventional language-learning activity, one that was fun and appealing to them. The whole project was done in an 8-week period. From an evaluation standpoint, the teacher observed that student reading skills and vocabulary improved. I observed an increase in students' self-confidence, responsibility, and communication skills as well.

A Literature Puppet Play

A second example of using puppetry for language development is my own experience with a kindergarten class of Russian-speaking students who performed "Goldilocks and the Three Bears" in English. When I started, I had in mind a crucial piece of advice from *Leading Kids to Books Through Puppets* (Bauer, 1997): "Think simple. Think lively. Think fun. Think books" (p. 5). I prepared the class by reading the folk tale "Goldilocks and the Three Bears" several times (over a period of 10 days) until students became familiar with the text. I also provided three copies of the book so that students could look through them during free time.

Next, I organized a book discussion during a whole-class session, asking questions and recording answers on a sheet of chart paper. Some questions involved literary elements and sequencing, such as "Who are the characters?" "Where does the story take place?" "What happened first, next, last?" Others, such as "What size were the bears, bowls, chairs, beds?" involved math and vocabulary. Next to students' answers, I drew pictures of what they said for reinforcement. For example, when they answered that the characters were Goldilocks and the three bears, I wrote the answer in English and drew a picture of the characters with their names under them. In this way, I helped students who had not yet learned the written form of English to relate the picture and spoken word to the written form.

I told students that we were going to prepare our first puppet show. "But we don't have puppets," one boy exclaimed. "You are going to make them," I replied. "You only need to think of what you just said about the setting, house, main characters, bowls, and other things in the story. You may also go to the chart and check what you will need for the puppet show. Now tell me what character you would like to play."

Assignment of characters was not difficult because only 11 students were in the class. The bravest chose the main characters. I asked students who did not choose a character role if they would take care of the props and requisites for the play. They were happy with that opportunity. After the roles were assigned, students made stick puppets of the characters. The only direction I gave was to draw, color, and cut out the character or object. I was ready to help students staple their puppets to the sticks (wooden sticks commonly used to mix paint). During this art time, students talked, made suggestions, and helped one another.

When the puppet-making was done, the excitement reached a high point. The teacher's aide served as videographer, and I took the role of narrator. The performance was a success and validated the use of puppets in the classroom for enhancing and developing oral-language abilities, social communication skills, and appreciation of literature.

Puppetry Beyond the Classroom

Moving beyond the classroom, I have attempted to engage students in puppetry by leading a puppet-making club at school in two 6-week sessions. Students in this after-school enrichment program create puppets that compete with the best of artwork. The club also performs a puppet show for peers, inventing the dialogue of the characters.

Building on this success, I received administrative and peer support at my school in Pasco, Washington, which led to the creation of Robert Frost Elementary School's puppet theater. The puppeteers, mostly English learners in grades 3–5, meet twice a week. The first show the puppeteers performed for schoolmates was inspired by the new self-discipline program at the school. I wrote the script to present the program in a more creative way. The characters in the play were either students who had engaged in discipline events and experienced consequences in the program or students who listened to teachers' expectations and utilized self-discipline. The second performance occurred at the Dr. Seuss reading celebration event at our school.

Feeling confident in their skills, the puppet theater group took the show on the road, visiting and performing at an elementary school in a neighboring city and at a local healthcare center for elders. In addition, the group gave three performances at a local bookstore as well as an hour-long presentation for the Kiwanis Club. These performances outside of school were especially rewarding for students because they felt positive support from the audiences. Such outreach activities promote oral-language development, reading and performance skills, and give students the confidence to be reading advocates in their schools, families, and communities.

Student Reactions to Puppetry

At the end of the school year, I conducted a short survey to determine how students perceived their involvement in puppetry, how it helped them master skills, what their favorite aspect was, and what they wanted to be different next year. The students' responses speak for themselves:

> I think that in puppet theater I learn how to read, to expressing, and how to learn English...to express more beter and communicate and talk beter. (José T., fourth-grade Spanish-speaking English learner)

> It is a very grate place to be. It helps me with better Inglish. (Tonya K., fourth-grade Russian-speaking English learner)

> I felt happy to join because I liked to perform to kids. I also liked all the puppets. And I should come each day or I would let my teacher and friends down.... Yes, I acquire more skills. I learned how to read and more and speak the language more better.... I like to stay in and practice to get better and more better and I like to prevorm to kids or adult. (Cristian G., fourth-grade English learner)

> It is part of my life because Mrs. Zuljevic really helped me understand how to not be afraid of proform on stage. She is one of my best friends. It helped me have an expressive voise. (Mandy B., third-grade native English speaker)

Teacher Reactions to Puppetry

Encouraged by my experiences, several teacher colleagues started using puppets in their teaching and have reported great success, including an improvement in student involvement and motivation, and increased development in reading, oral language, and general communication skills. One of these teachers shares the following comments about the use of puppetry with her students:

My students performed two puppet-plays for their families and friends. Not one student was late or absent from the performance. Afterward they talked about that evening for months. The puppet plays were the highlights of my students' year and an important part of their education.

I was a second-grade Spanish bilingual teacher in a school with many low-income families. I adopted the two puppet plays from Joe Hayes's [1987, 1988] bilingual stories set in the southwest of the United States. The Hispanic students connected to his storytelling style, which reflected their culture and traditions. One of my best performers was Crista, a student who arrived in the fall with almost no letter–sound recognition. Despite this lack of oral language, she shook her monster puppet with great expressiveness and lowered her voice to growl out the words. Performing with puppets definitely assisted Crista in her reading and fluency development.

My students and I had never used puppets before. Vida Zuljevic was our art teacher, and we had one hour of class time with her per week. One day, as I struggled with the idea of props in the two plays, Vida and I stopped to chat. As soon as she heard about the puppet plays, she suggested that the students learn how to use puppets and the puppet stage during art. In two or three art periods, Vida had taught my students many important skills. They learned how to enter and exit the puppet stage and how to use expressive voices and gestures, such as crying, singing, and dancing. They practiced moving the puppets' mouths and bodies properly, to sit, walk, or to talk.

Vida let us use her beautiful puppets, some of them bought and some homemade. Whether or not the puppet moved its mouth or other parts, Vida could make it come alive with acting. The students loved watching her act with puppets. They were waiting every week for art class to arrive. Vida became a true friend to our class and an important mentor to me.

In my reading and writing programs, I noticed significant improvements in the students' interest and abilities related to puppetry. I had tried many techniques for teaching fluency, and puppetry was most successful. In their reading, students began to attend to dialogue and punctuation. They changed their voices for expression and characterization. The students were excited about reading aloud to their friends and families. If the text did not sound right while they were reading, they would stop to reread for fluency.

Perhaps the most dramatic improvement was in the writing of Eduardo, a shy and quiet little boy. I decided that Eduardo, instead of talking, spent time looking at the world and making poetry about what he saw. His stories were full of images like "a bird floating overhead in the blue windy sky." However, none of Eduardo's stories had any organization. I worked with him to occasionally write a story with plot sequence. He was not transferring any of our work to his independent writing until after the puppet show. Suddenly, some of Eduardo's stories had structure that worked nicely. And then it occurred to me where his ideas had come from—the elements of plot were suspiciously similar to the sequence of the two puppet plays. Eduardo found meaning in the use of plot because of his experiences with puppetry.

After a year of puppet performances, students presented at the schoolwide recognition assembly. At recognition time, all but one of the puppeteers was called forward to receive an award certificate. Each student had not only reached a personal reading goal but exceeded it. Surely, part of this achievement was a product of their involvement in puppetry.

Suggestions for Using Puppets in the Classroom

How can teachers begin to integrate puppetry into their classrooms? Bauer (1997) is the perfect reference for ideas on how to start classroom puppetry. To learn more about puppet performance, *Making Puppets Come Alive: How to Learn and Teach Hand Puppetry* (Engler & Fijan, 1973), by the creator and director of Poko Puppets, is a "must-have" reference. Numerous books and websites offer ideas for scripts, as well as information about ordering puppets, stages, accessories, etc. Following are additional reflections for teachers to consider as they begin to use puppets with English learners:

- Keep in mind the advice given by Bauer: "Think simple. Think lively. Think fun. Think books" (p. 5). *Simple* means just that. Have a classroom mascot—a hand or stick puppet that is always there to introduce a new concept, read a book, report morning news, play a new game, announce new rules, or talk about conflict-solving strategies.

- Create a puppetry corner or station. It need not be elaborate; students need to feel comfortable using it. A big cardboard box (one that a refrigerator is packed in) works perfectly because it is inexpensive, foldable, and large enough to serve the purpose of a stage. A little work (e.g., cutting a hole for the main performing window; decorating it using markers, crayons, or paints; putting up a curtain) can produce a great puppet stage.

- Place a box in one corner of the classroom with some hand puppets or materials (such as construction paper, scissors, fabric pieces, beads, feathers, glue, paper bags, and wooden sticks) for students to make their own puppets if they wish.

- As students work together to create their characters, assess student understanding of story elements or concepts, a rule or lesson objective. Students' free play with puppets can be a window to observe students' feelings, possible traumas, conflicts, and understandings of just-introduced concepts, and thus, helpful in planning appropriate interventions.

- Before starting puppetry in the classroom, consider the goal you want to accomplish.

My focus as a kindergarten teacher is to use puppets to enhance curriculum teaching. I do not worry about what the puppets look like, how they move, or what voices students are using for particular characters. I focus on what the puppets say and how they reflect learning objectives and what I have taught. For example, if students perform a puppet show about the parts of a plant, I assess what the puppets say about their color and roles as part of a plant (root, stem, and leaf) rather than how students draw the leaf, root, or stem or what voices they give to the parts.

On the other hand, with the puppet theater group, I teach the skills of puppet performance—focusing on movement, voice expression, and gestures. During the puppet play about the parts of a plant, I encourage students to produce a stutter, a squeak, or any other voice they imagine these parts of a plant have. I teach them to add personality to each of the stick puppets they make (e.g., a leaf with charming eyelashes, roots with tiny shoes on each branch, a stem with a tie or lots of buttons). Next, students practice the basic skills of how to enter the stage with the puppets from the side of the stage; for example, the walking movement should be up and down rather than linear or sliding. After that, students practice dialogue and communication between two puppets on the stage. A little exaggeration in expression of a character's feelings is encouraged, to keep the attention of the audience.

These are just suggestions for using puppetry in teaching. Teachers need to adjust these ideas to their own situations and make them work for their students.

Conclusion

There is great potential in using puppets for developing language and reading skills of students, especially English learners. Puppets hold students' attention and draw out their ideas (Crepeau & Richards, 2003). Teachers should not hesitate to use puppets as much as they wish in their teaching, for puppets are open, honest, and trustworthy "friends" that can be of great help in their everyday work.

REFERENCES

Bauer, F.C. (1997). *Leading kids to books through puppets*. Chicago: American Library Association.

Crepeau, I.M., & Richards, M.A. (2003). *A show of hands: Using puppets with young students*. St. Paul, MN: Redleaf Press.

Engler, L., & Fijan, C. (1973). *Making puppets come alive: How to learn and teach hand puppetry*. Mineola, NY: Dover Publications.

Krashen, S.D. (1981). *Second language acquisition and second language learning*. Oxford, England: Pergamon Press.

Pokrivka, V. (1991). *Dijete i scenska lutka* [Child and theatrical puppet]. Zagreb: Skolska Knjiga.

Vygotsky, L.S. (1978). *Mind in society: The development of higher psychological processes* (M. Cole, V. John-Steiner, S. Scribner, & E. Souberman, Eds. & Trans.). Cambridge, MA: Harvard University Press. (Original work published 1934)

Wilson, F.R. (1998). *The hand: How its use shapes the brain, language, and human culture*. New York: Pantheon.

Young, T.A., & Vardell, S.M. (1993). Weaving Readers Theatre and nonfiction into the curriculum. *The Reading Teacher, 46*, 396–406.

Zuljevic, V. (2005). Puppets—A great addition to everyday teaching. *Thinking Classrooms, 6*(1), 37–44.

CHILDREN'S BOOKS CITED

Hayes, J. (1987). The terrible Tragadabas/El terrible Tragadabas. In *Tell me a cuento/Cuéntame un story*. Great Falls, MT: Trails West Publishing.

Hayes, J. (1988). *Mariposa, mariposa*. El Paso, TX: Cinco Puntos Press.

CHAPTER 12

Let's Read, Write, and Talk About It: Literature Circles for English Learners

Deanna Peterschick Gilmore and Deanna Day

> I like literature circles because you can really talk about the book with other kids. Share your
> thoughts and hear other kids' ideas about the book and what you wrote in your journal.
> Your connections, questions, what you think about, and what you feel. You can talk openly
> and no one will say anything against you or your writings. (Pavel, age 11)

Many students express the idea that literature circles are exciting and that they enjoy talking about books. As shown by Pavel's response, literature circles involve many facets of learning, such as asking questions and connecting books to their own lives. This chapter explores how literature circles work for students and in particular for English learners. The teaching practices can be applied to English learners as well as fluent English speakers. Literature circles are for all students.

Both authors of this chapter, former elementary teachers, wanted to discover the best ways to implement literature circles with English learners. We asked local public school teachers in Pasco and Battleground, Washington, USA, if we could work with students to introduce literature circles. Deanna Gilmore spent seven months, one day a week, working with English learners from Russia and the Ukraine. There were six boys and nine girls, ages 8–11, in grades 3–5. Some students had just immigrated to the United States, and others had been in the United States for up to three years. They had varying levels of English speaking and writing abilities. Gilmore read aloud books to the students and implemented various literacy strategies. She read quality books such as *Molly's Pilgrim* (Cohen, 1983), *When Jessie Came Across the Sea* (Hest, 1997), and two of Patricia Polacco's books, *Babushka's Doll* (1995) and *Rechenka's Eggs* (1996). Gilmore chose these books because they had a connection with students' Russian culture.

Deanna Day worked with an English teacher two to three days a week for three months, collaboratively implementing literature circles with sixth graders. The class was

Supporting the Literacy Development of English Learners: Increasing Success in All Classrooms, edited by Terrell A. Young and Nancy L. Hadaway. Copyright © 2006 by the International Reading Association.

a mix of English learners and fluent English speakers. The English learners were from Russia, Ukraine, and Mexico, and were at diverse proficiency levels in their learning of English. For one month, Day and the students read aloud and discussed picture books. The next round of literature circles consisted of one book and small groups, and the last round involved small-group literature circles around a theme.

In this chapter, we share different ideas and strategies to use in literature circles with English learners. We begin by defining literature circles and explaining the importance of scaffolding English learners. Next we discuss how to use literature circles with English learners and we present several strategies that work well with English learners. We address the monitoring of students in literature circles, making connections to real life, asking questions, and, finally, celebrating literature circles. In order to help teachers understand how English learners react to literature circles, the chapter includes quotations by students. (All students' names are pseudonyms.)

What Are Literature Circles?

Literature circles, also known as literature discussions, book clubs, or literature studies, are formed when a group of readers gathers together to talk about a book in depth (Strube, 1996). Literature circles are grounded in a sociopsycholinguistic view of the reading process, one that recognizes the way in which reading is a meaning-making process (Samway & Whang, 1996).

In literature circles, students usually read a selection of literature on their own and then discuss it in a small group of four to six students. These discussions are guided by students' responses to what they have read, rather than by a list of teacher questions (Schlick Noe & Johnson, 1999). Peterson and Eeds (1990) state that intensive reading occurs when group members share their thoughts, feelings, impressions, personal connections, ideas, and problems about the books. The talk in these discussions shifts to dialogue when students' perceptions are altered and their meaning is worked out and expanded with other readers.

Scaffolding English Learners

Teachers understand that they have to make many accommodations when they have English learners in their classrooms. Herrell and Jordan (2004) note that teachers should "scaffold" or help the learner understand English by using props, gestures, pictures—anything that can help them understand what is going on in the text. Teachers serve as scaffolds when they demonstrate a procedure, guide students through a task, break complex tasks into smaller steps, and supply information. According to Vygotsky (1978a, 1978b), as students gain knowledge and experience about how to perform the task, teachers gradually withdraw their support so that students make the transition from social interaction to internalized, independent function. This holds true in literature circle discussions.

Vygotsky also maintains that meanings arise in the mind of a student through inter-actions with other language users, and that students who use language as a tool for social interactions show increased cognitive growth. A student from Moldava unknowingly agreed with this research when he said,

> I really like to work with my partner because he helps me pronounce the words I don't know in English. (Sergei, age 10)

Using Literature Circles With English Learners

The benefits of using literature circles with English learners are many. When teachers facilitate literature circles, they help students develop community and increase students' understanding of different cultures (Owens, 1995). English learners hear natural oral language when native speakers talk about books. Literature circles help English learners gather stronger understandings of what they have read through written and artistic responses to the text. According to Brown (1994), English learners understand English better when they talk about books that mean something to them. He states, "Appropriate and meaningful communication in the second language is the best possible practice to engage in" (p. 69). Finally, literature circles are important for English learners because the students engage in natural talk about books.

The following comments from sixth-grade English learners support the idea that literature circles are important for acquiring oral language:

> What I liked about the literature circles is sharing the book with other people because I never shared in class my thoughts or ideas because I was always embarrassed about things and they helped me to talk in front of class. (Irina, age 11)

> In the literature circles I thought I would barely talk or just nod my head but no, I talked and talked. (Deli, age 10)

Note, however, that small-group discussions do not always just "happen" (Gavelek & Raphael, 1996; Lewis, 1997; Maloch, 2004). Teachers need to prepare students prior to the implementation of a literature discussion group (Maloch, 2004; Wiencek & O'Flahavan, 1994). Teachers can start by reading aloud quality picture books to students (in kindergarten through eighth grade). After reading several picture books and dis-cussing them, teachers move on to reading aloud quality chapter books.

Choosing Quality Books

Samway and Whang (1996) suggest that teachers choose books featuring rich language, interesting plots, and richly developed characters. They also recommend that teachers select books with lots of photos and illustrations for English learners, as these help stu-dents understand the plot. Samway and Whang state, "Selecting books is critical because it can change how students view books and themselves as readers" (p. 28). They also note that teachers should select books that are "based on the interests of their students" and that "lead them toward discussion" (p. 15).

When teachers read aloud books from other cultures, it helps English learners feel comfortable in the classroom. It also aids in teaching fluent English speakers about their classmates' countries of origin.

Resources for finding quality books include the professional books *Using Multiethnic Literature in the K–8 Classroom* (Harris, 1997) and *Multicultural Voices in Contemporary Literature: A Resource for Teachers* (Day, 1999). Professional journals are also helpful in finding quality literature. Two such journals are *Book Links* (American Library Association) and *Horn Book Magazine* (The Horn Book), as are the monthly columns in *The Reading Teacher* (International Reading Association), *Language Arts* (National Council of Teachers of English), and *Journal of Children's Literature* (Children's Literature Assembly of the National Council of Teachers of English).

Implementing Read-Alouds

One of the best ways for students to learn how to read is to hear others read books (Galda & Cullinan, 2000; Trelease, 1985). When students hear stories read aloud, their emotional development improves and their imagination is enhanced. Rasinski (1989) maintains that when students hear a quality book read to them, they develop a sense of story, their vocabularies improve, and they are motivated to finish reading the book on their own.

Rosenblatt (1938) advocates choosing books that hold some link with the readers' past and present preoccupations, anxieties, and ambitions. Some picture books that are particularly good for read-alouds followed by discussion are *Sister Anne's Hands* (Lorbiecki, 1998), *Wilma Unlimited* (Krull, 1996), *White Socks Only* (Coleman, 1996), *Richard Wright and the Library Card* (Miller, 1997), *I Hate English* (Levine, 1995), *La Mariposa* (Jimenez, 1998), and *Uncle Jed's Barbershop* (Mitchell, 1997).

After reading aloud a book, the teacher begins a whole-group discussion by asking students, "What do you think about the book?" and "How do you feel about the book?" Students voluntarily and informally share their feelings and thoughts. The teacher demonstrates by sharing his or her own thoughts and ideas. The teacher also tells the students that talking about a book is just like discussing a movie or a television program with friends. It is important to stress natural discussion or talk that occurs between family and friends— talk, laugh, give advice, disagree, sympathize, and share your inner thoughts (Smith, 1990).

Discussing Literature in Small Groups

There are many advantages to having English learners work in small groups rather than in a whole-class setting. Kucer, Silva, and Delgado-Larocco (1995) ascertain that English learners tend to respond more often in small-group settings than in whole-class situations.

Moreover, students pay more attention to the way their English-speaking peers use English when they are in comfortable settings, such as in a literature circle (Hadaway, Vardell, & Young, 2004). English learners agree:

> I like literature circles because when a class is talking about a book [whole group] there are too much people and you may not be called on. (Juan, age 11)

> In literature circles three to five people can take turns to share their ideas and everyone will get a turn. (Katrina, age 11)

One student shared this interesting insight:

> Not everyone is agreeable all the time in literature circles. It is sometimes hard to work in the groups with some people. (Valentin, age 11)

Once students understand how to share in verbal discussions with others, the teacher can organize books around themes, concepts, topics, or just based on a certain author or illustrator. One example of a theme is poverty. Books with this theme include *No Mirrors in My Nana's House* (Barnwell, 1998), *May'naise Sandwiches & Sunshine Tea* (Belton, 1994), *City Green* (DiSalvo-Ryan, 1994), and *Something Beautiful* (Wyeth, 1998).

The teacher introduces the theme and the books through book talks and invites students to browse through the texts. The teacher encourages students to read the back cover and to read one page in the middle of the book to determine if it is a good match for them. Next, students write their top three book choices on a secret ballot. The teacher forms the literature circle groups with four or five students, trying to honor students' first or second choices. The next day the teacher gives students their new books.

When they meet for the first time, the literature circle groups decide how many times they will read the book (if it is a picture book) before they will discuss it fully. If the book is a chapter book, students use a calendar to determine how many pages they will read each day to complete the book by the due date. The teacher supports English learners by giving them a large amount of time to read books in school. Students can read the books during reader's workshop or sustained silent reading.

Transitioning to Chapter Books

Once students are comfortable talking about picture books, the teacher transitions them to reading and discussing a whole-class chapter book or even various chapter books. During the literature circles, the sixth graders all read the same book: *The Music of Dolphins* (Hesse, 1998). This book was chosen specifically because of the brief chapters, large font size, and the gradual transition to smaller font. This helped the English learners feel more comfortable (most of them were reading below grade level). Choosing this text was important for the older students because it had the appearance of simplicity yet contained several engaging issues. The English learners in the class connected to the main character, Mila, because she moved away from her friends and also had to learn a new language.

Pairing Students for Partner Reading

To specifically help English learners, the teacher pairs every student in the class with a partner for the length of the whole-class chapter book. There are different ways to do this: The teacher may pair an English learner with a proficient English speaker or pair two English learners together. The key is to find two students who can work together, support each other, and complete the book. Teachers can use partner reading for the first chapter book and for the remaining books give students choice in how they read the books. If students are having difficulty reading the book on their own or with a partner, adult volunteers can read aloud the book to English learners. Another support for students is to have them listen to audiotapes of the stories they are reading in class.

Students like to work with partners:

> When we read the book I liked the way we read with partners because if we read by ourselves we could read too fast and not catch some things that were important. (Maria, age 8)

> I liked partner reading a lot because at the end of every chapter we got to go over what we had just read. (Bogdhan, age 10)

Strategies That Work Well With English Learners

Certain strategies help engage English speakers and English learners, including sticky notes, sketch to stretch, story hats, graffiti board, bookmarks, open mind portraits, and writing in journals. These strategies help students think about texts and prepare them for discussions about the book. The teacher introduces each strategy through a minilesson and demonstrates how to complete the strategies during a read-aloud—before asking students to use the strategies on their own.

Sticky Notes

One strategy that is beneficial for English learners is the use of sticky notes (Peterson & Eeds, 1990). As students read their books, the teacher has them mark the text they want to discuss with others in the literature circle. Students write on their sticky notes why they chose certain parts. The teacher has students mark pages that they learned from, loved, cared about, couldn't stop reading, connected to, questioned, puzzled over, thought were funny, or found surprising (Schlick Noe & Johnson, 1999). During a read-aloud the teacher demonstrates thinking and writing on sticky notes at the same time. The teacher posts the pages of the book to show English learners how to use the strategy. (Figure 12.1 shows several sample sticky notes in response to *The Music of Dolphins*.)

FIGURE 12.1
Student Sticky Notes

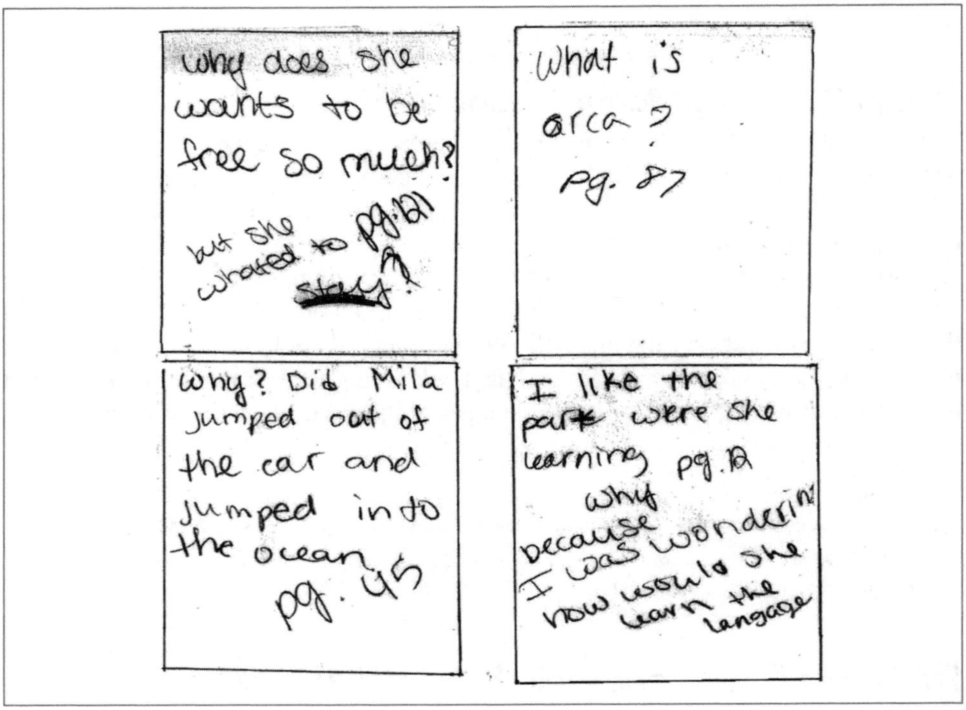

Sketch to Stretch

Sketch to stretch (Short, Harste, & Burke, 1996) is another strategy that is beneficial for English learners. After reading a book or during a read-aloud, the teacher invites students to make a sketch of what the story means to them—their feelings and thoughts about the story, *not* an illustration of the story. In literature circles, students share their sketches and their peers make comments.

Some English learners are more comfortable sharing their pictures with others in a knee-to-knee or eye-to-eye approach (Cole, 2003) because it helps them communicate through their drawings. After reading a chapter of *Bud, Not Buddy* (Curtis, 1999), for example, the teacher modified the sketch to stretch exercise by pasting colored cars on a paper and asking students to draw the man and Buddy in the car. Students also were directed to write dialogue for the story bubbles.

After completing the pictures, students come to the front of the room and share their pictures and dialogue. Figure 12.2 shows 10-year-old Ruslan's sketch based on *Bud, Not*

FIGURE 12.2
Student Sketch-to-Stretch Drawing

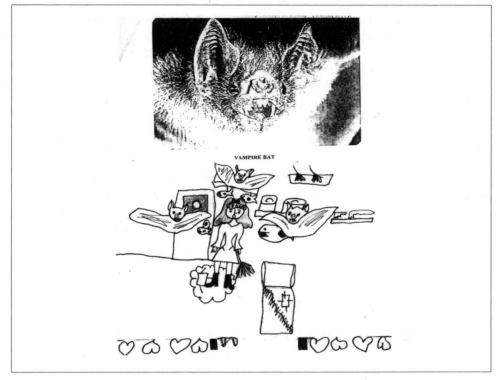

Buddy. He explained, "This is a picture of Bud in the car with a stranger. Bud thinks that he is a vampire, but I think he is just a man who works at a hospital and he is carrying blood to the patients."

Story Hats

Another technique is to have students make a story hat (Schlick Noe & Johnson, 1999). Students draw scenes from the story on an 11×14 sheet of construction paper while the teacher reads the book aloud. Students also write sentences to represent their thoughts about what is happening in the story. After they finish the drawings, students turn to their peers and share the pictures in a small literature circle. Students then fold the paper in the shape of a hat, staple it, and wear their story hats home. Elizabeth commented,

> I like to hear [the teacher] read the story to us. That way I can draw what I am thinking about the story at the same time.

Graffiti Board

One strategy that generates a lot of enthusiasm from students is "graffiti board" (Short et al., 1996). A large piece of chart paper is placed in the middle of the table; each member of the group takes a corner and writes and draws his or her thoughts about the book in graffiti fashion. Students can use pictures or words to express their thoughts, which are not organized in any particular fashion. The major focus is brainstorming, after which students share their graffiti with one another in small literature circles.

Bookmarks

Students also can prepare bookmarks as they are reading a text to share in literature circles (Samway & Whang, 1996). While the teacher is reading the book, students record the interesting or puzzling words they encounter and write questions for their groups on the bookmarks. During the research project, it was around Valentine's Day, so the bookmark was adapted to be a valentine for Deza, a character that Bud meets in the book *Bud, Not Buddy*. Students then shared their valentines with one another in small literature circles.

Open Mind Portraits

In this strategy, students have a precut face of a character in the book. In the inside there are two blank sheets of paper that are the same shape as the front page. All three pages have been stapled together. Students first draw the face and the hair of the character in the book. They are then instructed to open the book and write what is going on inside the mind of the particular character in the story (Tompkins, 2002). At times, teachers can include an outline of a particular building or setting where the story takes place. For instance, during the research project, this strategy was adapted for the book *Bud, Not Buddy*. Students were given a drawing of the outside of the shack that Bud was thrown into by his mean foster parents. They drew pictures of what was going on inside Bud's mind within the outline of the shack and also drew what was really happening. Because students might not understand the concepts of hornets or vampire bats, pictures of hornets and vampire bats were pasted on the shack. Students were allowed to choose between the hornets or vampire bats to respond to in their drawings. After students drew the pictures, they talked about what they had drawn in their literature circles.

Journals

Another strategy that is successful with English learners is the use of journals. Commercial notebooks or journals can be used, but students seem to take the writing more seriously if teachers make a special journal for the specific book they are reading. To make a journal, teachers can fold in half 5 to 10 pieces of paper (depending on how many chapters or the length of the book; include at least one page for every two to three chapters) and staple them together to form a 5-1/2×8-1/2 journal. The half pages are less intimidating then an entire page for students.

Students write after they have read one to three chapters. To help English learners specifically, the teacher brainstorms open-ended prompts that students can use to begin their journal entries, such as "I predict," "My favorite part," "I connect," and "I would change." Before discussing books in literature circles, students highlight areas in their journals that they want to share with the group. The teacher responds to each journal every few days, encouraging students in their reading, thinking, and understanding of the texts. (See Figure 12.3 for a sample journal entry in response to *The Music of Dolphins*.)

FIGURE 12.3
Student Journal Entry

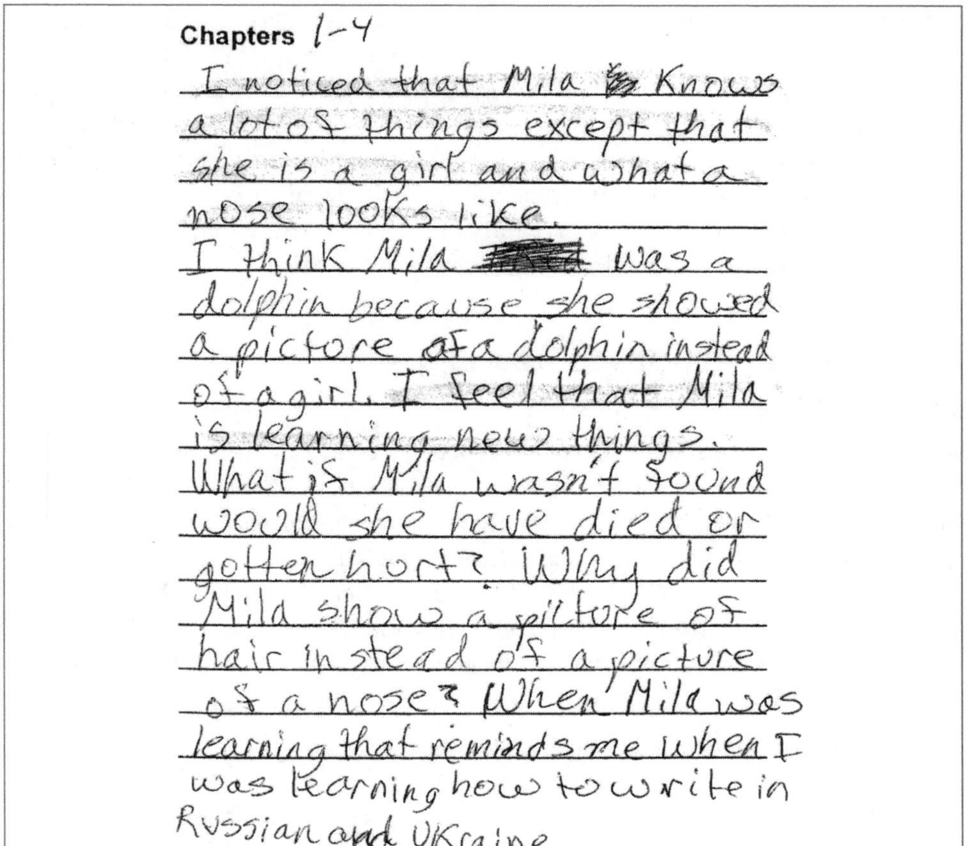

Chapters 1-4

I noticed that Mila Knows
a lot of things except that
she is a girl and what a
nose looks like.
I think Mila was a
dolphin because she showed
a picture of a dolphin instead
of a girl. I feel that Mila
is learning new things.
What is Mila wasn't found
would she have died or
gotten hurt? Why did
Mila show a picture of
hair instead of a picture
of a nose? When Mila was
learning that reminds me when I
was learning how to write in
Russian and Ukraine

Monitoring Students in Literature Circles

Teachers need to monitor the progress of English learners while they are reading their chapter books. As students are reading, the teacher listens to them and sits down with a pair to read along with them. The teacher takes "kid watching" (Owocki & Goodman, 2002) notes on a clipboard, listing the things that he or she is noticing about students' reading. When a student's partner is absent, the teacher places the student with another pair, if possible, or invites the student to read silently or with an audiotape. Sometimes the teacher becomes the student's partner for the reading period.

After all students have finished reading their books, the teacher sets aside time for the literature circles. Students usually complete the entire book before beginning literature circles. Some teachers prefer to read one chapter and discuss the book. English learners usually read slowly and need lots of reading support, whereas fluent English speakers sometimes read fast. Waiting until everyone has completed the book encourages students to read at their own pace, and the discussions are usually of higher quality. Eeds and Wells (1989) suggest that teachers take the role of literary guide and help students move toward "grand conversations." Teachers may play multiple roles in literature circles, including facilitator, participant, mediator, and active listener (Short, Kaufman, Kaser, Kahn, & Crawford, 1999). Short et al. (1999) discovered that the role of the facilitator is the most frequent and includes (a) asking students to extend and expand their ideas, (b) providing additional information to clarify details related to the story, (c) restating comments when others have missed something, (d) aiding with conversational maintenance, and (e) challenging a student's comment.

Making Connections to Real Life Through Literature Circles

One way to facilitate discussion is to ask students to connect something in the book to their own lives. If students see themselves in the characters of books, they may grapple with some serious issues and find solutions to their own problems. Students are able to do this by being allowed to make connections through discussions in literature circles (Harste, Short, & Burke, 1988). One student writes about a connection she made to the main character of Mila from *The Music of Dolphins* in Figure 12.4.

Sixth grader Isabelle commented on what it is like to make connections during literature circles:

> I liked that we could make connections with other people's connections.

The following transcribed conversation also indicates specific connections to the text *The Music of Dolphins*:

FIGURE 12.4
Making Connections Sample

Chapters 10- 14

A connection of my life to
Mila's, is when I just came
to America I couldn't
understand people when they
talked on English.
I think Mila will speak and
understand better after she
will live in this hospital
about a year.

Ruslan: I have a connection on page 66. When she first got her recorder, and
when I got my first recorder. I made a sound like that, too.

Katrina: Same here. When I got my recorder in fourth grade, I didn't know how
to play it because I'd never really seen it before, and I made a really
really loud squeak when I got it. It was really bad!

Students went on to discuss connections they had with fish, fishing, and eating fish.
Through this conversation, students more fully understand the text:

Steffan: I just can't think about eating raw fish.

Teacher: Yeah, but her perception is interesting, you know, that that's not good
fish because it is dead.

Michael: How would she know it was dead?

John: Because it's not flailing around or whatever.

Michael: Why did she only eat raw fish?

Steffan: Um, because that's the only thing she ate when she was growing up with the dolphins.

Teacher: It is kind of funny. But here is Sandy trying to give her a present, thinking, "Oh, she likes fish!" And then she says, "Yeah, if it's dead."

Asking Questions in Literature Circles

The teacher encourages students to ask questions about the text in the literature circles so that he or she can clear up any misunderstandings. During one literature circle about the book *Bud, Not Buddy*, a student asked, "What is a flyer?" Because this word was new to students, the teacher explained that in this case a flyer is a poster that is put up in the town to advertise Herman E. Calloway's band. The students interpreted the information from the story and drew their own posters (see Figure 12.5). Students volunteered to share their posters with others in the small-group literature circles.

When students are allowed to ask questions, they have the opportunity to think and gain greater understanding (Diaz-Rico & Weed, 1995). The teacher can also ask follow-up questions (e.g., "Why do you say that?") when participants use one-word or nondescript answers (Maloch, 2004). In one conversation, students ask questions about the book *The Music of Dolphins*:

Steffan: When Sandy brought Mila a fish, a dead fish, and she said it's not edible. I know that she didn't like the dead fish, but I don't understand, like in the sea, the dolphins would bring her fish and how could she eat the live fish that had to die?

Irina: Yeah, that's just weird.

Ruslan: It would be in the dolphin's mouth.

Steffan: Well, it's still dead.

Irina: I know, and how could you eat the eyeballs? The guts? The eggs? I think I would rather eat seaweed.

Ruslan: It's just like eating sushi.

Pavel: But all the sushi we eat in America is smoked.

Irina: Well, actually I had it from an Asian family and they did it by scratch and it was raw.

Students remarked about asking questions during literature circles:

FIGURE 12.5
Student Poster

What I enjoy about talking about the books in literature circles is that you catch some things that you didn't notice before. I get to ask questions about the book and my lit circle members will help me figure it out or give me ideas. (Katerina, age 10)

Some people had really good questions that took a while to answer. Most people in our literature circle got a lot of different and good ideas. (Ruslan, age 11)

Celebrating Literature Circles

To bring closure to a set of literature circles, teachers have a couple of possibilities. Sometimes the teacher brings all students together and lets the individual groups do a quick sharing or book talk. Other times the teacher has students plan and organize a presentation in which they connect their thoughts to share with others. Focus questions that are helpful are, "What do you want other students to learn about your book and discussion?" and "What do you think was most important about this book?" Through brainstorming, students decide the best way to share this information.

Students can make presentations through various sign systems, such as drama and visual arts (puppet shows, murals, ABC books, etc.). The teacher shares the many possibilities with students and allows the groups to decide which presentation would be best for their books. The teacher invites parents and another class to watch the literature presentations.

Conclusion

Students who are learning English feel more comfortable speaking in small-group settings. Literature circles are a wonderful way to scaffold English learners for this reason. Literature circles also allow fluent English speakers to learn more about students and their cultures in a more intimate way. Through literature circles, all students are able to share what they think and how they feel about books. Teachers invite students to make connections to their own lives and the world around them. Students hear diverse responses, and this helps them to think critically about books. Literature circles encourage a love for literature and positive attitudes toward reading for both English learners and fluent English speakers. Following are closing thoughts about literature circles from some English learners:

> I like to go "knee to knee and eye to eye" about the book, because I get to hear other people's ideas, and I like talking to my friend. (Ruslan, age 11)

> What I really think is good about literature circles is that you have time to draw pictures about the story. (Arena, age 10)

> I enjoy talking about a book because you get to talk with people not just yourself and your brain. (Pavel, age 9)

REFERENCES

Brown, H.D. (1994). *Principles of language learning and teaching* (3rd ed.). Englewood Cliffs, NJ: Prentice Hall.

Cole, A. (2003). *Knee to knee, eye to eye.* Portsmouth, NH: Heinemann.

Day, F.A. (1999). *Multicultural voices in contemporary literature: A resource for teachers.* Portsmouth, NH: Heinemann.

Diaz-Rico, L.T., & Weed, K.Z. (1995). *The crosscultural language and academic development handbook: A complete K–12 reference guide.* Boston: Allyn & Bacon.

Eeds, M., & Wells, D. (1989). Grand conversations: An exploration of meaning construction in literature study groups. *Research in the Teaching of English, 23,* 4–29.

Galda, L., & Cullinan, B. (2002). *Literature and the child* (5th ed.). Belmont, CA: Wadsworth.

Gavelek, J., & Raphael, T. (1996). Changing talk about text: New roles for teachers and students. *Language Arts, 73,* 182–192.

Hadaway, N., Vardell, S., & Young, T. (2004). *What every teacher should know about English learners.* Boston: Pearson.

Harris, V. (1997). *Using multiethnic literature in the K–8 classroom.* Norwood, MA: Christopher-Gordon.

Harste, J.C, Short, K.G., & Burke, C. (1988). *Creating classrooms for authors: The reading-writing connection.* Portsmouth, NH: Heinemann.

Herrell, A., & Jordan, M. (2004). *Fifty strategies for teaching English learners.* Upper Saddle River, NJ: Merrill/Prentice Hall.

Kucer, S., Silva, C., & Delgado-Larocco, E. (1995). *Curricular conversations: Themes in multilingual* and monolingual classrooms. New York: Stenhouse.

Lewis, C. (1997). The social drama of literature discussions in a fifth/sixth-grade classroom. *Research in the teaching of English, 31*, 163–204.

Maloch, B. (2004). One teacher's journey: Transitioning into literature discussion groups. *Language Arts, 81*, 312–322.

Owens, S. (1995). Treasures in the attic: Building the foundation for literature circles. B.C. Hill, N.J. Johnson, & K.L. Schlick Noe (Eds.), *Literature circles and response* (pp. 1–12). Norwood, MA: Christopher-Gordon.

Owocki, G., & Goodman, Y. (2002). *Kidwatching: Documenting children's literacy development.* Portsmouth, NH: Heinemann.

Peterson, R., & Eeds, M. (1990). *Grand conversations: Literature groups in action.* New York: Scholastic.

Rasinski, T. (1989). *Inertia: An important consideration for reading motivation.* East Lansing, MI: National Center for Research on Teacher Learning. (ERIC Document Reproduction Service No. CS009550)

Rosenblatt, L. (1938). *Literature as exploration.* New York: Modern Language Association.

Samway, K., & Whang, G. (1996). *Literature study circles in a multicultural classroom.* Portland, ME: Stenhouse.

Schlick Noe, K.L., & Johnson, N.J. (1999). *Getting started with literature circles.* Norwood, MA: Christopher-Gordon.

Short, K.G., Harste, J.C., & Burke, C.L. (1996). *Creating classrooms for authors and inquirers* (2nd ed.). Portsmouth, NH: Heinemann.

Short, K.G., Kaufman, G., Kaser, S., Kahn, L.H., & Crawford, K.M. (1999). Teacher watching: Examining teacher talk in literature circles. *Language Arts, 76*(5), 377–385.

Smith, K. (1990). Entertaining a text: A reciprocal process. In K.G. Short & K. Pierce (Ed.), *Talking about books: Creating literate communities* (pp. 17–31). Portsmouth, NH: Heinemann.

Strube, P. (1996). *Getting the most from literature groups.* New York: Scholastic.

Tompkins, G. (2002). *Language arts: Content and teaching strategies.* Upper Saddle River, NJ: Merrill/Prentice Hall.

Trelease, J. (1985). *The read-aloud handbook.* New York: Penguin.

Vygotsky, L. (1978a). Social origins of self regulation. In L. Moll (Ed.), *Vygotsky and education: Instructional implications and applications of sociohistorical psychology* (pp. 139–140). New York: Cambridge University Press.

Vygotsky, L. (1978b). Teaching mind and society: Teaching, schooling, and literate discourse. In L. Moll (Ed.), *Vygotsky and education: Instructional implications and applications of sociohistorical psychology* (pp. 195–196). New York: Cambridge University Press.

Wiencek, J., & O'Flahavan, J.F. (1994). From teacher-led to peer discussion about literature: Suggestions for making the shift. *Language Arts, 71*, 488–498.

CHILDREN'S BOOKS CITED

Barnwell, Y. (1998). *No mirrors in my nana's house.* New York: Harcourt Children's Books.

Belton, S. (1994). *May'naise sandwiches and sunshine tea.* New York: Simon & Schuster.

Cohen, B. (1983). *Molly's pilgrim.* New York: Lothrop Lee and Shephard.

Coleman, E. (1996). *White socks only.* Morton Grove, IL: Albert Whitman.

Curtis, C.P. (1999). *Bud, not Buddy.* New York: Scholastic.

DiSalvo-Ryan, D. (1994). *City green.* New York: William Morrow.

Hesse, K. (1998). *The music of dolphins.* New York: Scholastic.

Hest, A. (1997). *When Jessie came across the sea.* Cambridge, MA: Candlewick Press.

Jimenez, F. (1998). *La mariposa.* New York: Houghton Mifflin.

Krull, K. (1996). *Wilma unlimited.* New York: Harcourt.

Levine, E. (1995). *I hate English.* New York: Scholastic.

Lorbiecki, M. (1998). *Sister Anne's hands.* New York: Dial.

Miller, W. (1997). *Richard Wright and the library card.* New York: Lee & Low.

Mitchell, M. (1997). *Uncle Jed's barbershop.* New York: Simon & Schuster.

Polacco, P. (1995). *Babushka's doll.* New York: Simon & Schuster.

Polacco, P. (1996). *Rechenka's eggs.* New York: Putnam Juvenile.

Wyeth, S.D. (1998). *Something beautiful.* New York: Bantam Doubleday Dell.

AUTHOR INDEX

Note: Page numbers followed by *f* and *t* indicate figures and tables, respectively.

CHILDREN'S LITERATURE AUTHOR INDEX

Note: Page numbers followed by *f* and *t* indicate figures and tables, respectively.

V–W

Y

SUBJECT INDEX

Note: Page numbers followed by *f* and *t* indicate figures and tables, respectively.

COMMANDS, 140–141

COMMUNICATION. *See specific types*

COMMUNICATIVE LANGUAGE TEACHING (CLT): and cognitive load, 16–18; combined with content teaching, 15–16, 25; overview of, 30

COMMUNITY COLLABORATION, 11

COMMUNITY, SENSE OF, 158–159

COMPARE/CONTRAST ESSAYS, 161

COMPARE/CONTRAST TEXTS, 138, 139*t*

COMPREHENSIBLE INPUT, 30–31, 43

COMPREHENSION. *See* reading comprehension

CONFERENCES, WRITING, 160

CONSERVATION, 75

CONSIDERATE TEXT, 16

CONTENT AREAS: and benefits of poetry, 172; challenges of, 132–133; demands of teachers in, 16–18; importance of expository text instruction in, 133–135

CONTENT THEMES. *See* themes

CONTENT-BASED INSTRUCTION (CBI): combined with communicative language teaching, 15–16, 25; overview of, 8, 30; rationale for, 62

CONTEXT: and benefits of poetry, 172; for vocabulary instruction, 101, 108–109

CONTRAST FRAMES, 145–146

CONVENTIONAL WRITING, 159*f,* 162

CONVERSATION PRACTICE, 141

COOKING, 165*t*

COOPERATIVE LEARNING: benefits of, 14; drawbacks of, 15; for oral-language development, 169; in Vocabulary Improvement Program, 99–100

CUEING SYSTEMS, 114–1167

CULTURAL ADJUSTMENT, 11–12

CULTURE: role of, in learning, 11–12; and thematic instruction text selection, 65, 66*f*

CURRICULUM: for Vocabulary Improvement Program, 107–112

D

DADDY SAVED THE DAY (SHELF MEDEARIS), 71

DECISION MAKING, 11

DECODABLE TEXTS, 129

DEEP PROCESSING: activities for, 102–103, 110–111; overview of, 102

DESCRIPTION TEXTS, 138, 139*t*

DETAIL QUESTIONS, 49–53

DEVELOPMENTAL BILINGUAL PROGRAMS, 8

DEVELOPMENTAL WRITING, 162

DIALOGUE JOURNALS, 152–164

DIFFERENTIATED INSTRUCTION (DI): for expository text instruction, 140; in Four-by-Four Model, 34; overview of, 33

DIRECT EXPLANATION: overview of, 84; for reading comprehension, 84–85; in Vocabulary Improvement Program, 99–100

DIRECTION-GIVING, 141

DISCUSSIONS: in emergent guided reading, 116–117, 120–121; and instructional routines, 94; in literature circles, 195, 196, 197–198; for text structure instruction, 141; in writing instruction, 160

DOMAIN LANGUAGE, 134–135

DRAMATICS, 165*t,* 176

DUAL-LANGUAGE PROGRAMS. *See* two-way immersion programs

E

EARLY FLUENT READERS, 121–124

EARLY READERS, 116–117

EARLY WRITING, 162

EARLY-EXIT PROGRAMS. *See* transitional bilingual programs

THE EARTH AND I (ASCH), 75

ECHO READING, 173

ECONOMICS, 73–74

EL PARQUE DE PEDRIN (MONDRÍGUEZ), 73

ELABORATION, 90–91*t*; in dialogue journals, 158, 159*f*

ELD. *See* English-language development (ELD) instruction

ELECTRONIC POETRY CENTER, 178

ELEMENTARY AND SECONDARY EDUCATION ACT (1965), 7

E-MAIL, 152–153, 162

EMERGENT READERS, 116–117

ENGAGEMENT, 80

ENGLISH AS A SECOND LANGUAGE (ESL) METHODS: and content area success, 132, 135; types of, 8

ENGLISH LEARNERS: academic problems of, 6, 96; awareness of expository text structures, 135; characteristics of, 9–12, 41; factors affecting language acquisition of, 12–13; in

Four-by-Four Model, 35–38; goals of, 42–43; location of, 6; misconceptions about, 14–16; number of, 6; proficiency levels of, 81; projected increase in, 6; reading and writing problems of, 31–32; stages of adjustment for, 11–12; support for, 13–18; younger versus older, 42

ENGLISH-LANGUAGE DEVELOPMENT (ELD) INSTRUCTION: definition of, 26; in Four-by-Four Model, 34

ESL METHODS. *See* English as a second language (ESL) methods

EXCERPT, 46, 47

EXPECTATIONS, 88

EXPERIMENTAL WRITING, 162

EXPLICIT TEACHING, 43–44

EXPOSITORY TEXTS: challenges of, 135–136; common structures of, 3, 134, 138; importance of learning about, 133–135; instructional strategies for teaching, 138, 140–146; versus narrative texts, 136–137

F

FAMILY INVOLVEMENT, 10–11

FAMILY THEME, 70–72

FEEDBACK, 158

FIRST-LANGUAGE LITERACY, 12–13

FLUENT GUIDED READING, 124–127

FOUR-BY-FOUR MODEL: guiding principles of, 33–34; illustration, 29*f*; overview of, 26–28; structure of, 34–38; theoretical foundations of, 28–33

FRAME SENTENCES, 177

FRIENDS FROM THE OTHER SIDE/AMIGOS DEL OTRO LADO (ANZALDÚA), 72

FRONT LOADING. *See* preteaching

G

GEOGRAPHIC BACKGROUND, 10

GETTING TO KNOW YOUR NEIGHBORS (CHIN), 72

GLOBAL VILLAGE, 61, 68–75

GLOSSARIES, 142

GRAFFITI BOARD, 202

GRAMMAR: cloze procedure for, 51–53; and ideal input formula, 31; in writing instruction, 161

GRANDPARENTS, 71

GRAPHIC ORGANIZERS: for expository text instruction, 143–144, 145; and instructional routines, 93

GRAPHOPHONIC SYSTEM, 115–116

GREAT IMMIGRATION (1890–1920), 7

THE GREAT KAPOK TREE (CHERRY), 75

GREEN CORN TAMALES/TAMALES DE ELOTE (RODRIGUEZ), 72

GUIDED READING: cueing systems in, 114–116; early fluent lessons in, 121–124; emergent reader format for, 116–121; for fluent readers, 124–127; importance of, 113, 114; miscue analysis in, 116; overview of, 3, 113; sentence structures in, 129–130; teacher's role in, 3; text selection for, 127–129

H

A HANDFUL OF SEEDS (HUGHES), 73

HELPING EACH OTHER (RILEY), 74

HERRINGBONE TECHNIQUE, 53–55

HIGH SCHOOL COMPLETION, 10

HIGH-FREQUENCY WORDS, 129

HISPANIC POETRY, 181

HMONG: percentage of speakers of, 6

HOME ENVIRONMENT: and challenges to NCLB Act, 9; in Vocabulary Improvement Program, 100

HOME–SCHOOL COMMUNICATION, 11

HOMEWORK, 100

HUMAN HANDS, 185–186

I

IF THE WORLD WERE A VILLAGE (SMITH), 61, 69

IMAGERY, 86–87

IMMIGRANTS: background elements of, 9–10; factors affecting language acquisition of, 12–13; family involvement of, 10–11; high school completion rates of, 10; history of, 7–8; misconceptions about, 14–16; projected increase in, 6; stages of adjustment for, 11–12; support for, 13–18

IN MY FAMILY/EN MI FAMILIA (GARZA), 71

INCONSIDERATE TEXT, 16

INFERENCING SKILLS, 101, 107

INFORMAL READING INVENTORIES, 35

INFORMAL WRITING ACTIVITIES. *See specific types*

INSTRUCTIONAL ROUTINES, 93–94
INSTRUCTIONAL STRATEGIES: definition of, 84; for literature circles, 199–203; overview of, 81; for reading comprehension, 84–94; for teaching expository text structure, 138, 140–146. *See also specific types*
INTEGRATED ELD/ELA INSTRUCTION, 26
INTEGRATED THEMATIC INSTRUCTION. *See* themes
INTERACTIONS, 186
INTERACTIVE WRITING PROJECT: importance of, 159–160; objective of, 153–154; supportive environment in, 153–159
INTERLANGUAGE, 32
INTERNATIONAL READING ASSOCIATION (IRA), 150–151
INTERNET USE, 134
INTERPERSONAL COMMUNICATION, 2
INTONATION, 173
ITALICIZED WORDS, 47, 173

J–L

JOURNALS: in early fluent guided reading, 121–124; in literature circles, 202–203; value of, 3; for writing instruction, 152–165
KID WATCHING, 204
KOREAN: percentage of speakers of, 6
LANGUAGE: benefits of, 41
LANGUAGE ACQUISITION: factors affecting, 12–13; ideal input for, 30–31; stages of, 27
LANGUAGE ARTS, 164*t*
LANGUAGE DIVERSITY: benefits of, 41–42; challenges of, 113; history of, 7–9; misconceptions about, 15
LANGUAGE-PROFICIENCY RATING SCALES, 26–27
LAU V. NICHOLS (1974), 7
LEARNING: at home, 11; role of culture in, 11–12
LEARNING STYLES, 15
LETTER WRITING: value of, 3; for writing instruction, 152–165
LIMITED ENGLISH PROFICIENT STUDENTS. *See* English learners
LINGUISTIC PERFORMANCE GAP, 42
LINGUISTIC STRUCTURES: and instructional routines, 93; for reading comprehension, 89–90*t*
LINGUISTICALLY ISOLATED COMMUNITIES, 10
LINGUISTICS, 28
LISTENING CENTER, 177–178

LISTENING COMPREHENSION, 169
LITERACY: challenges to, 31–32
LITERARY TECHNIQUES, 174
LITERATURE. *See* texts
LITERATURE CIRCLES: benefits of, 196; closing activity for, 207–208; connection to real life through, 204–206; definition of, 195; discussion in, 195, 196, 197–198; function of, 4; instructional strategies for, 199–203; monitoring students in, 204; overview of, 194–195; partner reading in, 199; questioning in, 206–207; read-alouds in, 197; scaffolding in, 195–196; text selection for, 196–197

M

MAIN IDEA: questions for, 53–56; terminology for, 48
"MAKING TAMALES/LA TAMALADA" (GARZA), 72
MATH: thematic lessons for, 69, 70; writing activities in, 164–165*t*
MINILESSONS, 99, 161
MISCUES, 116
MODELING: definition of, 85; for expository text instruction, 141–142; for expository text reading, 136; and instructional routines, 93; poetry reading, 173–174; for reading comprehension, 86–87; in writing instruction, 156, 160
MOTHER GOOSE POEMS, 181
MULTICULTURAL POETRY, 181
MUSIC, 165*t*
MY FAMILY TREE (SCOTT), 71

N

NAMES, 12
NARRATIVE TEXT, 136–137
NATIONAL ASSESSMENT OF EDUCATIONAL PROGRESS (NAEP), 133
NATIONAL CENTER FOR EDUCATION STATISTICS, 9, 96
NATIVE AMERICAN POETRY, 181
NATIVE AMERICANS, 7
NEIGHBORS, 72–73
NO CHILD LEFT BEHIND (NCLB) ACT (2001): challenges to, 8–9; English-proficiency assessment in, 24; overview of, 8; standard

requirements in, 64; and standardized tests, 133

NURSERY RHYMES, 181

O

OBSERVATIONS, 204

OFFICE OF BILINGUAL EDUCATION AND MINORITY LANGUAGE AFFAIRS, 6

OPEN MIND PORTRAITS, 202

ORAL-LANGUAGE SKILLS: and benefits of poetry, 171–172; developmental stages of, 151–152; for expository text instruction, 140–141; in Four-by-Four Model, 36, 38; importance of, 168; literature circle benefits for, 196; poetry sharing activities for, 172–178; puppetry to develop, 185–186; and reading and writing skills, 26; supporting development of, 168–170

OUR BOOK OF MAPS, 69

P

PARAGRAPH, 46, 47

PARAGRAPH-WRITING FRAMES, 145

PARENTING SKILLS, 10

PARTNER READING, 199

PARTS OF SPEECH, 52

PASSAGE, 46, 47

PAST TENSE, 130

PERFORMANCE STANDARDS: VOLUME I ELEMENTARY SCHOOL, 68

PHRASING, 173

POETRY: classroom collection of, 180–182; overview of, 170–172; responding to, 178–180; sharing of, 172–178

POETRY CIRCLES, 180

POETRY MAGAZINE, 178

POETS & WRITERS WEBSITE, 178

POKO PUPPETS, 192

POSTERS, 206–207

POTATO HILL POETRY WEBSITE, 177

POVERTY, 198

PREDICTIONS: in emergent guided reading, 117, 119; in fluent guided reading, 125; questioning to check, 115

PREFIXES, 104

PREREADING ACTIVITIES, 142

PRETEACHING, 92–93

PREVIEW/VIEW/REVIEW TECHNIQUE, 65, 67–68

PREWRITING, 143, 160

PRIOR KNOWLEDGE. *See* background knowledge

PROBLEM SOLVING, 170

PROBLEM/SOLUTION OUTLINES, 143, 144*f*

PROBLEM/SOLUTION STRUCTURES, 138, 140*t*

PROFESSIONAL DEVELOPMENT, 9

PROFICIENT WRITING, 162

PRONUNCIATION, 12

PUPPETRY: beyond the classroom, 189–190; examples of, 187–189; goals of, 186–187; overview of, 185–186; students' reaction to, 190; suggestions for implementation of, 192–193; teachers' reaction to, 190–191

Q–R

QUESTIONING: to check predictions, 115; for comprehension, 49–59; for deep processing, 102–103; in emergent guided reading, 118, 119; and instructional routines, 94; in literature circles, 206–207; and organization of themes, 63–64; to respond to poetry, 179

RATE, READING, 173

READ-ALOUDS: and benefits of poetry, 171; for expository text instruction, 142–143; in literature circles, 197

READERS THEATRE, 176

READING COMPREHENSION: fluent guided reading for, 124–127; instructional strategies for, 84–94; and oral-language development, 170; overview of, 48–49, 80–81; questions for, 49–59; requirements of, 82

READING COMPREHENSION STRATEGIES: instruction in, 82; strategy starters for, 83–84; to support academic language, 80–81; types of, 82; visual cues for, 82

READING SKILLS: English learners' problems with, 31–32; in Four-by-Four Model, 34–38; and oral English development, 26

REFRAIN, 174–175

REREADING: and benefits of poetry, 171; in emergent guided reading, 121; and instructional routines, 94

RETELLING: for expository text instruction, 145; to summarize, 84–85

RISK TAKING, 157–158

ROOM FOR ONE MORE (JACOBS), 70

TRANSFERRING ACTIVITIES, 141
TRANSITIONAL BILINGUAL PROGRAMS, 8
TRANSITIONAL LIFESTYLE, 9
TWO-WAY IMMERSION PROGRAMS, 8, 24

U

UNDER THE CANOPY (CHERRY), 75
UNISON, READING IN, 174
UNIVERSITY OF CALIFORNIA AT SANTA CRUZ, 98
U.S. CENSUS BUREAU, 6
U.S. DEPARTMENT OF EDUCATION, 6

V

VENN DIAGRAMS, 143
VIETNAMESE: percentage of speakers of, 6
VISUALIZING, 86–87, 88*t*
VISUALS: for detail questions, 49–50; in expository versus narrative texts, 136; for reading comprehension strategies, 82; for vocabulary instruction, 18
VOCABULARY IMPROVEMENT PROGRAM: assessment in, 106; basis of, 97; content of, 98–99; development of, 97–98; features of, 99–100; organization of, 99; overview of, 96; results of, 96–97; sample curriculum for, 107–112; types of activities in, 100–105
VOCABULARY INSTRUCTION: for book parts, 44–47; characteristics of effective, 97; cloze procedure for, 51–53; cognate activities for, 103, 111–112; context in, 101, 108–109; deep-processing instruction for, 102–103, 110–111; in emergent guided reading, 117; in Four-by-Four Model, 34–38; and guided reading texts, 128–129; and ideal input for-

mula, 31; and instructional routines, 93; and linguistic structures, 89–90*t*; preteaching for, 92; strategies for, 18; structural analysis activities for, 104; themes for, 63, 91–92; in writing activities, 161
VOLUNTEERING, 11

W

WE'RE ALL SPECIAL (MAGUIRE), 70
WH WORDS, 49, 50, 84–85
WHO PUT THE PEPPER IN THE POT? (COLE), 70
WITHIN-GROUP SIMILARITIES, 15
WORD KNOWLEDGE, 96, 97
WORD SUBSTITUTIONS, 102
WORD WIZARD ACTIVITY, 100
WORLD WAR I, 7
WORLD WAR II, 7
WRITING ACTIVITIES: across curriculum, 163–165*t*; for expository text instruction, 145–146; recommendations for, 160–162; reduced emphasis on, 150; starting point for, 152–153; suggestions for, 151; supportive environment for, 153–159
WRITING CONFERENCES, 160
WRITING SKILLS: development of, 162; first- versus second-language learners, 151; in Four-by-Four Model, 34–38; learners' problems with, 31–32; and oral English development, 26

Y

YES, WE CAN! (COHN), 73
YOU CAN SELL (TRUMBAUER), 74